GERMANY IN WORLD POLITICS

VIOLA HERMS DRATH
Editor

CYRCO PRESS, INC., PUBLISHERS • NEW YORK AND LONDON

CONTENTS

FOREWORD

THIS VOLUME OF collected papers by leading American and German diplomats and scholars on Germany's new international authority and its increasingly activist role in world politics constitutes by no means an exhaustive study. The contributions, largely an outgrowth of a series of lectures at American University in Washington, D.C., are interdisciplinary in scope and because of their widely diverging approach and subject matter not rigidly compartmentalized.

No longer the proverbial "economic giant and political dwarf," the Federal Republic of Germany shoulders new responsibilities. As a prime component of the Western alliance, it exercises considerable leverage on the international stage. The introduction of differing accents and nuances into economic, political, and military policies makes it abundantly clear that thirty years after its defeat and division, the former client and junior partner has developed into a major force.

Significantly, the precepts of the generation that leads Germany in the seventies are untainted by Nazi indoctrination.

After the "economic miracle" ushered in by the largesse of the Marshall Plan, after Adenauer's westpolitik (the Western alignment that promised and delivered internal stability), and after the Social Democrats' and Free Democrats' ostpolitik (a formula for rapprochement, born in the fifties, that could only have been launched in the context of detente when Washington gave the signal), Chancellor Helmut Schmidt emerged as the representative of a government embodying the renewed self-assurance that accompanied the Federal Republic's impressive economic forward thrust. It is perhaps no accident of history that Schmidt's personal image blends so perfectly with the confidence that he seeks to project for his country in the world.

The overview of the political aspects is enhanced by highlights of social developments and intellectual concerns reflected in contemporary literature. This volume is meant to acquaint the student of German affairs with some of the problems confronting the Federal Republic in world politics as it endeavors to maintain equilibrium in its relations with the German Democratic Republic. Dealing with an ongoing political process of extraordinary complexity, some of the observations, approaches, and solutions concerning these fundamental issues, which may be summed up as the German question that dates back to Bismarck's time, are perhaps more stimulating and provocative than conclusive.

Obviously, Germany's prominent position as a medium class power is not without challenge. In their thoughtful presentations the experts point to some pressing questions concerning the impact of Germany's newly acquired power status on the Atlantic Alliance. For example, how will Bonn capitalize on its new role to serve its national interests? How much convergence and divergence are or can be tolerable within the German-American alliance—in the words of Professor Kelleher—"the critical element left in a somewhat stagnating Atlantic

alliance?" To what extent must or will the alliance change
to accommodate the objectives of a more independent German
Federal Republic? Will Germany's heightened independence
result in a challenge to or a rejection of United States leadership? If the balance of power were to tilt drastically against
the West, what are the chances that Bonn may decide that it
is to its advantage to maneuver West Germany into a neutral
position in the rivalry between the superpowers?

Ever since it was forged into a bulwark against the communist bloc, West Germany has evolved as the United States
most reliable ally in military and economic affairs. Although
Germany's foreign policy is firmly rooted in the European Community and the North Atlantic Treaty Organization, Bonn and
Washington have in effect become the two most important
links in the Atlantic alliance. Although bilateral cooperation,
especially in the military sector, has been strengthened markedly
during the last three decades, suggestions of a "bigemony," or
a "special relationship" between the two powers, tend to generate
old resentments and new fears among neighbors and little
resonance in Bonn. The political leadership of the Federal Republic long ago concluded that a German-American partnership
can succeed in the framework of extended American-European
relations.

No matter how self-confident West Germany may appear
because of its economic vitality, its political stability, and the
recognition of the inviolability of its eastern boundaries—the
status quo by way of ostpolitik and Helsinki—the fact remains
that the Federal Republic is a nonnuclear power and hence
dependent for its security on the viability of the North Atlantic
Treaty Organization. Moreover, its economic fortunes are closely
tied to a healthy European market, ready and able to consume
two-thirds of its exports. It is the consensus in Bonn that its
chances for survival and for attaining freedom of action can
be realized as a contributing member of the Atlantic community
and by assuming a fair share of responsibility in the conduct

of world affairs. Only a politically united Western Europe, it is also argued in influential circles in Bonn, can ensure the preservation of the liberal democracies and a sound partnership with the United States on the basis of equality. Beyond and above this, such a political entity could serve as an effective counterweight to the Soviet Union.

✻   ✻   ✻   ✻

The discussions in this volume range from an analysis of the meaning of state and sovereignty to current trends in German literature. Within this broad spectrum such questions as economic development, domestic and international issues, the role of the churches, and the rights of women are investigated.

Divided into three parts, this volume addresses itself to the political and economic dimension, the social dimension, and the literary scene. In the first part George Schwab touches on the essential characteristics of independent states; Niels Hansen and Catherine Kelleher speak from different perspectives on the significance that Bonn attaches to American-German relations, European cooperation, and the Atlantic Alliance; Peter C. Ludz and John Starrels treat the complex problem of intra-German affairs. The interdependence of economic power and political responsibility is discussed by Peter Hermes, and Ralf Dahrendorf offers a reassessment of the changing relationship between the United States and its European allies since the United States suspended unilaterally the convertibility of the dollar into gold as well as the lack of progress in European unification.

This juxtaposition of German and American points of view on future objectives and their possible ramifications for the alliance, the United States, and the balance of power is buttressed by an examination of some aspects of the social dimension. The second part illuminates the domestic background and the social problems, attitudes and behavior patterns not commonly understood that German society is confronting in the process of its emergence on the international chessboard of power.

Werner Steltzer approaches the ongoing debate on the German resistance against Hitler in an international context; Ferderick Spotts dwells on the still explosive question of the influence of the churches on such vital political issues as denazification and industrial impoverisation, and rearmament as well as the centripetal force that they exerted during the Federal Republic's recovery; Charles Foster discusses the problem of manpower from the perspective of primary, secondary, and higher education, and Wendelgard von Staden reflects on the impact that consciousness raising has had on German women; the debt that the Federal Republic felt compelled to repay, namely, the creation of a German Marshall Plan as an appropriate gift on the twenty-fifth anniversary of ERP, is sympathetically treated by Robert G. Livingston.

It is in the third part, devoted to the exploration and analysis of the literary scene, that the reader will discover the key to one of the most perplexing syndromes of the German-American relationship: Bonn's basic feeling of insecurity vis-à-vis Washington. In my review of contemporary literature I address myself, among other things, to the anxieties that are basic to the new literature. The expression of uneasiness, the profound self-doubt mingled with guilt, exasperation over the inhumanities of the past, the manifold, experimental efforts to purge the German language of authoritarian cliches and thinking patterns, the severity of the social critique, the fear of ideological overtones, the intensity of attachment to individual and social realities, and the inordinate concern over the issue of "private versus public virtue" in these writings leave little doubt that the persisting ruminations are not merely intellectual reflections on symptoms grown rampant in the minds of frustrated politicians in Bonn's hothouse atmosphere but of feelings of anxiety thoroughly embedded in the self-image of the average German. Hugo Mueller takes a close look at various forms of self-criticism, a tradition in twentieth-century German literature; how these traits manifest themselves in contemporary theater is shown by Jürgen Kalkbrenner and in political literature by Bruno Steinbruckner.

Notwithstanding imbalances and necessary omissions, notably, Germany's well-known social achievements and its visual arts, this volume presents an excursion into the multifaceted socio-political German landscape. As such it should add considerably to perspective and heighten curiosity, particularly if one shares or wishes to understand a belief widely held on both sides of the Atlantic that in contrast to the nineteen thirties and forties, there is a rejuvenation of the spirit of humanism in the Federal Republic.

In summary, it deserves to be noted that Germany is an extraordinary country with extraordinary problems that is trying to grope its way back to ordinariness.

For his generous support and continued professional advice during the preparation of this volume (fifteen papers had to be coordinated and assembled from various parts of the globe) I wish to thank my friend George Schwab, a professor at the City College of New York and the Graduate Center. Thanks are also due to Professor Bruno Steinbruckner for affording me the opportunity to conceptualize and develop for the liberal studies program at American University a course on German affairs, an idea that he originated. For his unflagging enthusiasm and encouragement my appreciation goes to Niels Hansen, Minister of the Embassy of the Federal Republic of Germany in Washington, who opened this lecture series.

I also thank Professor Hugo Mueller and Francis S. Drath for their ready counsel.

Above all, I express my gratitude to all the contributors. It was their expertise and willingness to give of their time and energy that endowed the project with its unusual scope, thus enabling us to proceed with its publication. Of course, I assume editorial responsibility for anything that appears in this book.

VIOLA HERMS DRATH

Washington, D.C.

PART I

THE POLITICAL
AND ECONOMIC
DIMENSION

THE GERMAN STATE IN HISTORICAL PERSPECTIVE: AN INTRODUCTION

George Schwab

AN INQUIRY INTO THE German state in historical perspective must of necessity be preceded by a discussion of the meaning of the word state. In common parlance, for example, it is not unusual to use state and nation interchangeably. Yet, as I hope to show, the two are not identical. In fact the conceptual distinction inherent in the two words is decisive for a proper understanding of the meaning of state.[1]

The Oxford English Dictionary (1933, reprinted in 1961) notes, among other things, that a nation is "an extensive aggregate of persons, so closely associated with each other by common descent, language, or history, as to form a distinct race or people." The definition includes the assertion that "in early examples the racial idea is usually stronger than the political [while] in recent use the notion of political unity and independence is more prominent."[2] Thus the word nation is not synonymous with that of state, especially not until more recent times.

3

This description of the word nation must be further circumscribed by associating a specific people with a specific territory. From this follows the dictionary's description of a "nationality" as a people "belonging to a particular nation." Whether a nation consists of one nationality or of several depends on the extent to which there exists a community of language, religion, custom, and so forth. The fact that a nation can contain three distinct nationalities, for example, does not negate the fact that it is a nation, however heterogeneous. Conversely, extrapolating from the aforementioned criteria, a territorially enclosed unit consisting of an integrated community is a homogeneous nation, that is, a nation based on one nationality.

Although every nation must by definition consist of a nationality or of a series of nationalities, this need not yet imply a link between the words nation and nationality. The Israelites, for example, despite their fervent attachment to the Holy Land, were geographically far removed from it for several thousand years. Still the Israelites survived as a nationality outside the territory that they considered to be theirs.

What is characteristic of the brief description of the words nation and nationality is that a specific political connotation cannot be associated with either word. The Israelites in the Diaspora, on the one hand, and India in 1910, on the other, although as much a nation as the Philippines or Egypt, neither functioned in the arena of power politics. In other words, neither a nation nor a nationality is politically autonomous. By existing outside the framework of an organized state,[3] the highest goal of both, that is, a nationality or a nation, is to attain statehood.[4] Hence a nationality possesses the potential of becoming a nation, and the latter, in turn, of becoming a state. Conversely, when a state is dismembered by war, for example, it reverts to the status of a nation, and should its people be dispersed as well, it even loses that status.

From an organizational perspective, a state is a more developed form of entity than is a nation. It is an enormous administrative apparatus.[5] To enforce laws, decrees, and the like a state relies on law-enforcing machinery, on a bureaucracy that includes a police force. Yet such an attribute need not necessarily be absent from a nation irrespective of the extent to which a foreign power may control a nation's law-enforcing machinery. Thus a hallmark of an independent state always is its possession of an autonomous administrative apparatus and of an armed force free of foreign domination or supervision.

Only in possession of these characteristics does a state legitimize itself as such and qualify to enter and begin operating in the global arena of power politics. This linkage between state and politics still leaves us in the air to an extent. What is actually meant by a state operating in the power-political sphere? A state, after all, is not an abstract entity, one that floats among other such states somewhere in outer space. Viewed from the perspective of power-political relations, and this is the perspective from which this topic is briefly approached, a state is a politically autonomous entity, one that has concrete political interests and in the most extreme case is prepared to pursue them with the force of arms. Hence the question: Who decides what these power-political interests are?

We thus arrive at another attribute of the state, namely, that of sovereignty. State, politics, and sovereignty are indivisible. Irrespective of who the sovereign is, in the final analysis it is the sovereign who concretizes what the interests of state are and decides on the power-political course to be pursued.

From the perspective of history, the state assumed its specific political shape in Europe only recently. Although some of its features can be traced as far as ancient Greece and Rome, the modern state, according to Joseph Strayer, "is based on the pattern which emerged in Europe in the period between 1100 and 1600."[6] It was also during that period that the word state gradually became associated with a specific territory,[7] and it was not until the sixteenth and seventeenth centuries that the notion of sovereignty became indivisibly linked with that of the state. Medieval doctrine, according to Otto Gierke, had not made law dependent on the state for its existence,[8] had limited sovereign power to precepts of natural law, and had adhered to the idea that sovereignty "by no means excludes an independent legal claim of nonsovereign subjects to participate in the power of the state."[9]

Events particularly brought about by the Reformation accelerated a process that culminated, in the sixteenth and seventeenth centuries, in the emergence of what we commonly call the modern European sovereign state.[10] With regard to the German state specifically, its immediate emergence is always traced to the Thirty Years War between 1618 and 1648, a war that was terminated with the peace of Westphalia. Although a multitude of events that occurred during that period was crucial to the emergence of the German state, here we need be detained only by several that were decisive from the perspective of our topic.

As is well known, Protestant–Catholic rivalry was at the root of this conflict in the territory known today as Germany. But as the conflict unfolded, the religious components gradually faded in favor of territorial ambitions on the part of most princes. In proportion to the fervor with which these ambitions rose, power-political interests of state assumed ever greater significance, so much so that they began to take precedence over interests of religion.[11] Thus during this conflict a series of states emerged that were governed by almost completely independent princes.[12] The new political reality that emerged was codified by the peace of Westphalia. Article 64 of the treaty stipulated, for example, that "the princes . . . are so established and confirmed in their ancient rights, prerogatives, liberties, privileges, free exercise of territorial right . . . that they never can or ought to be molested therein by whomsoever upon any manner of pretence." This was further reinforced and elaborated in Article 65. Accordingly, princes were given the right in their territories to interpret laws, "to declare war, to impose taxes, to levy or quarter soldiers, to erect new fortifications . . . [and] to make alliances."

Notwithstanding the fact that the treaty emphasized that a "link existed between the princes or states and the Empire ... events," according to Pagès, "quickly demonstrated that the princes could make treaties with foreign sovereigns without breaking the articles by which they were bound, even though the treaties, without being directed against the emperor, took no account of his interests."[13] Thus despite the nominal allegiance to the emperor, the princes were in fact, if not strictly speaking in name, sovereign. Hence it was they who defined the power-political interests of their states and in extreme situations decided who the enemy was and acted in conformity with that decision.

With the framework provided on the essential attributes of a sovereign state, we may now proceed to inquire into the evolution of the German state from the perspective of power politics. To this end I will leave out the period between 1648 and January 18, 1871, the day the Prussian king William I was proclaimed emperor. Eighteen seventy-one is a convenient demarcation line, for a united Germany then began to play a crucial role in the foreign policy calculations of all relevant sovereign states. To put it another way, the German Empire assumed the status of a premier political power.

Germany's territorial size and geographic location in the heart of Europe were, of course, important in lending it political weight. Three additional factors contributed to that end, namely, (1) the population of the German Empire by 1871 had already surpassed that of France, (2) its economy had become as strong as that of France, and (3) Germany was also rapidly closing the gap between its industrial development and that of Great Britain. In short, the German Empire was swiftly emerging as an economic and industrial giant with the distinct prospect of surpassing Great Britain (something that did happen not long after the turn of the century).

The German Empire thus unquestionably possessed attributes that are decisive for assuming a powerful posture in the arena of power politics. As important as these attributes are, they must also be correlated with the political coherence of the state.

According to the constitution of 1871, the empire was sovereign. Speaking concretely, the constitution stipulated that the sovereign authority in the empire belonged to the king of Prussia, who was also the German emperor, and with the chancellor whom he appointed. Because of the constitutional requirement of countersignature, the chancellor, technically together with the emperor, determined the power-political interests of the state, including that of going to war.[14] As such the sovereign authority was constitutionally able to commit the state to actions commensurate with the decision taken. Moreover, because of the basic commitment of the people to the state, the sovereign authority was not hindered from carrying out policies that it considered necessary. The preservation and strengthening of this harmony between state and society were Bismarck's foremost domestic aims during the period of the empire in which he dominated the scene, namely, between 1871 and 1890.

But in the process of orchestrating society to the needs of the state, Bismarck did not display the acumen that characterized his foreign policy. This maladroitness emanated from his insensitivity to some of the problems that the empire had inherited.

Although manageable at the time, these problems gradually became so formidable that they finally undermined the cohesiveness of the state and thereby its ability to effect policies in the power-political domain deemed necessary to the well-being of the state. Of particular significance in this context was the rise of political parties that were inimical to the state. Irrespective of size, the most ominous ones to the state were the ideologically inspired parties, those movements with militant doctrines that claimed to embody the true will of the people.[15] Based on this claim they challenged the state's monopoly of politics, that is, the sovereign's right to define the interests of the state and to act accordingly in the arena of power politics, including the sovereign's judgment in the extreme case of who the enemy or foe was.[16]

Bismarck's confrontations with the Center party and with the Social Democratic movement anticipated the political polarization of society that, for example, in Weimar Germany undercut the effectiveness of the state in pursuing its national interests. At different stages in his career Bismarck perceived these political forces in German society as inimical to the strength of the German state. By receiving their inspiration from outside Germany they were, in his view, corroding the state and the positive national spirit on which it rested. Thus he first attacked the Center party, the party that championed the Catholic church in Germany. His intention was nothing less than crushing this Catholic power structure through a number of measures, including the "pulpit paragraph" that was added to the criminal code (December 1871), the law concerning the order of the Society of Jesus (July 1872), the Prussian "May laws" (1873), and the "expatriation law" (May 1874). These laws provided the government with the necessary legal tools to impose penalties on bishops and priests, to imprison and expel bishops, and to prohibit those clerics deprived of their positions from practicing their priestly functions elsewhere.

Despite these measures Bismarck failed to crush the Catholic power structure. In fact, the repressive measures had no visible impact on the Center party. It survived undiminished in popular strength. Realizing his failure, Bismarck finally helped to bury most of the antichurch legislation and contributed to reorchestrating German Catholics into the fiber of the state. Although the *Kulturkampf* did succeed in redividing Germany along denominational lines, German Catholics, by not challenging the foundations of the state, did not undermine its posture in international politics.

The case was different with the Social Democratic movement, particularly that segment that had received its inspiration largely from Marx and Engels. Based on an erroneous perception of this overt movement's danger to the state, Bismarck was instrumental in having a severe anti-Socialist law passed in 1878. In its twelve-year existence the law succeeded in destroying the party's structure, but it failed to destroy the party's popular base. Because the law often forced members to operate clandestinely, a popular comradely spirit emerged in the underground days that helped to forge a cohesive movement whose aim became, in accordance with the tenets of Marx and Engels, the destruction of the bourgeois state. Given the not inconsiderable popularity that the movement enjoyed, it certainly evolved into a state within a state, and as such it began to constitute a politically centrifugal force in Germany.

The impact that the extension of the franchise had on the growth of negative movements did not become evident until the Weimar period. Nevertheless the door was open for parliament to be exploited as a springboard by ideologically inspired political movements in conquering the state. An important turning point in subjecting the state to parliamentary influence occurred during World War I.

Discontent with Germany's annexationist policies and the insensitivity and high-handedness of its military establishment, a number of parties in parliament, including the powerful Center and Social Democratic parties, coalesced to pass in the Reichstag a peace resolution on July 19, 1917, that stipulated among other things, that the peace to follow must be one that would not be accompanied by "forced cessions of territory and political, economic, and financial impositions." The political parties thus undercut in the middle of the war the prerogative of the sovereign authority to determine the power-political interests of Germany. Furthermore, with the deterioration of economic conditions in Germany and of its military posture, a far-reaching constitutional amendment was passed on October 28, 1918, that stipulated that the chancellor was subject to the confidence of the Reichstag and that that body had to consent to such policies as declaring war, concluding peace, and entering treaties with foreign powers. In short, this amendment drastically contributed to splitting up and dividing the powers of the sovereign authority. The political cohesiveness of the German state was thus further impaired.

The German republic was established on the ashes of Germany's military defeat, and a liberal democratic constitution was adopted shortly after the German government unconditionally signed the Versailles Treaty. Although the new Germany reflected the liberal democratic *Zeitgeist*, the political reality that had emerged in the wake of its military defeat and the war-guilt clause of the Versailles settlement was inimical to the institutionalization of the republic. Speaking of the English constitution, for example, the Earl of Balfour once noted that the whole English

political machinery presupposes a people so fundamentally at one that they can safely afford to bicker; and so sure of their own moderation that they are not dangerously disturbed by the never-ending din of political conflict.[17]

Because a majority of Germans lacked such a commitment to liberal democratic ideals, despite the movement toward liberal democracy that was visible during the empire and even before, the Weimar republic was not incorrectly dubbed *eine Republik ohne Republikaner*. Thus from the very outset of the republic's existence it contained buds that were distinctly malignant to the liberal democratic development of Weimar Germany.

Despite the fact that the new Germany rested on a flimsy republican foundation, the state as such survived for some years largely intact. Because the war did not destroy it physically and no occupation comparable to the one that followed World War II occurred, Germany's economic, industrial, and, to some extent also, military base remained unharmed. In short, however relegated by the victors to the outer fringes of the community of states, Germany retained the status of a state and acted accordingly. Rapallo (April 1922), Locarno (December

1925), the Treaty of Berlin (April 1926), and Germany's entry
into the League of Nations (September 1926) are but a few
examples of the vigor with which Weimar Germany pursued
in the arena of power politics its national interest of destroying
the shackles that Versailles had imposed on it.

But the Weimar constitution that was legalistically interpreted
and bound the government to the Reichstag encroached ever
more on the state's ability to perform effectively in the arena
of power politics. This encroachment became particularly pronounced in the wake of the depression when parties of the
right and the left succeeded in paralyzing the working of the
Reichstag, and to an extent also the government, in their attempts
to capture power. Even the constitutional law of March 27,
1930, that enabled a newly appointed chancellor to countersign
his own appointment as well as the dismissal of his predecessor,[18]
and as such made him more independent of the whims of the
Reichstag, did not prevent the collapse of the Weimar state,
something that could probably have been avoided by the popu-
larly elected president. Burdened by age, by dubious advisers,
and by a strictly legalistic interpretation of the constitution that
inhibited him from ruling effectively by decree (Article 48),
President Hindenburg failed to fulfill his constitutional duty to
eliminate the centrifugal political forces that were undermining
the ability of the state to maintain order, peace, and stability.
Hindenburg's appointment of Hitler as chancellor of Germany
on January 30, 1933, and the Reichstag's passage of the enabling
act of March 24, 1933, destroyed the Weimar state.

The state that Hitler forged on the foundations of Weimar
is too well-known to need much elaboration. On his appointment
as chancellor Hitler moved swiftly to crush all opposition and
thereby solidify his powers. The emergency decree of February 28, 1933,[19] that was passed immediately following the Nazi
instigated Reichstag fire became one potent tool in Hitler's
arsenal of weapons used to destroy all opposition. In addition,
the enabling act[20] that legally liquidated the Reichstag's legis-

lative power to participate in the lawmaking process further helped to eliminate society as a counterpoise to the state. Thus, for example, Hitler outlawed in June and July 1933 all political parties save his own. This proscription was followed by the SA purges that occurred between June 30 and July 2, 1934. Finally, upon the death of President Hindenburg in August 1934, Hitler capped his power by merging the offices of chancellor and president.

Hitler's moves to crush all opposition and thus solidify his powers were accompanied by his policy of conditioning the German people to his militant ideology. Because of his successful synchronization of the German people and his rearmament policies Hitler's Germany became for a while the most powerful political entity on the Continent. It was precisely because of the militant ideology that he injected into politics that one can no longer speak of Hitler's Germany as a state in the strict sense of the word, certainly not from the perspective of the political interrelationship of states.

In contrast to the totalitarian one-party state that Germany became under Hitler, the traditional modern European sovereign state that emerged in the sixteenth and seventeenth centuries was an entity based on a secular or nonideological conception of politics. Precisely such a conception facilitated the *jus publicum Europaeum* to emerge.[21] The basic assumption on which this order rested was the genuine acceptance of the natural law precept of *pacta sunt servanda*. By subscribing to certain rules and regulations that were applicable in time of war and peace sovereign states were able to interact with one another on an equal basis. Such coexistence was possible only as long as the power-political interests of state were limited in scope, a fundamental characteristic of states underpinned by a secular or nonideological conception of politics.

Hitler's militant ideology, which he had outlined in *Mein Kampf*, was global in scope, and as such it was incompatible with the notion of the limited power-political interests of state. Because of Hitler's determination to dominate the world and hammer it into the image of his ideology the principle of *pacta sunt servanda,* for example, became for him nothing more than a tactical device to gain specific advantages, as was the tactic of legality that he used in his quest for power in the second half of Weimar.[22] Hitler's militant ideology finally brought about the clash of two irreconcilable conceptions of politics and culminated in World War II, his suicide, and, in May 1945, the total collapse of his Germany[23] and of its dismemberment as a state.

In contrast to Germany's military collapse in 1918 and the Versailles settlement that followed, the victors in 1945 assumed all the prerogatives that are characteristic of a sovereign state. Thus all decisions that the victors thought necessary with regard to their respective zones of occupation were made, and Germany was thereby relegated to the status of a nation.

But events in the world soon compelled the United States, the most powerful state at the time, to reassess its strategic interests. Because of the intransigent behavior of the Soviet Union in 1945 and in view of Stalin's declaration on February 9, 1946, on the impossibility of capitalism and communism coexisting genuinely, thus alluding to the inevitability of war,[24] Washington became fearful that Moscow would escalate the war of nerves into a hot confrontation.[25] Washington's apprehension that the Soviet Union would march toward the Rhine and the English Channel was crucial in its decision to forge the western part of Germany into a viable first line of defense. It was thus in the context of the cold war that that part of Germany under American, British, and French military occupation received a lease on life as a nation with the distinct possibility that Germany, however truncated, would be permitted to reassume the status of a state.

Yet the United States was compelled to move cautiously. The cessation of hostilities in 1945 was not accompanied by an appreciable decline in the hatred of Germans by those in the West that had suffered most under their occupation. This hatred was further fueled in the immediate postwar years by the full documentary disclosure of the enormity of the crimes that Germany had perpetrated. There was therefore widespread aversion to everything German, and people were genuinely afraid of a revived Germany that could again embark on an expansionist course. Therefore any move to forge West Germany into a viable member of the Western community so soon after the conflict had to be handled very delicately.

Nevertheless, the first significant step took place in May 1946. The decision was then made to suspend reparation shipments from the western zones to the Soviet Union. Shortly thereafter, on September 6, 1946, Secretary of State Byrnes publicly revealed the United States position on Germany. In a major foreign policy statement at Stuttgart he committed the United States to a policy of "maximum possible unification" that would in effect obliterate zonal barriers as "far as economic life and activity in Germany are concerned." Despite widespread denunciations of his speech, particularly by Poland and France, the United States refused to be deflected from its course. Following the American lead, a German economic council was established early in 1947 for the purpose of bringing about the economic fusion of the American and British occupation zones. This was followed in 1948 by the first in a series of massive infusions of Marshall-fund aid that helped to accelerate the rapid rebuilding process of German industry. Nineteen forty-eight was also the year of the German currency reform in the three western zones.

The Berlin blockade that was imposed by the Soviet Union in that summer reconfirmed Washington's perception of the correctness of its policy of rebuilding West Germany so that it could play a role in the East-West conflict. To hasten this process the Western allies issued in April 1949 the "Occupation Statute" that turned over to selected German authorities con-

siderable legislative, executive, and judicial powers. This enabled Germans to "enjoy self-government to the maximum
possible degree consistent with the occupation." The "Occupation Statute" was followed immediately by the creation of the
Federal Republic that rested on a new constitution commonly
known as the Basic Law. The steps taken within the short span
of three years thus provided a solid foundation for West
Germany to reemerge as a political entity.

Yet it took a while before the Federal Republic gained autonomy. An important step in this direction occurred in May
1952. The "Occupation Statute" of 1949 was then replaced by
the so-called Bonn Conventions. According to these conventions,
the American, British, and French military occupation was
reduced to a contractual arrangement between the Federal
Republic and the Western powers. Although these conventions
restored autonomy to the Federal Republic, it was not until
May 1955 that the three powers terminated their military occupation, recognized West Germany as autonomous, and admitted
it to membership of the North Atlantic Treaty Organization.[26]

Because a criterion of politics in power-political relations is
the distinction between friend and enemy or friend and foe,
the following question must be asked: Is the autonomous authority in Bonn able to decide in an emergency who the enemy
or foe is and act accordingly? By virtue of the status acquired
in 1954 Bonn is entitled to make this decision.[27] But the ability
to implement such a decision is an entirely different matter.
This ability depends on a number of factors, including the
resources in being rather than potential.

Given today's rivalry between the superpowers, Bonn's ability
to decide who the enemy or foe is and to act in accordance
with that decision is dubious. This is not to say, however, that
the Federal Republic possesses no room in which to maneuver
politically. Because of the fact that West Germany has emerged
as an economic and industrial giant it enjoys considerable
political leverage and thus even incidental political decisions,

decisions that do not involve emergencies in the domain of power politics but may turn out to have political implications that are global.

A few examples will suffice to illustrate this point. Dependent as West Germany is on world markets, a political decision to export its advanced fast-breeder nuclear technology to states that are anxious to go nuclear may contribute to undermining the already precarious balance of power between the superpowers. Similarly, a political decision not to aid substantially those liberal democracies that are faltering economically, and possibly thereby also politically, may contribute to the further political and military erosion of the West of which the Federal Republic is a part. And there is always the possibility that under certain circumstances, for example, if the balance of power were to shift against the West, Bonn may decide that it is to the Federal Republic's advantage to maneuver West Germany into a neutral position in the rivalry between the United States and the Soviet Union.

Thus although the concept of sovereignty has not changed in the epoch of the modern European state, West Germany's power-political role has. Because of the altered global political configuration since World War II, Bonn's ability to decide on the enemy or foe and to act accordingly is academic.[28] Because the Federal Republic depends today for its survival on the United States it can therefore be concluded that West Germany currently enjoys in the arena of power politics the status of political autonomy in the shadow of the sovereignty of the United States.[29]

NOTES

1. For a survey of various interpretations of the meaning of state and nation see Louis L. Snyder, *The Meaning of Nationalism.* Foreword by Hans Kohn (New York, 1968), pp. 17–40.

2. The dictionary still relies here on the traditional and hence unscientific use of the word race.

3. Carlton J. H. Hayes, *Essays on Nationalism* (New York, 1966), p. 5.

4. Hans Kohn, *The Idea of Nationalism: A Study in Its Origins and Background* (New York, 1961), p. 19.

5. For the constituent parts of the state and their development see the informative volume edited by Charles Tilly, *The Formation of National States in Western Europe* (Princeton, 1975), *passim*.

6. Joseph R. Strayer, *On the Medieval Origins of the Modern State* (Princeton, 1970), p. 12.

7. For a discussion of the meaning of the word state in antiquity and the Middle Ages see Paul-Ludwig Weinacht, *Staat: Studien zur Bedeutungsgeschichte des Wortes von den Anfängen bis ins 19. Jahrhundert* (Berlin, 1968), *passim*.

8. Otto Gierke, *Political Theories of the Middle Ages*, trans., intro. by F. W. Maitland (Cambridge [England], 1958), p. 74.

9. *Ibid.*, p. 93.

10. On the emergence of the modern European sovereign state and some of the implications of this development, see the following important works by Carl Schmitt: *The Concept of the Political*, trans., intro., and notes by George Schwab. Comments by Leo Strauss (New Brunswick, [New Jersey], 1976), pp. 19–68; Schmitt's preface (1971) to his *Le categorie del 'politico,'* ed. Gianfranco Miglio and Pierangelo Schiera (Bologna, 1972), pp. 23–25; *Der Nomos der Erde im Völkerrecht des Jus Publicum Europaeum*, 2nd ed. (Berlin, 1974), pp. 112–189; "Staat als ein konkreter, an eine geschichtliche Epoche gebundener Begriff" (1941), *Verfassungsrechtliche Aufsätze aus den Jahren 1924–1954: Materialien zu einer Verfassungslehre* (Berlin, 1958, 1973), pp. 375–385.

11. G. Pagès, *The Thirty Years War, 1618–1648* (New York, 1970), p. 149.

12. *Ibid.*, p. 230.

13. *Ibid.*

14. The fact that the *Bundesrat* (Federal Council) had to approve a declaration of war if the empire were the initiating party was a mere formality because the presidency of the *Bundesrat* and the conduct of its business belonged to the chancellor.

15. See my article entitled "Legality and Illegality as Instruments of Revolutionaries in Their Quest for Power: Remarks Occasioned by the Outlook of Herbert Marcuse," *Interpretation*, Vol. 7, January 1978, pp. 74–89.

16. On the friend-enemy criterion of politics see Schmitt, *The Concept of the Political*, pp. 26–37. The conceptual distinction inherent in the words "enemy" and "foe" and some of the implications of

this distinction are treated by George Schwab in "Enemy oder Foe: Der Konflikt der modernen Politik," trans. J. Zeumer, *Epirrhosis: Festgabe für Carl Schmitt*, ed. H. Barion *et al.* (Berlin, 1968), II, pp. 665–682, also Ion X. Contiades, " 'ΕΧΘΡΟΣ' und 'ΠΟΛΕΜΙΟΣ' in der modernen politischen Theorie und der griechischen Antike," *Griechische Humanistische Gesellschaft*, Zweite Reihe (Athens, 1969), pp. 5ff.

17. Introduction to Walter Bagehot, *The English Constitution* (New York, 1955), p. xxiv.

18. Sections 2 and 13 of the "Gesetz über die Rechtsverhältnisse des Reichskanzlers und der Reichsminister (Reichsministergesetz)," *Reichsgesetzblatt*, I, No. 9, 11 (1930), pp. 96, 97.

19. "Verordnung des Reichspräsidenten zum Schutz von Volk und Staat. Vom 28. Februar 1933," *Reichsgesetzblatt*, I, No. 17 (1933), p. 83.

20. "Gesetz zur Behebung der Not von Volk und Reich. Vom 24. März 1933," *Reichsgesetzblatt*, I, No. 25 (1933), p. 141.

21. By far the best discussion on the evolution of the *jus publicum Europaeum* is contained in Schmitt's *Der Nomos der Erde.*

22. See section 2 of my "Legality and Illegality." Also George Schwab, "Appeasement and Detente: Some Reflections," *Detente in Historical Perspective*, ed. George Schwab and Henry Friedlander, (New York, 1975), pp. 141–143.

23. On the impact that ideology had on Hitler's conduct of foreign policy, see John H. Herz, "Power Politics or Ideology? The Nazi Experience," *Ideology and Foreign Policy: A Global Perspective*, ed. George Schwab (New York, 1978), pp. 14–34. Also Klaus Hildebrand, *The Foreign Policy of the Third Reich*, trans. Anthony Fothergill (Berkeley, 1973), esp. pp. vii–ix, 135–140.

24. "Speech Delivered by J. V. Stalin at a Meeting of Voters of the Stalin Electoral Area of Moscow, February 9, 1946," *The Soviet Union and World Peace* (New York, 1946), pp. 5–7.

25. The apprehension of the United States is well documented in numerous studies, including that by John Lewis Gaddis, *The United States and the Origins of the Cold War, 1941–1947* (New York, 1972), pp. 282–284, 296–315, 318–337.

26. In fact, the details of West Germany's accession to NATO and the Western European Union had already been worked out at the Nine-Power Conference in London between September 28 and October 3, 1954. The agreements were signed in Paris on October 23, 1954. For a historical outline of West Germany's emergence as

an autonomous entity see Keesing's Research Report on *Germany and Eastern Europe Since 1945, From the Potsdam Agreement to Chancellor Brandt's 'Ostpolitik'* (New York, 1973), *passim*. Because of the emergence of two Germanys in the postwar period a two-state theory emerged in the context of the unity of the nation. See *Materialien zum Bericht zur Lage der Nation 1974* (Bundesministerium für innerdeutsche Beziehungen, 1974), pp. 16–19. The questions that this theory raises have provoked a lively discussion on the meaning of state, nation, and people. *Ibid.*, pp. 66–129. For a discussion of the official interpretation of the word nation in East Germany see Peter C. Ludz, *Die DDR zwischen Ost und West: Politische Analysen 1961 bis 1976* (Munich, 1977), pp. 227–242.

27. There are those who rightfully question Bonn's ability to make such a decision. See, for example, Helmut Rumpf, *Land ohne Souveränität*, 2nd ed., (Karlsruhe, 1973), pp. 70–72, *passim*.

28. *Ibid., passim.*

29. For a discussion on the extent to which the United States is still in the position to act as a truly sovereign state, see my article "The Decision: Is the American Sovereign at Bay?" in *Revue europénne des sciences sociales. (Cahiers Vilfredo Pareto)*, Tome XVI, No. 44, 1978, pp. 67–76.

1

U.S.-GERMAN RELATIONS WITHIN THE AMERICAN-EUROPEAN PARTNERSHIP

Niels Hansen

AT THE BEGINNING* it would seem appropriate to dwell on an aspect of American-German relations that is obvious but often overlooked: That they are embedded in—and in effect influenced and often determined by—a broader relationship between America and Western Europe or even—more generally—within the community of all the industrialized democracies, including, above all, Japan.

In a world that has undergone dramatic political-social changes in the third quarter of our century, this group of comparatively few countries not only has largely identical interests but also shares fundamental moral values.

When the present international structure emerged after World War II, no more than three dozen countries played roles.

---

*Niels Hansen opened the lecture series on the Federal Republic of Germany at American University in February 1977.

21

Nowadays the comity of nations is comprised of some 150 states. But only 30 or so are still democracies in Western terms. The crisis of liberal democracy results, as Zbigniew Brzezinski maintains, from a cultural and spiritual crisis that has placed in jeopardy two basic principles having governed our world since the nineteenth century, the ideas of progress and individual liberty. In Europe, during recent years this conflict has shifted from some formerly authoritarian right-wing regimes to certain liberal democracies that are confronted with the problem of including communists in government. The democracies of the West indeed share identical interests in coping with this ideological antagonism.

Related to this crisis are the tremendous differences in percapita income among the nations of the world. The Western industrial countries are far ahead, the Federal Republic of Germany and the United States ranging in the top group. The continuous growth of population in the developing countries aggravates this imbalance. The existing international system is, therefore, subject to heavy pressure. Because we shall be confronted with the increasing effects of this conflict during the next decades, the Western industrial nations must strive in common for an evolutionary solution that will preserve our free enterprise system and generate, nevertheless, acceptance on the part of all.

And last but not least: The military ratio of power between the United States and the Soviet Union, and between the two pact systems in general, has slowly shifted. I do not need to elaborate on this point. The Soviets have caught up.

These profound changes, the main aspects of which I have tried to summarize, make close cooperation among the Western industrial democracies vital. Bilateral relations among members of this group will have to be adapted and adjusted accordingly, all the more as our experience has shown in the last decade or so that the economies of the Western industrial democracies are heavily interdependent: Sound economic growth and recovery on the one hand and inflation, recession, and unemployment on the other have become international phenomena, spilling over from one country to the other—the most powerful one, the United States, generally taking the lead.

Those sitting in the same boat are bound to row in unison. However, this metaphor requires some institutional differentiation. In the Atlantic Alliance Americans and Western Europeans boarded the same boat. The nine partners of the European Economic Community (EEC) launched a boat of their own in the economic sea, whereas the other European and non-European countries of the West are navigating different ships. It is important indeed that the various boats be steered in a coordinated manner and that collisions be avoided. There are other organizations working within their respective jurisdictions for the urgently needed harmonization, for instance the Paris based Organization of Economic Cooperation and Development (OECD) to which—and this is of special relevance—Japan, Australia, and New Zealand also belong.

Because my topic is the European context of the German-American partnership, I shall have to deal mainly with our cooperation in the framework of NATO in the field of security and common defense as well as with the relationship between the United States and Germany as the economically strongest member of the EEC. If I now leave aside—mainly for practical reasons—Japan (as well as Australia, New Zealand, and the Western European countries that belong neither to NATO nor to the EEC) this does not invalidate what I said before: The industrialized democracies as a whole—whether situated in North America, Western Europe, or in the Pacific—share common interests and values and, above all, their economic policies require careful coordination. Let me mention in this context the so-called trilateral concept, aimed at a more institutionalized relationship among the United States, Western Europe, and Japan.

Let's take a look now at the two areas in which American-

European cooperation is most vital for all concerned—defense and the economy, the two being obviously interlocked in various ways and having "political" implications—and consider the role of the Federal Republic of Germany in both of them.

This is not the place to enter into a detailed discussion of detente. It must and will go on. However, it will continue to be possible only on the basis of a strong defense posture supported by all members of the Alliance. There is no longer uncertainty about the extent of the Soviet armament effort in the recent past, especially as it pertains to Europe and to naval forces. Unilateral American force reductions in Europe are no longer seriously considered. The process of decreasing Western defense expenditures has more or less come to a halt on both sides of the Atlantic, but that does not exclude rationalization in certain areas. Not least, we should aim at strengthening NATO's conventional capabilities in order to compensate for the armament efforts in the East and to avoid increased dependence by the Alliance on nuclear weapons.

American-European defense and security cooperation takes place within NATO. It has preserved the strategic balance in Europe for the last three decades by maintaining a credible deterrence in which the United States is—for obvious reasons— primus inter pares.

All decisions concerning security require close coordination. They are made generally on a multilateral basis in Brussels. It is in Brussels that the United States also consults its allies about the SAL II negotiations.

And it is within the Alliance in Brussels, for instance, that the 15 NATO countries harmonize their views with respect to the CSCE—the Conference on Security and Cooperation in Europe—in which the Europeans have, for evident reasons, placed strong emphasis on the participation of the United States.

This multilateral cooperation in NATO time and again transcends the sphere of defense proper and extends to matters of foreign policy as such, the two areas being indeed very much intertwined anyhow. The 15 consult frequently on various matters of foreign policy, a process that sometimes creates procedural problems because the 9 EEC countries possess a foreign policy consultation mechanism of their own, the European political cooperation meetings. The CSCE has proved, however, that the two institutional frameworks can be interrelated successfully.

The strategic concept of the Bundeswehr is integrated into the strategy of NATO based on the political framework of the Alliance. The Federal Republic of Germany cooperates actively in all NATO bodies. Of the 13 European members, Germany has the strongest conventionally armed forces. The bulk of the Bundeswehr's combat elements is earmarked for NATO assignment. Germany's contribution to NATO is the second highest within the Alliance, both in absolute terms of defense expenditures and expenditures per capita, and is surpassed only by that of the United States.

As to the jointly financed NATO infrastructure projects, we are (with 26.4 percent) in first place, ahead of the United States (18.8 percent) and the United Kingdom (16.6 percent). (That is why it is so important that the force reductions aimed for in the Vienna talks on mutual balanced force reductions pertain to both pact systems in their entireties and not to individual member nations.)

All this seems plausible as the Federal Republic of Germany is the only NATO member that borders on the Warsaw Pact countries in the decisive central sector. We would be the first to be attacked and would face massive destruction. It is not by chance that 213,000 of the total of 317,000 American soldiers in Europe are stationed in Germany. Psychologically, too, we perceive the threat most strongly, not least because of the presence of Soviet troops in the GDR. I want to stress, however, that the NATO partners agree that considering the present state of weapons technology, all members of the Alliance are subject to the same threat, which has to be manifest in the individual defense efforts.

Let me return to what I emphasized before: the German-American partnership is sensible and feasible only in the framework and in the perspective of extended American-European cooperation. The geographic and power dimensions suggest this extension. Look, for instance, at the vital question of the American military presence in Europe. In the long run, America's interest in continuing this presence would weaken if it were not considered worthwhile for the protection of all or most partners of the Alliance. This is why we Germans must place so much emphasis on not only maintaining our own strength and stability but also on the maintenance by our European partners of their strength and stability. It is thus in our own interest to contribute to the realization of this goal. I shall come back to this point.

Of course, defense cooperation within the Alliance has also produced bilateral agreements in the area of German-American relations. I am thinking, among other things, of the training of German soldiers in the United States. You may not be aware of the fact that about 2,500 members of the Bundeswehr are trained annually in your country in courses lasting from two weeks to three years.

Let me also mention our cooperation in the armament field. In recent years we have bought American military equipment at the rate of 500 million dollars annually, which, of course, is much more than the United States has bought from us. This brings me to our bilateral cooperation in the development of a new battle tank. As you may know, the tanks built by both countries—the XM 1 and the Leopard II—are expected to contain a number of common components, an important step in the effort to achieve more armament efficiency within the Alliance.

Turning from the field of security to economics, it is relevant for German-American relations that the Federal Republic of

Germany is a member of the EEC, whereas the United States and six other NATO countries—Canada, Norway, Iceland, Greece, Turkey, and Portugal—do not belong to it. (The European countries, however, are tied to the Community by agreements of more or less intensive association or cooperation. On the other hand, Ireland, a non-NATO country, belongs to the EEC.) While defense cooperation between both our countries is performed within the same institutional framework (NATO), this does not apply to economics—apart from the regionally far-reaching OECD, having to some extent a consultative character, the International Energy Agency and the like. The European context of German-American partnership has, in this field, a different character already with regard to institutionalization.

As you know, the nine EEC countries—beyond the economic aims of the Rome treaties—do strive for the political unification of Western Europe. A step in this direction is their continuing effort to institute an overall economic and monetary policy for the Community, conceived in the early seventies, for instance, in the so-called Werner Plan, with the final objective of an economic and monetary union.

The Federal Republic of Germany has always supported this political goal of the EEC, and Western Europe's political unity continues to be a high priority for us Germans. It is true that the desired degree of progress in attaining this objective has not been made during years past and that the Community, mainly because of growing economic and social disparities among the partners, has been subject to critical developments that appeared to jeopardize the goals so far achieved. Slow progress, however, should not obscure the fact that the EEC long ago passed the point of no return.

Let me mention five developments as examples of the vitality of the Community and its objective of political unity, examples that appear to be even more remarkable because of the requirement of "digesting" the accession of Great Britain, Denmark, and Ireland in 1973: the freedom for medical doctors of all nine countries to practice within the Community; the Lomé convention of 1975 on cooperation with the developing countries of Africa, the Caribbean, and the Pacific; the decision to hold direct elections to the European Parliament; the inauguration of the European University in Florence, Italy; and the increasing foreign policy cooperation of the nine partners. Thus the Community continues to be a reality extending beyond common economic and trade policies, the latter being, however, for practical considerations, an essential element in European-American relations.

The dialogue with the United States on how to keep the Western world from sliding into a new recession will therefore be conducted from the German side with due consideration for the situations prevailing in the other EEC countries. This brings me to the so-called economic summit meetings that first took place in Rambouillet in November 1975 and in Puerto Rico in June 1976. These summits are attended by the "major nations" only—the United States, Japan, Germany, France, Great Britain, Canada (1976), and Italy—indicating that in multilateral economic relations the criterion of "weight" is definitely present and even of institutional relevance. In the past the five smaller EEC members had raised the question of their participation; however, the problem has been solved by the four major EEC nations' undertaking to represent the interests of the nine after consultation and coordination. It is of importance that as a result of regular attendance by Japan, the trilateral concept has now been realized in this field and at the summit level. The German-American partnership so far is not only taking place in a Western European transatlantic context but also in a trilateral one. This seems all the more significant because the summit conferences have also dealt with important economic problems arising from our relationships with the third world (raw materials, adjustment of debts, and so forth).

A word concerning the German position with regard to the world economic situation. The Germans are especially interested in it, because of all countries, the Federal Republic is exporting by far the highest percentage of its GNP (23 percent), as compared with 7 percent for the United States, and it is— in absolute terms—the most important world trade power after the United States. Therefore, our economy reacts more sensitively than does any other to international fluctuations. We welcome—let me mention it as an example—the 31 billion dollar economic stimulation program introduced by the Carter administration and anticipate that it will boost world-wide recovery. This program will have a positive impact on the European economies. Increased confidence in an American economy on the upswing will be even more important than the immediate expansion of international trade. Experience has taught us that the state of American business has a marked influence on the expectations of businessmen in Europe. There is the familiar saying that if America catches a cold, Europe will come down with the flu. This is true in a positive sense, too: If America recovers from its cold, then Europe has a much better chance of getting rid of the flu.

As far as Germany is concerned, the government has always pursued an active economic policy. It is in the process of shaping a medium term investment program that will influence favorably the business cycle. It may not be as far reaching as some would hope because our unemployment is now running at about 5.5 percent. Our success in controlling inflation—at present around 4 percent—has overshadowed the fact that the government has resorted to heavy deficit spending over the last three years to combat the economic slowdown. If we add the deficits of the federal and state governments to those of the municipalities, their total percentage of the GNP is considerably higher than in the United States.

Let me return to trade policy. It constitutes a "Community matter" for the nine EEC countries, and all responsibilities rest with the Commission in Brussels. In this sector there generally are no German-American but only European-American dealings. Decisions are made by the Community as such. The Commission maintains representation with diplomatic status in Washington. This EEC delegation deals with the State Department and other departments on questions pertaining to anti-dumping, countervailing duties, and the like, and the nine embassies simply assist wherever necessary. This coordinated system is also employed in important matters other than trade policy, e.g., for the procurement of enriched uranium.

It is in the area of trade policy that conflicting interests between the countries on the near and far sides of the Atlantic Ocean emerge most frequently. Although I have stressed the general identity of interests existing among the Western industrial democracies in reference to the Eastern bloc as well as the third and fourth worlds, this does not exclude conflicts of interests on certain less essential but often still quite important issues. Such conflicts develop in the private sphere among relatives, even between brothers and sisters, and certainly among the West Europeans, even EEC members, as well as between the United States and Europe. The differences grow out of a wide spectrum of domestic policies and social and economic conditions of the partner nations, their different histories, constitutions, geographic locations, and so forth. They exist, and we cannot shrug them off. However, we can make efforts to settle them in a solidary way, taking into account deep-rooted common interests.

Conflicts over trade policy also emerge from time to time in the area of European-American relations, which, as already mentioned, have been multilateralized; that is, they are dealt with by the EEC on the one hand and by the United States on the other—possibly within the scope of OECD and GATT. Remember the so-called chicken war and the difficulties arising from the export of other agricultural as well as industrial products from Europe to the United States and vice versa. In this context, it must be realized that Europeans and Americans have the same supply structure in many fields. During times of recession and resulting unemployment, such difficulties are accentuated, especially during election years. We have a number of issues on the agenda. However, Europeans and Americans agree in principle—and this consensus has been reiterated during the recent talks between your Vice President and EEC President Jenkins in Brussels—that a liberal trade policy, especially in regard to the developing countries, is a goal of mutual interest.

All things considered, we can say that with the readiness of each side to make compromises, success has so far been achieved in restricting the adverse effects of conflicting interests in the commercial and monetary sectors.

The trade balance between America and the EEC has always been in favor of the United States, which had a surplus in 1976 of 7.6 billion dollars. Bilateral trade between our two countries is more or less balanced right now, which means that each German spends more than three and a half times as much on American goods as each American on German goods.

Lacking is a generally binding concept on the part of the West covering the predominant issues of economic policies, for instance in the field of raw materials, in reference to the countries of the third and fourth worlds. Despite some encouraging progress, for example at the Conference on International Economic Cooperation, a great deal of important work remains. However, the positions of Germany and the United States in this complex area are quite close.

Before leaving the economic field, let me comment on America's approach toward the European unification process, a process, as I have pointed out, that will continue and that has a high priority in German policy. During the fifties and sixties the United States provided active support. It did so in the hope that a united and thus strengthened Europe would, in terms of a division of responsibilities, take some of the burden from its shoulders. A prerequisite of this support, of course, was and is that Europe would agree not to apply the power gained by unification against its Atlantic partner but rather would continue acting with it in a concerted manner. Germany—already as a consequence of its geographic location, the situation of Berlin, and its awareness of the importance of the American shield—has always stressed the need for a strong Atlantic orientation within the Community and the closest possible link of the nine with America. On this premise (which is above question), the Americans have been willing to advocate the process of unification. We are gratified to note that President Carter—in an interview before his election—assured the Europeans of his support, stating that a more unified, strong, prosperous, and dynamic Western Europe would be advantageous to the United States and that there are many fields in which even closer cooperation would be possible. Vice President Mondale unequivocally confirmed this attitude in Brussels.

The misunderstandings and tensions connected with the 1973 initiative of the "Year of Europe" have generally been settled. Nowadays relations are relaxed in the best sense of the word. The Atlantic relationship has become more balanced. More than ever before it is recognized as a partnership of giving and taking.

I have tried to demonstrate in two related fields—namely, defense and economic policies—that United States-German relations must be understood in the context of a larger American-European partnership and that these areas, each in a different way, are marked by a strong multilateral orientation. This, however, does not mean that bilateralism has become nonexistent. It is still present in a variety of fields: There are multiple areas not immediately related to security and economic policy. Think of the personal ties between our two peoples that became particularly evident during the Bicentennial. In the 1972 census not less than 25 million Americans professed their German origin—the second largest ethnic contingent—outnumbered only by those of "Anglo-Saxon origin," some 30 million. A recent poll in the Federal Republic showed that 69 percent of all Germans hold that the friendship with the United States is the most important one, the next country in this popularity test attaining only 17 percent. There were probably more Bicentennial celebrations in Germany than anywhere else in the world outside the United States.

Think, for instance, of the intense German-American cultural exchanges and of our scientific and technological cooperation. In the latter field, the Helios solar probes, one of the most ambitious international scientific projects, were developed in German-American cooperation. It would seem, however, that cooperation in space demonstrates the need for conducting projects of a certain size and scope in a still more extended framework, for example, the European-American space lab project in which Germany participates by bearing 53 percent of the cost. Remember also the numerous bilateral agreements between our two countries in such fields as double taxation, extradition, and environmental protection, among others, and the successful cooperation resulting therefrom.

Occasionally bilateral problems do emerge. Fortunately, this is not often the case. For some time we have had on the agenda our proposed delivery of an entire nuclear fuel cycle to Brazil. The restrictive approach of the administration toward reprocessing and the fast breeder in general will constitute a difficult problem for the United States-European relationship as a whole. Despite intensive consultations, agreement has not yet been achieved on all points. Further consultations will take place, hopefully leading eventually to a solution of this thorny and complicated matter.

Special bilateral arrangements exist even within the broader framework of the (wholly or partially) "multilateralized" American-European partnership, some, as we have seen, in the defense area. As far as the economy is concerned, think, for instance, of mutual direct investments. By the end of 1976 American investments in the German economy had reached approximately seven billion dollars. Some of the largest firms in Germany (Ford, Opel, IBM) are American owned. German investments in the United States amount to about 2 billion dollars. For many years capital moved along a one-way street from America to Europe. Now we see the street beginning to accommodate two-way traffic. Not only Volkswagen but other German companies are expected to invest in production facilities in the United States. However, there is little chance that their profits made here will approach the sums earned by American industry in Germany.

A country such as the Federal Republic of Germany that demonstrates economic and political "weight" as well as political and social stability (in our last general election, with a voting participation of 91 percent, 99.1 percent of the votes went to the three main democratic parties, whereas communists and the extreme right scored only 0.7 percent) is bound—and obliged—to play a particular role and to assume particular responsibilities. This role obviously gives a particular dimension to our bilateral relations with comparable countries (like France and Britain) and especially with the leading power of the West, the United States. This aspect was referred to when I mentioned the economic summit conferences in which not all but only the major Western countries participate. Obviously, President Carter could not phone his colleagues in all Western states in mid-January, only some of them. The recent trip of your Vice President—indeed highly welcome—signifies the close ties between the United States and its allies and the priority given to them by the Carter administration. The fact that Mr. Mondale visited the four major Western European countries (and Japan) as well as the NATO and EEC headquarters in Brussels reflects precisely the bilateral and multilateral character of the American-European partnership.

The fact that "Germany steps up"—to use the title phrase of a recent, significant article by Gerald Livingston in *Foreign Policy*—creates certain problems insofar as the political balance of Western Europe is concerned. This balance is an essential element in the process of European unification to which my country is strongly committed. We Germans must use much care and tact in asserting our new position so that old wounds are not torn open again. Germany's position is not always understood here. Some still think that the image of Germany as an "economic giant and political dwarf" holds true. I do not think so. In recent years we have made efforts—and it seems to me successfully—to shoulder a fair share of responsibility not only by our contributions to the joint defense effort but also by our economic sacrifices within the EEC for the sake of European unification (in 1975, for instance, we paid approximately 1.3 billion dollars more than we received, thus accounting for four-fifths of net transfers within the community) and in our endeavors to assist some of our European partners in overcoming their economic difficulties. Let me mention our 2 billion dollar loan to Italy in 1974 and our very substantial participation—23 percent as compared with 28 percent by the United States—in the recent IMF loan to Great Britain, a multilateral framework being deemed by us, for evident reasons, preferable. Last but not least: We have made considerable political sacrifices for the sake of detente and believe that thereby we have served the interests of the West in general.

In 1973, after having settled our basic relationship with Eastern Germany, we became a member of the United Nations. Since January 1977 we occupy a seat on the Security Council but only on a two-year basis, not permanently as in the case of the United States, Britain, and France. This indicates that economic importance does not automatically transform itself into political "clout." As to the latter, it should be added that the United States, Britain, and France are nuclear powers, that they exert particular rights in Berlin (this fact being of the greatest importance to us), and that Britain has special relationships within the Commonwealth and France with the French-speaking countries of Africa. These facts should not be forgotten in discussions about whether Germany still behaves as a "political

dwarf." As I said before, we do live up to the political responsibilities imposed by our "weight," and we endeavor to exercise
them in solidarity with our European and American allies. We
do it perhaps in an unspectacular way and sometimes in low
key, knowing that this approach is in the overall interest of
the West.

Let me conclude by quoting from Chancellor Schmidt's policy
statement before the Bundestag on December 16, 1976, "A
relationship of mutual confidence never before known has
developed between the United States and the Federal Republic
of Germany," and from Vice President Mondale's press conference a week ago: "Relations with Germany are as good as
they could possibly be." And let me add that the quality of
German-American relations essentially depends on the state
of relations between the United States and Western Europe.
They are determined by a partnership based on common values
and interlocked interests, and they are, therefore, very good.
Nobody knows better than we Germans that this is vital in
the proper sense of the term. Consequently, we shall do everything in our power to maintain and strengthen the close Atlantic
partnership and thus contribute to peace and stability.

2

GERMANY AND
THE ALLIANCE

Catherine McArdle Kelleher

1. *Introduction*

In 1977 the Federal Republic is the second state of the Western
alliance. Thirty years after its defeat and division, it ranks
second only to the United States on every major dimension of
state power except nuclear weapons capability. Its preeminence
in Europe is disputed only at the margins. And although official
German style is often muted in recognition of past events and
present fears, Bonn now exercises significant influence, especially in the economic sector throughout the developed world.

In many respects Germany's reemergence as a major power
represents the fulfillment of earlier alliance plans. From its in-
ception NATO, and especially the United States, sought to
harness a rebuilding Western Germany against the East.[1] German
forces, German territory, German expenditures—all were needed
for Western defense. The price was full German political re-

habilitation, however grudgingly given by France, Britain or the United States. Indeed, by the mid–1960s the "Bonn connection" was clearly the successor to the special relationship that Washington had once had with a waning Britain and had denied to a Gaullist France.

Similarly, the Federal Republic can view its new status as proving the success of Adenauer's bargain of necessity.[2] Alignment with the West brought not only security, "equality," and internal confidence and stability, but it also allowed greater legitimacy for German foreign policy maneuvers in the sixties and seventies—an ostpolitik based on a secure westpolitik, a Europe relancée in a continuing Atlantic framework.

But this success is not without drawbacks from the perspective of either Americans or Germans. Washington has spent much of the past decade in self-absorption—over Vietnam, domestic unrest, economic downturn, and strategic accommodation with the Soviet Union. Its leadership, and therefore the alliance as a whole, has faltered, characterized as often by a policy of benign neglect as by focused initiatives or responses to the broader questions of defense in an era of detente. The United States has thus viewed Germany as a junior partner able (if not very willing) to shoulder some of the heavier burdens within the alliance and throughout the global economic system.

For the Federal Republic the question of the appropriate German role is equally significant but requires a quite different definition. How can the Federal Republic capitalize on its emerging position as first among the middle powers (not an incipient global actor) to serve all of its national interests?[3] Its military dependency on the United States will remain significant; but unlike the 1950s and 1960s this dependency no longer guarantees Bonn's support for all NATO or American policies or even grudging acceptance of former "let the Germans pay" formulas. How much convergence and divergence can be tolerable within the German–American alliance, the critical element left in a somewhat stagnating Atlantic alliance. And how must or can the alliance itself change to accommodate (or perhaps offset) the interests of a more powerful, self-assured Germany?

In this brief essay I can only attempt to survey these critical questions, not suggest the answers that Bonn, Washington, and Brussels will eventually offer. The essay will turn first to a brief review of the evolution of Germany's role, the critical phases of alliance development that have both shaped and constrained present options. A second focus will be on outstanding issues on which German positions are as symptomatic of long-range policies as they are of current German–American irritations. A final section will suggest a range of scenarios that may define both future German policies and the evolution of NATO itself.

II.   *Germany in NATO: the Evolution of an Essential Actor*

An epigrammatic summary of Germany's evolution within the alliance over the past two decades could be "from object to secundus in pares in only twenty years." Little has happened secretly; the maturation of German political sensibilities was heralded by Germany's economic and military capabilities, long superior to its European allies. Germany has indeed benefited directly from their weaknesses—the political liabilities of an economically troubled Britain and those of a France struggling first to achieve and then to mitigate the Gaullist challenge of global grandeur.

The argument here is not simply that the past is a prologue or that present policies grow out of perceptions of past constraints. Rather it is that the evolution of German influence is inextricably linked with the evolution of the NATO alliance and the role of the United States within it. Accordingly, this review will divide the familiar postwar period into four critical phases, treating in turn: 1) the state of the alliance itself; 2) the developing German role, particularly vis-à-vis the United States; 3) the impact of domestic political factors on Germany's definition of its role in the alliance, and 4) the present state of affairs within the alliance.

A. *Phase I. West Germany as Object*

In what now appears to have been the critical years of NATO's formation, 1949 to 1955, Germany's primary role was that of the object of alliance actions and planning. At stake were not only the securing of West German territory and resources but also the erection of barriers against possible future German misbehavior. Even at the height of the perception of a direct Soviet threat, Europeans preferred a European Defense Community to German membership in NATO. A rearmed Germany so desired by the United States must be subject to continuous, discriminating European control to ensure in the words of a popular witticism, "a Germany strong enough to frighten the Russians but not the French." Years of negotiation and the ultimate failure of the EDC softened but hardly reduced European fears and the resolve of NATO members (especially Britain and France) to hold fast to the national roles and responsibilities secured in the initial organizational stages (e.g., the Standing Group, the command structure, Council procedures).

Adenauer's strategy throughout this period was simple and consistent: 1) inextricable involvement with the West; 2) acceptance of the proffered rearmament bargain and rhetorical "equality" in the hope of future payoffs, and 3) primary reliance on the American connection to secure German interests. His own preference clearly was for a smaller, integrated European entity, one perhaps without extensive military capability or organization. But his fears of communist expansion, of congressional moods, and of the political volatility of his own people made him believe an Atlantic security framework was critical, however costly in the short term to European unity.

Adenauer's views were not shared by some in his own coalition and clearly not by the opposition Social Democrats, massively opposed in descending order to rearmament, operational inequality, and an Atlantic grouping. The resulting parliamentary and electoral battles were among the most emotional in German history; for many the issue was the fate of the German nation. The chancellor shrewdly traded on this turmoil, making the alliance with the West the touchstone of his drive to secure his domestic leadership. He also used domestic unrest to convince his Western negotiating partners that only he and the concessions that he demanded stood between them and a neutral (or a revanchist) Germany.

B. *Phase II: Germany—the Increasingly Critical Member*

In the decade that followed, 1955 to 1965, the Federal Republic became an increasingly critical alliance member in both military and political terms. The slowly building Bundeswehr soon outnumbered either the British or the French ground contingent and clearly bore a "made in the U.S.A." stamp. With a succession of Berlin crises to shake any remaining faith in the doctrine of massive retaliation and the American shift to a flexible response strategy, the significance of these German forces increased. German political influence was still limited and largely dependent on the strength of the German–American link, less strong than it was in the days of automatic Dulles–Adenauer understanding. Yet Bonn weathered a number of major disagreements with Washington—over strategy, diplomacy vis-à-vis the East, Franco–German friendship, and nuclear control sharing. It remained Washington's strongest and most cooperative European ally.

Bonn's role within NATO reflected both growing recognition of the increasingly important German contribution and increasing German willingness to press for full alliance rights. Formal and informal coalitions with the French over Berlin and a European "force" increased German leverage in Washington: pressure for a broader participation in alliance nuclear control led to a series of responses—the Norstad Plan, the multilateral nuclear force, and the Nuclear Planning Group. Yet this increasing self-confidence was at least matched by German concern about American threats of withdrawal from Europe and potential Soviet–American hegemonic agreement on Germany's permanent division and constraint.

Domestic German attitudes toward NATO reflected a related ambivalence. Politically, allegiance to NATO and a credible stance vis-à-vis Washington were the *sine qua non* of electoral success, as the SPD "conversion" of the late 1950s attested. Yet it was also increasingly apparent to the small, concerned elite that NATO strategy and forces could result in the dreaded loss and reconquest of substantial amounts of German territory, probably with tactical nuclear use. An increasingly bitter Adenauer and the few German Gaullists argued that it was not at all clear that German and American interests in war or at peace, in alliance nuclear control and in economic burden sharing, were convergent or congruent.

C. *Phase III: Germany Emerges; NATO Declines*

The period 1966 through 1973–1974 led perhaps to the clearest definition of Germany's alliance role. On the one hand, this definition meant the final recognition of German preeminence—in the NATO reorganization that followed French withdrawal, in the obvious pattern of Washington's communications and consultations with the alliance. On the other, it meant greater German responsibilities in an increasingly fragmented Western camp—the United States absorbed in Vietnam and in Soviet–American relations; the increasing economic weakness of both Britain and France; the general Western disarray in an era of perceived detente; and of pervasive domestic agitation and unrest. The NATO force structure itself showed signs of severe strain, a lowering of capabilities, and increased pressures for further cuts, with mutual balanced force reductions or without.

Germany's role was that of the relatively stable, cool partner, critical of United States mistakes but loyally shouldering its responsibilities despite major domestic pressures. In part, this role represented the new, official consensus, the consolidation of the foreign policy commitment that the grand coalition signaled. But it was also a relatively safe base from which Brandt could launch the initiatives of ostpolitik, the efforts to unfreeze relations with the East. Internal and external critics were assured of Germany's continuing commitment to the West; the parallel actions of the United States and France lent greater legitimacy.

Perhaps the only flashpoints were in the highly polarized responses of a troubled West German population. Counter-culture demonstrations, student political demands, the limited but perceptible crises of continuing inflation—all led to greater introspection and revealed deep societal cleavages. The young saw the alliance as largely irrelevant, if not anachronistic, and the possibility of a major war virtually nonexistent. Older generations and more conservative groups saw detente as another stimulus to American withdrawal and the eventual Finlandization of Europe under Soviet pressure. Normalization of ties with the East and greater social welfare programs would not substitute for an American security guarantee or for an assured channel into the American decision-making process—both provided at a minimum through a strong NATO.

D. *Phase IV: the Present Condition*

It is difficult to pinpoint a particular point at which the Federal Republic entered the present phase, emerging as a more independent ally both within NATO and in extra-Atlantic forums. A number of specific events have been cited: the German refusal to permit unauthorized American overflights during the 1973 Middle East war; Germany's steadfast rejection of American demands for reevaluation during the recurring monetary crises; German insistence on the appropriateness of the German–Brazilian nuclear equipment agreement. The critical point is that particularly under Chancellor Schmidt, Germany's emergence as something more than America's primary ally is complete. The difference is in a new sense of national self-confidence, a new tone of voice that insists that NATO must be "a two-way street." The Washington connection is still of primary importance, and security dependence is as great as ever, leaving much of the leverage in the relationship still on the American side. But Bonn demands new respect for its alliance contributions, new consideration for its economic convictions, and greater American tolerance for its determination neither to accept excessive alliance burdens nor to let Atlantic needs determine all of its foreign policy choices.

The costs involved in this role definition have so far seemed manageable to Germany and the alliance. German willingness to accept major, selected burdens has helped; Bonn is now the daily banker for Italy and Britain and has provided critical financial support to others for short periods. Acting as a major socialist leader, Schmidt has taken a major role in promoting Iberian stability and in guiding constructive north–south dialogue. Within the alliance itself the Federal Republic has taken the lead in increasing its defense expenditures, reorganizing its reserve capability, and reviving MBFR consultations. Nonetheless, the degree of disagreement and mutual irritation, especially in the Washington–Bonn channel, has at times resembled the level of the Adenauer–Kennedy disputes.

Popular disagreement with the Schmidt stance is muted or lost among the dominant economic and social concerns of the moment. The perception of a new Soviet military buildup is widespread and worrisome but once again is not generally viewed as justifying a major counter program that would constrain needed social welfare improvements. A CDU–CSU victory in the next election would perhaps mean greater defense efforts and more enthusiasm for alliance relations but would probably involve few major policy shifts on specific issues.

III. *Present Issues*

A. *Short-Range Disputes*

In many respects current issues in the alliance reflect the impact of a more independent and self-confident Germany. Most of the issues are short-range disputes, the latest manifestations of basic problems that have concerned NATO at least since the mid-1950s.[4] In some respects, too, German concerns are not new—as before, they are the clear results of the FRG's position as the front line of defense, of its traditional caution vis-à-vis negotiation with the Russians, and of the pervasive German belief that domestic prosperity and stability are as important to national security as are increased defense expenditures. The Federal Republic presses its claims with greater force and skill, without the shrillness and anxiety of the past. Moreover, Bonn is less content to have Washington take all the initiatives or to wait for France to shoulder the burden of complaining about American policies or practices.

Four specific issues serve to delineate the range of disagreement and dispute. They neither approach in seriousness past points of alliance crises (as over nuclear sharing) nor do they threaten alliance cohesion or the substantial measure of present cooperation. Yet they represent continuing irritations and are to a degree symptomatic of larger conflicts.

1. *The "neutron bomb" dispute*

The current dispute involves an American decision to develop and deploy a new weapons technology for central front defense. American military and political leaders argue that the eventual deployment of neutron bombs largely on West German soil will give NATO a credible answer to the question of how to use tactical nuclear weapons to offset the conventional superiority of an attack from the East. These weapons, they predict, would leave the West German battlefield with substantially less radiological contamination and property destruction than would the tactical nuclear weapons now in place, thus ensuring a greater chance of swift recovery of lost territory. Critics, who include several West German political leaders, suggest that such weapons will greatly enhance the probability of rapid nuclear use because they blur the critical conventional-nuclear threshold for *both* sides and promise territorial gain or defense at the cost of "only" military and civilian lives.

Viewed from a broader perspective, however, the issue is only the latest questioning of the rights of American decision makers to set the direction of Western defense and therefore determine the risks under which Europeans live. In the past the German flurry was intense but brief—whether the subject was the diffusion of tactical weapons, the stationing of medium-range missiles, the limitation on missiles and weapons sold to the Europeans, or the right of the Europeans to veto the use of weapons launched from or stored on their soil. American preferences generally prevailed then and may continue to do so, if only because American forces constitute such a large component of central front capability (35 percent) as well as set the standard for "equality." But Bonn is now pressing hard for greater consultation at the early stages of the decision process and in the extreme case for the right to challenge particular deployments in Germany. The eventual compromise will cost Washington more than in the past and may involve new guidelines for future decisions.

2. *The question of defense expenditures*

The issue of higher German defense expenditures is less a single dispute than several crosscutting conflicts. The specific topics vary—licensed European production of specific weapon systems, a NATO AWACS system, reinforcement of northern flank capabilities, more reserve manpower. In each case, however, the argument reduces to three familiar assertions: 1) It is on German territory that the first defense will occur; 2) the German economy is the strongest in Europe; and 3) the West Germans still must bear—as junior partners or former enemies—the residual burden.

The claims are not new, nor are the proposed or actual divisions of shares (for example, the German share in MLF or the F-104 program versus that in the AWACS arrangement or the initial MRCA project). What is noteworthy is the German willingness to say no or to demand explicit tradeoffs and the often equally explicit American pressure for an "appropriate" German role. Again, in many cases the German share may well be greater than Bonn considers appropriate, and American interests often will be served. But as Schmidt's Bundestag speech in December 1976 made dramatically clear, this will not characterize all or even most cases; it will not occur without a major German role in relevant decision making; and it cannot involve a disproportionate sacrifice of the social and economic welfare benefits available to West German citizens.

3. Standardization: the demand for the two-way street

A related issue obviously is the dispute over standardization, an issue of particular significance for the Germans. In part because of the dreams of former Defense Minister Strauss for recovering lost ground in weapons technology, in part as a political necessity, the FRG has consistently supported NATO production and multinational purchase. It has participated in every major alliance effort and in many bilateral projects (especially with France) as well. It has thereby suffered repeated losses—of resources, as in the F-104 Starfighter fiasco, of political face, as in the Main Battle tank project and in the recent American rejection of the Leopard tank.

The German position on standardization is similar to that on defense expenditures but with a peculiarly European flavor. The burden of standardization practices, Bonn has argued, now falls on the United States, which can no longer claim either exclusive technological preeminence or extra-Atlantic requirements. The United States must therefore either buy from European production or allow its major European allies to build consortia (as though the Eurogroup) that will maximize their returns, financially and technologically. Without such efforts Washington must face growing European and national resistance to all arms sales and reequipment pressures.

4. *The Future of MBFR*

Bonn's concern with the progress of alliance efforts on MBFR springs from several sources. At the simplest level, criticisms of the talks, whether from a Brandt or a Dregger, reveal continuing German ambivalence about any Western dealings with the Russians, even those emphasized in ostpolitik. Perhaps the stronger strand evokes an image of a poorly coordinated West giving away too much to the wily, patient Russians who need only wait. Perhaps the greatest danger would be an assured Soviet voice in and therefore control over Western security affairs—in numbers of force, types of equipment, or whatever. But there is also the sense that the West has not pushed the East hard enough to negotiate on its terms and on a timetable appropriate to its decision-making needs.

A comparatively new theme is Bonn's explicit impatience with the American decision-making process. It was largely due to German pressure that NATO consultations and positions have played such a significant role in the MBFR process, a role that has generally proved satisfactory despite the lack of progress.[5] But many of these gains have been vitiated by the seeming impermeability and indecisiveness of intra-Washington debates and bargaining. There have been recent improvements, but many in Bonn talk of the need for a more assured allied channel and an American commitment to broader negotiating interests and timetables.

B. *Long-Range Issues*

It is important to repeat that none of these four disputes will undermine NATO's existence in the short run or the general stability of the German–American connection. The alliance will survive as long as the United States finds it compatible with its security interests and the Europeans find it a useful lever over American policies. And Washington's need for a "second ally" and Bonn's interest in a cooperative superpower ally and guarantor seem hardly likely to diminish.

What is critical is that each of these disputes turns in some degree on an appropriate new balance between Germany and the United States not only within the alliance but also outside it. How much of its decision-making independence is the United States willing to give up and under what conditions? What impact will this decision have on popular and congressional interpretations of the alliance guarantee? How much responsibility and policy initiative is the Federal Republic willing or able to assume? And at what risk in terms of the future of the German nation and of domestic political stability?

Over the past decade American decision makers have expressed intermittent preferences for two different German roles.[6] Broadly sketched, the first would require that Bonn take the explicit role of Washington's European partner, the other NATO "pole," the synthesizer, coordinator, and if necessary, the makeweight of European alliance commitments and contributions. The United States would continue its force contributions in the short run and would remain the leader. But it would emphasize its responsibilities for securing the wider framework of Western security as set forth in the Nixon Doctrine. This would include the security of oil resources, the stability of the Middle East, the forging of economic ties to emerging regional middle powers, the keeping of the broad balance in Asia as well as the maintenance of strategic parity with the Soviet Union. How the reformed Eurogroup under Bonn's leadership would function would be left to time, the progress of Franco–British–German cooperation, and Bonn's skill and opportunity. But Bonn would be assured of major decision-making influence in Washington and fundamental American support for its foreign policy efforts outside the alliance. There will be divergences in specific interests and areas but not in overall goals, especially within the Atlantic area. And the division of labor presumably would lower the political and economic burdens of both states.

The second is an even more ambitious scheme: the adoption of "bigemony," reflecting the combined predominance of the two states in international economic affairs. This relationship would not only ensure more favorable, effective action vis-à-vis the continuing international monetary crises, the critical question of financing international trade flows, and the problems of creating a new international order more responsive to the south, but it would also provide a broad global role for an increasingly active, assured Federal Republic without posing a direct threat to the existing European balance, East and West. Present economic and political constraints, although worrisome in the short run, would be gradually transformed along with temporary competitive frictions between the United States and Germany on trade, monetary policy, and technology transfers.

Bonn, particularly under Chancellor Schmidt, has reacted to these broad suggestions as either illusionary or totally beyond West Germany's national scope. Schmidt has been quick to emphasize present West German economic difficulties, its continuing political vulnerability, and its unwillingness as well as its inability to attempt activism where others will not follow. The development of a different German international role will be a slow process, one building on quiet diplomacy and German preferences for mediation and short-run involvements beyond its basic Atlantic and European commitments. Moreover, Germany's emergence as a more independent actor does not change its need for a fully unfolded American nuclear umbrella or for the United States fundamental trusteeship over the German nation.

Many of Schmidt's arguments may simply represent the expression of good instead of real reasons. His administration enjoys too narrow a margin for bold foreign policy initiatives, however attractive they may superficially appear. The political weaknesses and liabilities of most other European states are at least as apparent, and there is considerable uncertainty about the implications of even minimal leftist electoral victories in France, in Italy, and in Spain. Schmidt and the apparent CDU leadership find the international status quo quite tolerable, particularly given domestic economic woes. This position, after all, represents a new consensus and the fruits of a hard-won fight.

IV.   *Future Possibilities*

However well Schmidt's words may express the present German consensus, the question of future German objectives to be sought with increased national capabilities remains open. Much will depend on the evolution of German–American relations particularly now under the more activist, more European oriented Carter administration. A second factor may be the growing importance of a German right wing in domestic politics, one attracted less to Strauss and general conservatism than to policies and roles, domestic and international, that express German national aspirations and attainments.[7]

But of at least some interest are international developments that may force choices or the recognition of role constraints long before either Bonn or Washington wishes to face them. A range of probable scenarios could include:

1. A dramatic breakdown in Soviet–American detente in which the recent Soviet military buildup is seen to pose an

overwhelming threat to European security (for example, a "quick win" war with little or no warning). Only the United States and the Federal Republic are, however, willing and able to respond.

2. A continuing European economic and political crisis that both brings further stagnation to the alliance as a whole and ensures the electoral triumph of an explicitly anti-German left coalition in France and perhaps Italy and an anti-German Conservative majority in Britain.

3. A Polish crisis precipitates Soviet intervention and major East German unrest, resulting in a breakdown of European detente and MBFR.

4. A truncation of NATO through the a) the withdrawal/ expulsion of Greece and Turkey or b) the gradual attenuation of northern flank ties under conditions of broad Soviet–American cooperation and direct Soviet pressure or c) the effective withdrawal of several smaller European states.

These four scenarios hardly exhaust the list or suggest all of the factors that in various combinations could serve as catalysts for ending the international status quo.[8] But they do highlight the critical significance of the present balance in the German–American relationship. All that would be needed would be 1) a shift in America's international position, particularly vis-à-vis the Soviet Union and 2) a shift that would produce Adenauer's nightmare: Soviet–American hegemony, NATO in disarray, and Bonn isolated within Western Europe.

It is highly probable that the Federal Republic will have the time to develop a new role without undue pressure. As Gerry Livingston has argued, there is much that the United States can do to facilitate and participate in the process. But this development will at a minimum require a rethinking of Germany's NATO bargain in Washington as well as in Bonn. And that alone portends a new, perhaps more painfully achieved division of NATO's political, economic, and military labor.

NOTES

The author thanks Alan Levy for his aid in the preparation of this essay.

1. See Robert McGeehan, *The German Rearmament Question* (Urbana: the University of Illinois Press, 1971).

2. For a more detailed development of this argument see Catherine M. Kelleher, *Germany and the Politics of Nuclear Weapons* (New York: Columbia University Press, 1975).

3. Two somewhat different views are Gerald Livingston's "Germany Steps Up," *Foreign Policy,* no. 22, Spring 1976, pp. 114 ff., and Gebhard Schweigler, "A New Political Giant? West German Foreign Policy in the 1970s," *The World Today,* April 1975, pp. 134–140.

4. For background see Kelleher *op. cit.,* Roger Morgan, *The United States and West Germany, 1945–1973* (London: Oxford, 1974), and Warner R. Schilling, William T. R. Fox, Catherine M. Kelleher, and Donald J. Puchala, *American Arms and a Changing Europe* (New York: Columbia University Press, 1973).

5. See Christoph Bertram "The Politics of MBFR" in *The World Today,* January 1973, pp. 1–7, and John Newhouse "Western Europe: Stuck Fast" in *Foreign Affairs,* January 1973, pp. 353–366.

6. A critical source here is Peter J. Katzenstein's "Die Stellung der Bundesrepublik Deutschland in der amerikanischen Aussenpolitik: Drehscheibe, Anker, oder Makler" in *Europa-Archiv,* no. 11, June 10, 1976, pp. 347–356, from his longer chapter of the same title in Richard Rosecrance's edited volume, *America as an Ordinary Country* (Ithaca: Cornell University Press, 1976).

7. A third factor, of course, would be a major positive shift in the intensity and orientation of France's role in the alliance and in Europe. One who argues this will not happen is Jean Klein in his "France, Nato and European Security" in *International Security* vol. 1, no. 3 (1976), pp. 21–41.

8. A more systematic presentation of possible European futures is contained in Schilling *et al., op. cit.,* Chapter IV.

FOREIGN POLICY IN GERMANY: IDEOLOGICAL AND POLITICAL ASPECTS OF INTRA-GERMAN RELATIONS

Peter C. Ludz

1. *A Point of Departure*

ANY ANALYSIS OF THE ideological and political dimensions in the future development of intra-German relations will have to assume a series of factors as "constant":

(a) No serious deterioration in East-West relations will occur in the foreseeable future. A stable Europe is needed by the United States and the USSR—as much as by the FRG and the GDR. Although weakened, it may be assumed that detente will continue. Such an assumption appears to be valid even though there is doubt about or opposition to the concept of detente.

(b) The FRG and the GDR will continue to form the focal point of East-West confrontation and rivalry in Europe.

(c) A wide spectrum of opinions relating to the "German question" has developed in Western Europe since political and ideological relations between the two German states have become increasingly complex. This spectrum ranges from pragmatic attitudes concerned with what is relevant to attitudes based on the principle of friend-foe polarization.

(d) Numerous opinion polls have testified to the fact that over the long run there is in the FRG declining interest, especially by large segments of youth, in the issues of intra-German relations and German reunification. In the GDR, on the other hand, interest in these matters remains strong.

(e) The FRG has worldwide obligations. It has to assume greater international responsibilities. For these reasons the German question now ranks lower on the FRG's governmental roster than it did formerly. To a much lesser degree this is also true for the GDR.

2. *The Current Situation of Intra-German Relations*

Before the conclusion of the "Basic Treaty on Relations Between the Federal Republic of Germany and the German Democratic Republic," intra-German relations had unquestionably intensified in many areas despite altered conditions. After the treaty went into effect (on June 21, 1973), a number of agreements, accords, protocols, and arrangements were signed. Among them:

—arrangements covering working possibilities for East German journalists in Bonn and West German journalists in East Berlin;

—accords concerning emergencies in border areas;

—a protocol on the establishment of permanent representations between the government of the FRG and the government of the GDR, which on June 20, 1974, led to the assumption of activities by representatives in East Berlin and Bonn;

—accords on the transfer of bank balances in certain cases and on the transfer of alimony payments;

—a health agreement;

—an accord concerning the Luebeck Bay, regulating fishing rights and defining the boundary of the coastal waters;

—accords on the development of access roads to West Berlin and on the lump sum to be paid for transit;

—an agreement on postal services and telecommunications;

—an accord concerning the mining of soft coal deposits in the borderland at Helmstedt/Harbke.[1]

Furthermore, the three standing commissions (the Border Commission, the Transit Commission, and Traffic Commission) authorized to resolve unsettled treaty problems and controversies have been continuing their work.

However, concerning other matters the respective FRG and GDR delegations have been unable to reach agreements—although the resolution of these matters had been provided for in the Basic Treaty. The state of negotiations on these ideologically loaded matters varies:

A legal aid agreement is not in sight, despite more or less regular negotiations. Among other things, the GDR insists that the FRG recognize GDR citizenship. Up to now the 1973 decision of the Federal Constitutional Court has prevented the FRG from complying with this demand.

The conclusion of a cultural agreement has been delayed mainly because of the GDR's demand for the return of cultural objects now in the custody of the Prussian Cultural Foundation in West Germany. This demand implies massive claims to an ideological monopoly: The GDR, as the "socialist German nation-state," regards itself as the legitimate custodian of the cultural heritage of Germany. Furthermore, it has thus far rejected the inclusion of West Berlin in such an agreement.

Nor is there any end in sight for the—presumably—greatly advanced negotiations on scientific-technical cooperation. Up to now the two states have not agreed on the meaning of the concept of science on which the agreement should be based. Despite the general approval in the Final Act of Helsinki of the Ten Principles and of specific areas of science for which cooperation appears meaningful, the SED leadership evidently has no clear idea of how the GDR can best handle "the expedient implementation and improvement in organization, including programs, of international visits of scientists and specialists" as well as "the exchange and dissemination of scientific and technological information among the parties interested in scientific and technological research and cooperation."[2] Furthermore, the GDR has been trying to inject general political principles into the science agreement. Finally, following the example of the FRG-USSR agreement, the inclusion of West Berlin causes difficulties that are still unresolved. (If the FRG were to make further economic concessions, the GDR would probably be inclined to conclude a treaty on scientific-technical cooperation.)

Nor is it likely that negotiations concerning environmental protection will be resolved in the foreseeable future. The GDR not only rejects the inclusion of West Berlin, it also opposes—partly for reasons of cost—the environmental protection measures that the FRG government deems necessary.

The sequence in which these unsettled issues earmarked for subsequent negotiations within the Basic Treaty is listed reflects various degrees of political difficulty encountered in the search for solutions. This suggests in the event that a legal aid agreement can be reached, other negotiations still pending may also lead to satisfactory conclusions.

In addition to the intra-German activities that fall within the framework of the Quadripartite Agreement on Berlin and the Basic Treaty, a special point must be made of IDH (*Innerdeutscher Handel,* that is, intra-German trade). In 1975 IDH reached a total figure of DM 7.4 billion (from the GDR to the FRG: DM 3.4 billion; from the FRG to the GDR: DM 4 billion). The most recent figures show that in 1977 a total volume of DM 8.4 billion may be achieved.

It is no secret that the GDR would like to expand its economic relations with the FRG. This expansion could be accomplished through a broader security pledge (spring 1977: DM 2.3 billion) by the Federal government for deliveries from the GDR to the

FRG. Moreover, the GDR is attempting in various ways to get badly needed Western exchange or credits (Eurodollars).

Intra-German relations are thus proceeding at various levels. (Follow-up government negotiations on agreements and IDH have already been mentioned.) In addition, there are relations at the level of nongovernmental organizations (for example, German Labor Union Federation–Free German Labor Union Federation; German Sports Association–German Gymnastics and Sports Federation).

Conflicts at the party level are also important factors in intra-German relations. One must certainly regard as highly relevant to current intra-German relations the noticeable sparks of rivalry between the SPD and the SED arising from the framework of the European communist and socialist movements;[3] the role of the SPD in the FRG and in the "socialist international;" the activities of the SED controlled DKP; as well as the ideological-political stand on the issues of socialism and communism taken by all parties represented in the Bundestag.

In the end perhaps the most important aspect of the present intra-German scene may well be personal encounters between the people of both German states that have been facilitated in the course of the new ostpolitik through the negotiated relaxation of travel restrictions. Such meetings, and there are millions, are affecting the ideological-political dimension of intra-German relations, although their influence cannot as yet be precisely assessed. Nevertheless, influences come into play through the mere fact that people in Germany realize the differences between the two states and societies on German soil.

These various intra-German relations do exist in spite of strong ideological reservations in the West and what amounts to ideological-political antagonism in the GDR. It ought to be mentioned that in the actual negotiations the FRG expresses rather too few ideological reservations, whereas the negotiating postures of the GDR delegations, at least for the time being, are ideologically loaded.

3. *Ideological Tensions between the Two German States*

Ideological tensions are part and parcel of political relations. No analysis can possibly sort them all out, nor would such an attempt seem sensible in the given context.

There are "global," "regional," and "local" dimensions of current ideological-political relations. The political and economic membership that the FRG holds in the Western alliance stems from sharing political, military, and economic policy and ultimately from fundamental political-ideological convictions. The grounding of the GDR in the East bloc, is based on commonly held Marxist-Leninist ideas. We shall not go into detail at this point about the fundamental ideological tensions that result from the global conflict between West and East. Only one basic fact need be mentioned: The political elites in the FRG and the GDR view one another as "negative reference groups" in all conceivable sets of arguments, be they military-strategic, political-psychological, political-ethical and so on. This fact implies that all of one's own attitudes and actions are anticipated as positive and those of the other side as negative.[4] This negative field of reference is one of the reasons why the FRG has maintained a stable domestic policy and the SED leadership, in insisting on its own legitimacy, has a need to see the FRG as the "class enemy."

In the present context we are concerned with particular aspects of ideological-political relations and ties, with "regional" aspects that have come into prominence particularly since 1973. It must be admitted, of course, that the concept of nation combines global and regional dimensions. It must be pointed out further that even the term "intra-German relations" carries ideological implications. Consistent with the identity theory maintained from 1949 to 1969 by the FRG (which, in terms of international law, implies an identity between the FRG and the German Reich in its 1937 boundaries), the FRG views the GDR as nonforeign and since the signing of the Basic Treaty, simultaneously as a foreign country, the latter insofar as the FRG recognizes the GDR as an equal, sovereign, second German state on German soil.[5] The GDR has maintained since the early seventies that the FRG is a "foreign country," a thesis that it had previously denied.[6] Thus East German official terminology does not use the term "intra-German." Rather relations with West Germany are regarded and designated as "foreign" relations.

The Basic Treaty skirted fundamental ideological reservations, especially those pertaining to the unity of Germany and the question of one German nation. The FRG merely made a record of them in its "Letter on German Unity," which the GDR acknowledged as a document relevant to the treaty. One of the consequences of that evasion is that ideological issues now arise more often in specific forms. Among those issues burdened by ideological antagonisms that are likely to make them unresolvable, the following are most topical: (1) the problem of citizenship;[7] (2) the claim of each state to be the legitimate representative of the spiritual-cultural heritage of Germany; (3) clashing outlooks on policies designed to cope with the sociopolitical problems of the modern (educational) welfare state; and (4) different views on the meaning of "science."

The first three problems shall serve as points of departure for the following considerations. We shall not deal here with the debate about science and science policy, important though it may be for future intra-German relations, because it can add nothing to the understanding of our basic theme.

4. A Methodological Digression

The subject matter under discussion is thus a small and relatively clearly definable segment of political-ideological realities as they concern relations between the two German states today and in the near future.

The term intra-German relations is deliberately given a relatively narrow meaning here in view of the fact that we are limiting it more or less to government contacts and the ideological response that such contacts evoke. This term excludes important aspects of intra-German relations, such as contacts among associations, party disputes, and personal encounters between people of the two states.

The term ideology will hereafter be used fairly loosely as it relates to practical affairs. Without attempting to use an accurate and, of necessity, complicated definition of the concept of ideology, a few characteristics must be pointed out that in the ongoing social science debate (insofar as it abides by the rules of critical rationalism) usually are relegated to the phenomenon of "ideology."[8] There are five characteristics that within political realities, of course, do not always appear in their ideal types or in purity: A dichotomous scheme of interpretation (for example, the concept of totalitarianism on the one hand and the doctrine of class struggle on the other); an absolutist claim to truth (for example "socialist triumphs"); a monopoly on cognition (as given in dialectics and historical materialism); a frequent use of empty formulas (for example, "freedom," "progress"); and the friend-foe stereotype (for example, "democratic" versus "communist" states on the one hand and "fraternal people's" versus "imperialist monopoly capitalist" states on the other).

We are not interested at this point in further details of the extensive ideological debate between West and East. Rather we shall proceed from two hypotheses that appear realistic enough: (A) Both German governments in their political stances—above and beyond the facts—are committed to certain basic values that evoke vacuous dichotomies. (B) Ideology is disintegrating in both German states but mainly in the GDR. No compendium of empty statements couched in the language of Marxism-Leninism can make up for a fading ideology. Lack of capital, over-drawn credits, improving the standard of living, and the self-awareness of citizens who in tens of thousands are applying for emigration permits seem to play much greater roles in the GDR's attempts to find its own identity than do the ideological postulates and programs of the SED.

In spite of this complex state of affairs, comparisons can be made because there are in both German states ties that may be called ideological and that have political impact. This article is thus based—to use a term from social science methodology—on a "functional" interpretation of ideological phenomena.

5. The Ideological and Political Attitudes of the SED Leadership: General Aspects

In principle the SED leadership has brought its attitudes toward the FRG into line with the concept of "peaceful coexistence" through coordination with the ideological strategy of the CPSU.

For the short and medium range,[9] the SED leadership has repeatedly signaled and practiced, if not always in a politically consistent manner, an inclination toward "living peacefully side by side." This has been true particularly when for political raison d'etre (the Bundestag elections in October 1976) or for important economic policy reasons it has seemed to be the appropriate position to take. As the CPSU and the SED see it, taking such a position expresses the "cooperation" aspect of the principle of peaceful coexistence.

With respect to the political-strategic dimension, both the CPSU and the SED leadership continually stress the growing importance of ideological-political confrontation with the "capi-talistic" West—and especially with the FRG as the economically strongest and politically most stable power in Western Europe. This emphasis takes into account the principles of peaceful coexistence from the vantage point of the "ideological-political class struggle."

The doctrine of "peaceful coexistence" is designed in such a way that arguments and emphases can always be combined in a different "mix" as the political situation changes. The ideological substance of the principle of peaceful coexistence, however, has by and large remained unchanged.

The "foe image" belongs among the ideological fundamentals. The foe image of the FRG that prevails in the GDR must be distinguished from SED assessments of the political situation in the other Germany. Although the foe image in its basic features has continued unchanged, the SED's estimate of the political situation in the FRG has, of course, changed frequently since 1969. What is thus ambivalent here is not the concept of "peaceful coexistence" but rather the official SED estimate of the West in general and of the FRG in particular. As to their judgment of the situation, the 1976 SED program as well as the SED leaders' speeches at the ninth party congress (May 1976) demonstrate that a realistic view of the militarily and economically vital Western world, especially of the FRG (in spite of all the crisis manifestations), competes with an interpretation that places emphasis on the crisis ("the steady sharpening of the contradictions in the capitalist countries").

In the first instance, it is not the basic ideological concept that makes cooperation with the West possible. It is the fluctuating and vague yet operationally focused ideological estimates of the FRG that provide the SED, on general principles and at a moment's notice, with the possibility of justifying a wide range of domestic and foreign policy attitudes for internal and external consumption and chiefly vis-à-vis the Soviet Union.

This kind of distinction between the "core dogma" and an "operational ideology" is recommended because it can explain two different matters: the ideological flexibility of leading SED politicians and the increasing vacuity of the phraseology of the core dogma. The ritualistic use made of it and the ever widening area of sociopolitical facts with which its axioms have to contend mitigates the possibility of even the SED leadership explaining anything in terms of ideology.

The operational flexibility that in principle exists often does not take effect in practical GDR foreign policy. Why not? The GDR's dependence on the USSR is too strong, and the hierarchial stratification and bureaucratization of the decision-making process are too pronounced for ideological flexibility even though flexibility does exist in principle. With all the emptiness of the core dogma that, together with fluctuating operational estimates, should allow for a certain ideological flexibility, Marxism–Leninism in its political references remains as unwieldy as ever. Time and again this is evidenced when compromise is an issue in actual negotiating situations.

6. The Ideological and Political Attitudes of the SED Leadership: Particulars

(A) Attempts at Demarcation (Abgrenzung)

Almost from the start of the FRG's new ostpolitik, that is, since the fall of 1970, the SED leadership, through new approaches and by using the power instruments of the party and state apparatus, has been seeking the most extensive political-ideological "demarcation" possible between the GDR and the FRG—in the sense of defining the FRG as a foreign country and moreover a hostile foreign country. Only in the economic area does the GDR at times admit the "special" nature of intra-German relations.[10]

The GDR's insistence on the most rigid demarcation from the FRG may be related to the "two-state theory" that had become the dominant view in the 1950s. In his government declaration of September 1955, Otto Grotewohl, addressing the GDR's People's Chamber after the signing of the GDR–USSR Sovereignty Treaty, for the first time explicitly referred to the "two German states." That thesis then elicited further political interpretation in Ulbricht's 1956/57 New Year's message in which he enunciated the concept of a confederation of the two German states. Finally, the SED program of January 1963 became the first document to combine the confederation thesis, based on the two-state theory, with the concept of "peaceful coexistence."

As a consequence of the two-state theory, the postulate of "GDR citizenship" must be mentioned. It was first codified in the GDR Citizenship Law of February 20, 1967.

Some additional strategies have been developed by the SED, especially in recent years. Among them:

Orders forbidding contacts of certain politically and socially exposed persons with West German citizens, even if family ties exist;

Intensified ideological training for SED cadres, the main features of which are a more serious study of Western political and sociological theories and methodologies combined with an extensive if rather pragmatic training in GDR state and party organization;

The development and increased propagation of the thesis—supported by the doctrine on classes and the class struggle—of the "socialist nation" (workers class) in the GDR versus the "capitalist nation" (bourgeoisie) in the FRG.

The doctrine on the emerging socialist nation in the GDR—the vague beginnings of which go back to the late 1940s—has been reformulated time and time again. Although Ulbricht held on to the idea of the unity of the German nation until 1970, Politburo member Albert Norden, for instance, announced as early as the end of 1967 that by joining NATO the FRG had disrupted "the German national affiliation once and for all." Several concepts of the German nation were thus competing within the SED leadership. It was Honecker's achievement at and after the eighth SED congress (June 1971) to have brought together these concepts of the German nation, diverse as they were and with all of the confusion that they had created in the

SED itself, into a formal and superficially cohesive doctrine; even though on the whole it is not consistent even in terms of the self-image of Marxism-Leninism. This doctrine has literally been imposed on the leadership of the SED.

What makes this concept of the nation untenable, even for generating a power of conviction in the SED? For one thing, it relies too strongly on Stalin.[11] Also it is not capable of appealing to the working masses either in the GDR or in the FRG. But the main reason that this concept is unacceptable to vast segments of the population is that it contradicts the feeling of national solidarity and appears to seal the division of Germany.

It was consistent in 1971 for Honecker to reject as "mere talk" the "unity of the German nation," to emphasize the emergence of a new "type" of nation ("the socialist nation"), and to make a point of the stronger and deeper contrast to be expected in the future between the two German states.[12] Although the prognosis for these contrasts encompassed generally "all areas of public life," Honecker indicated—not only in his ninth SED congress speech but principally there—specific aspects of these contrasts, that is, their topical significance primarily in the "spiritual-cultural" realm. Again and again, a point was made of the "rich spiritual-cultural life of great ideological impact" that exists in the GDR but not in the FRG.[13]

Although this development reveals an ideological-strategic trend, the socialist nation doctrine, as already mentioned, has until now been repeatedly subject to reinterpretation. Even for the SED leadership it had apparently not been elaborated and formulated with sufficient conviction.

Between 1972 and 1974, for example, the word German was deleted wherever possible (the German Academy of Sciences became the Academy of Sciences of the GDR in October 1972). Since 1975–76 official statements have differentiated among "nation," "nationality," "nation-state," and so forth. The "socialist nation in the GDR" is being contrasted with the "capitalist nation in the FRG." Both are "German" in terms of their "nationality." But there are presumably "two historically different types of German nation." The attribute "German" is thereby acknowledged for the nation of the FRG. Of course, in the eyes of the SED "the concept of 'German' within the real context of the developing socialist nation (the GDR) is acquiring a richer and more varied content."[14]

The claim that is rooted in such ideas enables the GDR to think of itself in terms of cultural policy—and despite its demarcation from the FRG—as heir to a certain part, the future oriented part, of German national history. Thus the GDR claims the sole hereditary title to certain cultural traditions or, in concrete political terms, to specific works of German culture.

From time to time the FRG has not properly appreciated how much political vitality that claim contains possibly because, inter alia, in West Germany the argument runs much more along legalistic lines—even in matters of culture.

(B) Attempts at Stabilization

The SED's demarcation policy referred to in conjunction with the nation concept must be understood essentially as an attempt at immunization and legitimization by an ideological and political regime that even today has by no means been stabilized. The draconian party measures taken against artists in disgrace (Reiner Kunze, Wolf Biermann) are moving testimony.

7. The Ideological and Political Attitudes of the FRG Government: General Aspects

With respect to the matters at hand, the FRG seems committed to two definite policies:

(a) Pursuing ostpolitik under the aegis of detente. With regard to the concept of detente, one may proceed from a consensus among leading political forces in the Western world: For instance, there is at present, as Henry A. Kissinger has reiterated, no alternative to the policy of detente. Resting on this basic consensus, one finds also in the FRG, the most diverse nuances: from a negative evaluation (detente avoids a policy of strength) to a positive evaluation (detente is a means for containing Soviet power).

In terms of intra-German relations, detente has led to: Negotiations, agreements, and accords with the GDR about matters for common disposition and of common concern as reflected in the Basic Treaty; humanitarian relief, with special reference since Helsinki to the Final Act of CSCE; and an interpretation of the Quadripartite Agreement on Berlin in the sense of maintaining the status quo.

(b) Pursuing further the reunification task of the Basic Law as it was last emphasized in the decision of the Federal Constitutional Court (July 31, 1973) on the constitutionality of the Basic Treaty and explained in the light of intra-German relations.

Although in principle the decision of the Federal Constitutional Court commits the political forces in the FRG to "preserving the national and political unity of Germany," it leaves the way open for whatever political approach those forces may decide to take in meeting that task. Approaches do in fact differ greatly—mainly because contenders move in separate ideological and political directions in their approaches toward the "solution" of the German question.

Also, and especially in the FRG, conflicting ideological interpretations of the GDR and of the political situation in Germany ("unity of the German nation") can be found. The FRG government itself is in part ambivalent in its interpretation of the concrete domestic and foreign policy situation in the GDR, as shown by a recently published study of the FRG chancellery.[15] On the one hand, the lack of political legitimacy on the part of the SED leadership, its dependence on the USSR, and the continuing problems of the economy are clearly recognized. On the other hand, too much is made of what attitudes the GDR population may adopt and of the degree to which it will in the future be bound to the GDR regime.

Finally, there are differences in how political circles in the FRG interpret the demand for reunification as set forth in the Basic Law.

None of these interpretations is embedded in any core dogma, making the spectrum of interpretations of the GDR in official and unofficial circles in the FRG appear diffuse.

A certain rigidity attaches to this diffuse state of ideological interpretation: position versus position. And alignments change slowly. Yet precisely because ideology and policy are rarely intertwined, the FRG government's attitude toward the GDR could in principle be more flexible. In spite of the task of reunification, it has a broad ideological-political margin for pragmatic negotiations and decisions relating to the GDR.

8. The Ideological and Political Attitudes of the FRG Government: Particulars

(A) Humanitarian Relief

The "human rights" issue has been a factor in intra-German relations since World War II; "humanitarian relief" is the pragmatic formula that has been used in more recent FRG–GDR dealings. Since 1969 FRG governments have chosen achievements in the field of "humanitarian relief" as the measure of their policy toward Germany (for example, the Twenty Points of Kassel in 1970).

The present aims of "humanitarian relief" are: improving intra-German travel (between the FRG and the GDR, the FRG and West Berlin, West Berlin and the GDR); lowering the age limit for GDR citizens who wish to travel to the FRG; reuniting families; regulating certain family affairs (matters of inheritance, alimony payments, personal assets); easing postal and telecommunications restrictions; exchanging literature and information in the widest sense possible; and establishing contacts in the field of culture and in areas of science and technology.

In the matter of "humanitarian relief," ideological ties are considered because from the Western standpoint the GDR continually violates human rights. Recently, as a result of President Carter's campaign on human rights, the political and moral dimensions of this concern have been reactivated.

The most blatant violation of human rights by the GDR is the so-called *Schiessbefehl*, that is, the order given to GDR border troops to shoot at anyone who tries to cross the fortified border between the GDR and the FRG.[16] The CDU/CSU opposition in the West German parliament persists in stressing this issue in public, whereas the SPD/FDP governing coalition has remained silent in public in order not to burden intra-German negotiations. However, now as before, the *Schiessbefehl* is one of the reasons why the negative image of the GDR as an essentially unchanged police state remains firmly established.

(B) Demarcation

No generally binding concept of nation—let alone of a German nation—exists in the FRG despite attempts made by all political parties represented in the Bundestag (Gerstenmaier, 1965; Brandt, 1969, 1970; Scheel, 1969, 1970; Schmidt, 1974) and by many scholars.[17] This fact can also be traced historically. Those who drafted the Basic Law rejected any kind of crude nationalism, which is why by and large the FRG has spurned any national symbols since it was founded.

Since 1970 the concept of nation has been qualified as *Kulturnation* (nation in terms of a specific culture), *Staatsnation* (state-nation, that is, nation in terms of a specific state) and *Bewusstseinsnation* (nation in terms of a specific consciousness of the people).[18] For historical reasons Germany did not follow the practice of its Western neighbors and avoided identifying the "political" with the "cultural" nation. In most recent political discussions, "nation" has increasingly been reduced to its volitional or emotional component. The "sentiment of solidarity" and thus recourse to an at least latent will not to abandon the unity of the nation have been and with good reason will remain in the forefront of all official, unofficial, and academic statements on this theme, as has the widely proclaimed slogan *Vom Nebeneinander zum Miteinander* (from living side by side to living together) since more visitors began pouring into the GDR.

For the last 10 years discussions in the FRG of the concept of nation have been generally motivated by the desire to preserve a guideline for German unity: "nation" as a pure concept. The volitional-emotional quality of the concept of nation (nation as a community of the will and of consciousness)—as demonstrated in particular by Willy Brandt's reflections—is not without romantic elements. How such elements are to combine with new democratic concepts—with a new sense of responsibility for a constitutional democratic welfare state—has thus far not become at all clear in the discussions that are continuing in the FRG.[19]

Before discussions about the concepts of the "nation" and the "German nation" come to any conclusion, the FRG, regardless of which forces form the government, will continue to seek a "demarcation" from the GDR. This quest has brought about three major points of emphasis: a rejection of the ideological and political claims formulated by the GDR on the basis of its two-state (or three-state) theory and the theory of the socialist versus the bourgeois nation; a political conviction that there are two mutually exclusive social systems in Germany; and steady improvements in living and working conditions in the FRG not only to keep ahead socially and politically in the contest between the systems, thereby bolstering the loyalty of the people in the FRG, but to remain attractive to the people in the GDR.

The absence of generally acceptable ideas about the concept of a German nation facilitates as well as encumbers the FRG's conflict situation vis-à-vis the GDR. It facilitates it because there is no need for any recurring readjustment in ideology as would be necessary in reconciling topical political issues with political conditions in the FRG. It encumbers it in so far as the absence of national ideas has the consequence that, above and beyond the constitutionally vested demand for reunification, no politically or strategically applicable consensus of all political forces appears feasible for the time being.

9. *Short-range and Long-range Ideological Perspectives*

(A) *From the Vantage Point of the GDR*

The SED is likely to carry on its ideological and political confrontation with the FRG primarily in the field of cultural policy, and it will then also enter a sociopolitical contest with the FRG. The SED will seek continually to demonstrate that it offers the more secure, just, and freer social system, the one more strongly rooted in the German tradition. Even back in 1970, when the concept of "social policy" was still relatively rare in the GDR's political semantics, reference was made to the influence exercised on the FRG by the "exemplary social conditions in the GDR." The GDR press, for example, claimed that the right of codetermination (*Mitbestimmungsrecht*—the right of workers to take part in management), as introduced in the FRG by the Schuman Plan (1951) and the law on industrial organization (*Betriebsverfassungsgesetz*) 1952—was a reaction to influences originating in the GDR.[20]

This political line will also affect relations with the FRG. Since 1970 cultural, social, and welfare policy has contained a basically aggressive thrust against the FRG, however fluctuating in intensity. The ideological-historical interpretation of the GDR's official concept of "culture" proves a special challenge to the FRG. The FRG must also come to grips with recent German history. For too long it has failed to take any effective measures that could promote a politically responsible awareness of German history and culture and, in particular, a democratic reevaluation and interpretation of recent German history. This gap could be filled too easily by obscurantists and ideologues.

Although the GDR is advocating its doctrine of the "socialist nation" rather defensively, its latent aggressive core remains. For it is this very definition of nation that makes it possible for the GDR to treat the FRG as a "foreign country" and a "class enemy." Ultimately, it is only the "working class and its party," the SED, that has the mission for today and tomorrow to revitalize the German nation on its true foundation in the GDR. And along with that mission, the GDR can always increase its appeal to the "solidarity" of the "class brothers" in the FRG.

However, a political intensification of the class struggle doctrine is likely to become noticeable only if the international political situation relaxes and the GDR grows to depend less in its economic policy on the FRG. Right now the GDR's economic weakness and general conditions within the scope of detente prevent the GDR from exceeding a certain degree of aggressiveness in ideology and propaganda.

(B)   From the Vantage Point of the FRG

At present and for the foreseeable future the actual ideological-political confrontation with the GDR will by and large remain outside ongoing intra-German relations. That is, the FRG will not accept the ideological challenge posed by the SED. The FRG government under Helmut Schmidt has an overriding pragmatic interest in coping as best it can with the points set down in the Basic Treaty and in the Final Act of Helsinki for its relations with the GDR. It continues to seek cooperation in fields in which it assumes common interests could exist and engages in the task of "humanitarian relief" as much as possible. The margin provided by the vagueness of the nation concept and the still "open" German question is evidently to be met pragmatically and gradually by treaties, agreements, and rules of conduct. Moreover, by assuming worldwide political obligations and by taking part in coping with urgent international problems, the FRG is now less dependent on progress on the German question—and thus also on its relations with the GDR— than it was in the years from 1969 to 1973.

Sometimes one hears the view expressed, especially by the FRG's neighbors,[21] that sooner or later the FRG government will have to accommodate itself to two separate German citizenships and for that reason it would be well advised to take the initiative in this regard (with the speculative claim added that the GDR could thereby more rapidly consolidate itself politically and ideologically). However, in view of the political constellation in the FRG after October 3, 1976, this is not a pressing matter.

For short- and medium-, and also for long-range, it will continue to be important for any FRG government to develop the West German democratic and social *Rechtsstaat* (constitutionally-governed state). For one thing, this will make the FRG population politically and ideologically immune to appeals from the GDR. Moreover, it will enhance the FRG's political and social attractiveness to the people in the GDR.

In the long run, the aim of reunification of the German nation within the scope of a European order of peace remains a perspective that receives frequent emphasis. No parties represented in the Bundestag have given it up, nor can it be given up, as it is vested in the Basic Law. What one must ask, however, is how much political weight German reunification carries with the population of the FRG. Demands and claims derived from that goal are rarely voiced by people in the FRG any longer; they only come from certain social and political groups that are hardly typical of the FRG population at large. To be sure, no definite prognosis can be given because too many diverse factors determine and are in the future likely to affect public opinion in the FRG.

At present one can neither affirm nor deny any general trend in the FRG toward a revival of a genuine national consciousness—a consciousness that would transcend the people's allegiance to democracy, welfare state policy, and constitutional government and would thus be strong enough to affect seriously FRG relations with the GDR.[22]

NOTES

1. We refer here to the following agreements, accords, protocols, and arrangements between the FRG and GDR governments: *Vertrag über die Grundlagen der Beziehungen zwischen der Bundesrepublik Deutschland und der Deutschen Demokratischen Republik (Grundlagenvertrag)* (21. 6. 1973); *Vereinbarungen über Grundsätze zur Schadensbekämpfung an der Grenze sowie zur Instandhaltung und zum Ausbau der Grenzgewässer* (both: 20. 9. 1973); *Protokoll über die Errichtung der Ständigen Vertretungen* (14. 3. 1974); *Vereinbarungen über den Transfer aus Guthaben in bestimmten Fällen und über den Transfer von Unterhaltszahlungen* (both: 25. 4 1974); *Gesundheitsabkommen* (25. 4. 1974); *Vereinbarung über den Fischfang in einem Teil der Lübecker Bucht und Protokollvermerk über den Verlauf der Grenze zwischen dem Küstenmeer der Bundesrepublik und dem Küstenmeer der DDR* (29. 6. 1974); *Vereinbarungen über den Ausbau der Verkehrswege nach Berlin-West sowie über die Transitpauschale* (19. 12. 1975); *Abkommen auf dem Gebiet des Post- und Fernmeldewesens* (30. 3. 1976); *Vereinbarung über den Abbau des grenzüberschreitenden Braunkohlevorkommens* (19. 5. 1976).

2. Conference on Security and Cooperation in Europe, Final Act, *The Department of State Bulletin*, vol. 73, no. 1888 (1. 9. 1975), p. 3133.

3. See below.

4. For an attempt at describing large ideological groups by means of a critique of ideology based on critical rationalism and a social psychology oriented toward a critique of ideology, see Kurt Salamun, *Ideologie, Wissenschaft, Politik: Sozialphilosophische Studien* (Graz: Styria Verlag, 1975). See also Peter C. Ludz, "Entwurf einer Typologie des Ideologiebegriffs," in Peter C. Ludz, *Ideologiebegriff und marxistische Theorie* (Opladen: Westdeutscher Verlag, 2nd edition, 1977), pp. 82 ff.

5. In terms of international law, the FRG government can no longer regard the GDR as *Inland* (homeland), and yet after the 1973 decision by the Federal Constitutional Court, it cannot treat the

GDR as *Ausland* (a foreign country). Mainly in trade policy and customs law, one maintains the fiction that the GDR is *Inland*. Cf. Reinhold Biskup, *Deutschlands offene Handelsgrenze: Die DDR als Nutzniesser des EWG-Protokolls ueber den innerdeutschen Handel* (Berlin [West]: Ullstein Verlag, 1976), pp. 22 f.; as well as Peter C. Ludz, *Die DDR zwischen Ost und West* (Muenchen: Beck Verlag, 1977), pp. 317 ff.

6. See Jens Hacker, *Der Rechtsstatus Deutschlands aus der Sicht der DDR* (Köln: Verlag Wissenschaft und Politik, 1974), p. 401.

7. See Ulrich Scheuner, "Die staatsrechtliche Stellung der Bundesrepublik: Zum Karlsruher Urteil über den Grundlagenvertrag," *Die Öffentliche Verwaltung*, vol. 26, no. 17 (September, 1973), pp. 581 ff.

8. Salamun, *Ideologie, Wissenschaft, Politik* (*op. cit.*, n. 4), pp. 16 f.

9. See Hermann Axen's analysis of the outcome of the Final Act of CSCE in *Neues Deutschland*, 3 October 1975, also in *Deutschland Archiv*, vol. 8, no. 11 (November 1975), pp. 1207 ff.

10. Honecker in an interview with *New York Times* columnist C. L. Sulzberger in East Berlin, see *Neues Deutschland*, 25 November 1972.

11. See Ludz, *Die DDR zwischen Ost und West* (*op. cit.*, n. 5), pp. 224 ff.

12. Erich Honecker (rapporteur), "Bericht des Zentralkomitees der SED an den VIII. Parteitag der SED," *Protokoll der Verhandlungen des VIII. Parteitages der Sozialistischen Einheitspartei Deutschlands, 15. bis 19. Juni 1971*, 2 vols. (Berlin [East]: Dietz Verlag, 1971), vol. I, pp. 55 f.

13. Erich Honecker (rapporteur), *Bericht des Zentralkomitees der SED an den IX. Parteitag der SED* (Berlin [East]: Dietz Verlag, 1976), p. 103.

14. Alfred Kosing, *Nation in Geschichte und Gegenwart: Studien zur historischmaterialistischen Theorie der Nation* (Berlin [East]: Dietz Verlag, 1976), p. 180.

15. See *Der Stern* (Hamburg), no. 38/1976, p. 30.

16. The West German Ministry of Intra-German Relations has publicized statistics on murder along the border between West and East Germany: In the period from August 1961 (construction of the Berlin Wall) through the beginning of 1974, 94 persons were killed at the GDR-FRG border and 70 more at the borders in Berlin. Most had been shot by soldiers of the National People's Army.

17. See, for example, Waldemar Besson, *Die Aussenpolitik der Bundesrepublik* (München: Piper Verlag, 1970); also Lutz Niethammer and Ulrich Borsdorf, "Traditionen und Perspektiven der National-staatlichkeit," *Aussenpolitische Perspektiven des westdeutschen Staates* (München-Wien: R. Oldenbourg Verlag, 1972), pp. 13 ff.; also Karl W. Deutsch, *Nationalism and Social Communication: An Inquiry into the Foundations of Nationality*, 2nd edition (Cambridge, Mass.: The M.I.T. Press, 1966).

18. See Gebhard Ludwig Schweigler, *National Consciousness in Divided Germany* (London and Beverly Hills: Sage Publications, 1975), pp. 16 ff.

19. See Joerg Gabbe, *Parteien und Nation: Zur Rolle des National-bewusstseins für die politischen Grundorientierungen der Parteien in der Anfangsphase der Bundesrepublik* (Meisenheim am Glan: Anton Hain, 1976).

20. Article on "Sozialpolitik," *Sachwörterbuch der Geschichte Deutschlands und der deutschen Arbeiterbewegung*, 2 vols. (Berlin [East]: Dietz Verlag, 1970), vol. II, p. 584.

21. See, for example, Curt Gasteyger, *Die beiden deutschen Staaten in der Weltpolitik* (München: Piper Verlag, 1976), pp. 168 ff.

22. This point must be emphasized, in disagreement with Schweigler (*op. cit.*, n. 18) and his analysis of the nation concept and of national consciousness in the two German states.

4

THE GDR's
RELATIONS WITH
THE ADVANCED
INDUSTRIAL
SYSTEMS OF
THE WEST

John Starrels

AMONG MATURE COMMUNIST systems East Germany stands alone for the simple reason that it continues to possess a "Western" identity. Having been created on the foundations of a shattered German society at the end of World War II, having experienced the special severity of the cold war in Europe from the late 1940s to the early 1950s, and having capitulated to the economic nationalism of West Germany by making the decision to construct the Berlin wall on August 13, 1961—the German Democratic Republic continues to live within a context of Western economic, political, and sociological dynamics. This paper examines some of these realities in the framework of what I label East Germany's "westpolitik."[1] Once a conception of "westpolitik" is put forward, attention is shifted to the multilateral dimension within which the GDR operates as an industrial socialist system along with its Eastern European and Soviet

78

allies; consideration is then shifted to its special bilateral relationship with the Federal Republic of Germany, with some comments on several patterns of regime response to the attractions and dangers inherent in increased engagement with the West.[2]

I. Westpolitik

A large amount of attention has been given to the conduct of West Germany's ostpolitik since it was inaugurated during the first Socialist/Liberal government under Willy Brandt and Walter Scheel. Most analysts agree that the Federal Republic's attempt to balance its westward and Atlantic orientation by engaging the communist part of Europe in an extended dialogue—now in what one could term a consolidation, if not a retrenchment, phase—was—and is—both historically appropriate and politically intelligent. But what about East Germany's relations with the West? In one sense, of course, the German Democratic Republic has always had a foreign posture toward the West, broadly defined to include Western Europe, North America, and Japan, particularly contacts with the first two groupings. This posture—hardly a policy—sprang from several related sources. First, communist authority in the GDR emerged within a context of a common German past. Even though regime historians in East Germany attempt to demonstrate that the GDR enjoys separate "revolutionary legitimacy," which somehow removes East Germany from the burdens (Nazism for one pertinent and unexpungeable example) imposed by an all-German past, the past continues to determine both the behavior and the perceptions of East German leaders, especially in their dealings with the West Germans and the Soviets.[3] Admittedly, the memories of a common German and common European history will begin to fade as older generations pass from the leadership scene.[4] Nonetheless, the residue of historical experience unavoidably forces the GDR to think and behave in a manner that distinguishes it from other socialist regimes in Eastern Europe. Second, and in an operational sense of greater significance, the East German struggle for recognition was waged within the context of cold war politics and in a more personal sense within the framework of an intra-German confrontation that initially ranged the two German systems in direct ideological and political confrontation. And until the German Democratic Republic was finally able to achieve the coveted goal of de jure diplomatic recognition, the West was able to halt the East German regime's attempt to build a foundation of legitimacy within its borders.[5] Finally, as long as it displays a sense of geographic insecurity, explained in large degree by the traumas (in some measure, self-imposed) visited upon the regime by the massive outflow of people to West Berlin and the Federal Republic before August 1961, East Germany's relations with the West will always be of a special nature. This point deserves additional expansion.

At the core of East Germany's orientation toward the West is the regime's sense of geographic insecurity and the simultaneous attempt by its leadership cadre to create political conditions favorable to the gradual dissipation of these fears. But in what manner are such concerns reflected in this sense of geographic insecurity? Two basic considerations are of special significance here. In the first and larger instance, the German Democratic Republic gradually developed a westpolitik as an initial, yet enduring, response to the insecurity of its geographic situation in the heart of central Europe. One could even label such concerns "border psychosis." But they flow out of a realistic conviction that unless the regime is able to gain international validation for its geopolitical sovereignty, the status of communist authority in East Germany will remain questionable as well as compromised. Linking the idea of geographic security with the pursuit of political sovereignty, the secretary general of East Germany's ruling Communist party (the SED, Socialist Unity party of Germany) went on record during the first *Conference on Security and Cooperation in Europe* to make these observations within the context of a multilateral gathering:

Only if security and the sovereignty of states are guaranteed can there be fruitful, beneficial and mutually advantageous cooperation. The lessons of history and the current requirements of European politics make respect for, and recognition of, the principle of the inviolability of frontiers the decisive factor. Security for the European states has always meant, first and foremost, security for their frontiers. The terrible wars that devastated our continent in this century were the result of a policy which, whatever the pretext, started from the violation of existing frontiers, from disregard for the sovereignty and territorial integrity of other states.[6]

With special relevance for the future status of Berlin, it has been the sole responsibility of the Western occupation powers, along with the Soviet Union, to guarantee the German Democratic Republic that essential element of diplomatic and political legitimacy that it has finally achieved.

As a second consideration, the East German regime's sense of geographic insecurity relates to its ongoing competition with the Federal Republic. In the wake of both the Quadripartite Agreement of September 3, 1971, and the follow-up cooperative accords contained in the intra-German treaties (the Basic Treaty) of 1972–73, the juridical aspects of East German sovereignty appear to have been settled according to the predilections of the SED. But the expanded range of contacts between the two German systems, although advantageous to the GDR in terms of economic and financial aid, is highly disadvantageous in terms of its impact on the broad population of East Germans who are now able to come into sustained contact with West German (including West Berlin) friends and relatives.[7] And although the East German government has continued to pursue a pragmatic approach toward this "fait accompli" visited upon it by the Basic Treaty—for example, by opening additional luxury shops that explicitly cater to individuals carrying West German currency—the specter of peaceful penetration by a larger and more dynamic German society is viewed with understandable concern by the East German authorities.

These general elements of a westpolitik are combined with a final element involving the ideological and political goals of a mature communist system that, like many of its Western (but few of its Eastern European) neighbors, has already experienced the dilemmas and complexities of full-scale industrialization, the proliferation of a consumer oriented life style, and the most recent demands visited upon it by the claims of applied technology and its ability to create and solve social ills. But along with these broad structural commonalities that link the fate of East Germany with systems of the liberal democratic West are the recent challenges made by increasingly self-confident parties in Italy, France, and Spain, that are able to carry the banner of Marxism-Leninism in the spirit of democratic, in contrast with bureaucratic, transformation.[8] This side of the issue was sharply illustrated by an Italian journalist writing in the January 19, 1973, edition of "Unita" who traced a critical profile of the CPI's relations with the German Democratic Republic:

Along with other political forces . . . we have been consistently in favor of recognizing the GDR without being complaisant about the manner in which leadership was exercised by the communists in Berlin. We are obviously satisfied that a socialist solution has been found within a society which has moved from a most difficult beginning to a system which has developed a positive answer to many of the important questions facing modern societies in their search for peace and security. The central purpose of the CPI has been the generation of an Italian contribution to the goal of security and cooperation in Europe and in this regard the recognition of the GDR was a necessary step.[9]

Such considerations are touched upon at a later point in this discussion.

II. Multilateralism and Westpolitik

The GDR has occupied an ambiguous geographic status in Europe since its founding in late 1949. These special considerations have already been touched upon. Nonetheless, a certain paradox growing out of East Germany's strange—if simultaneously understandable—situation deserves mention. On the one hand, and especially since the eighth party congress of the SED in the spring of 1971 (subsequently reaffirmed at the ninth congress in the spring of 1976), the East German leadership has become the foremost proponent next to the USSR of accelerated integration into the Soviet bloc. On the other hand, its special competitive relationship with the Federal Republic has transformed East Germany into what one observer calls a transnational society, a system forced to be responsive to complex trends and processes emanating from both parts of Europe.[10] Regarding the GDR's response to the industrial system of the West, there are three elements composing the multilateral dimension that deserve mention.

European Security. The GDR occupies one of the most exposed positions within the European strategic military environment. In the event of a conventional or nuclear exchange between respective alliance organizations, it would be the East Germans who would suffer the most immediate and visible (and assumedly fatal) damage. As did the former SED leader Walter Ulbricht, Erich Honecker and the SED's national security apparatus have developed two different policies on matters relating to military security vis-à-vis engagement with the West. One, the regime currently devotes 8 percent of its national budget to military security matters, including border patrols and fortifications for East Berlin (the GDR capital) and the expanse of territory separating the East German system from the Federal Republic, secret police, and, of course, contributions to the Warsaw Treaty Organization.[11] Two, the German Democratic Republic has continued to play an active part in publicizing the Soviet sponsored

Conference on Security and Cooperation in Europe. For East Germany the most important element of that conference concerns geographic security in the context of territorial integrity. This position is fatefully linked to the generalized SED concern that West Germany's commitment to "peaceful" boundary changes in the future *within* Germany may be employed to undermine the regime's political authority within the GDR. Whereas the Soviet Union has attempted to use the conference as a forum for the final legitimization of Soviet hegemony in Eastern Europe (including the GDR), East Germany has made every attempt to employ this forum as a multilateral means of blunting West Germany's challenge to the GDR's newly won sense of territorial and political legitimacy.

From the East German vantage point, an implicit linkage now binds the fate of the Helsinki–Belgrade discussions with the less ambitious future surrounding the Conference on Mutual Balanced Force Reductions (MBFR). Few areas of East German politics are less discernible to the outside observer, but an *ipso facto* argument can be made that the SED is aware of what one foreign policy analyst calls the GDR's "special interest" in European security issues as they directly relate to the fortunes of the GDR in Europe:

While the GDR does not have a different interest which would presumably distinguish us from other socialist states on these matters, we certainly do have a special interest (spezielles Interesse). This interest flows from the realization that tensions within Europe invariably and directly effect the domestic situation within the GDR. In terms of our geographic position and the common border we share with the Federal Republic, which is also the border separating NATO from the Warsaw Pact, questions relevant to immediate security . . . involve us.[12]

Intrabloc Economic and Technological Cooperation. East Germany has an equally enduring interest in expanding its economic and technological links with the industrial West. On the trade front the regime has experienced the usual currency problems that confront nonmarket economies when they attempt to expand economic intercourse with the industrial West. Export–import data for 1974 puts the current account deficit—figured in East German marks—at 3,108,000,000 (East German exports of 8,328,000,000; imports from the industrial West at 11,426,000,-000). These data are not completely accurate, for it is nearly impossible to determine realistic exchange relationships between market versus nonmarket currencies. Nonetheless, they are at least illustrative of the problem facing East Germany. And even in view of such trade deficits, one should not lose sight of the fact that the GDR's trade with advanced industrial systems in the West has expanded tremendously on both the import and the export sides, with the important exception of North America and Japan.[13]

In terms of intrabloc cooperation in the aligned areas of economic and technological intercourse, East Germany has increasingly become supportive of wide ranging proposals for both technical and economic–financial cooperation between the Soviet directed Council for Mutual Economic Assistance (CMEA) and the European Economic Community. One GDR analyst put forward six general proposals in this substantive policy area: 1) creation of an all-European infrastructure, particularly in the realms of energy sharing and transportation; 2) substantial increases in all-European trade and a simultaneous decrease in tariff and other "market restrictions" (meaning the refusal of EEC countries to accept currency from the CMEA systems); 3) long-term cooperative treaties in the field of technology exchange; 4) a common European market research system devoted to gathering and analyzing data pertinent to the economic needs of the ECC and CMEA; 5) activation and extension of work done by international organizations *within* Europe such as the UN sponsored Economic Commission for Europe; 6) within a multilateral framework, the lifting of trade restrictions against CMEA products and the establishment of permanent agreements

governing the purchase and delivery of industrial products between the two parts of Europe.[14]

Eurocommunism and "Loyal" Opposition. For the Soviet bloc
as a whole and for the East German leadership in particular, the
specter of political dissent in their own societies and the growth
of European communist movements in various Western countries
(especially, France, Italy, and Spain) pose serious challenges
to the domestic and international ("proletarian internationalism") claims of legitimacy made by bureaucratic communist
regimes. Some initial comments on the GDR's perception of
multilateral cooperation with the Soviet Union are germane.

In a probing discussion devoted to the phenomenon of
hierarchic control in the European communist world, Roy
Macridis makes some especially relevant observations on the
meaning of supranational authority. Although these remarks
are for the French specifically, they have at least equal—and
this is an understatement—relevance for the SED's perception
of organizational loyalty to the Communist party of the Soviet
Union. Soviet control over the affairs of subordinate parties
means . . . "(T)hat when the Soviet leadership commits itself unequivocally to a course of action in the international arena, a
complex set of psychological, ideological, political, and cognitive
mechanisms, as well as bureaucratic constraints, is set in motion
and results in the alignment of the course of the PCF with that
of the Soviet Union."[15]

The issues of Eurocommunism and domestic political dissent
within the Soviet bloc, particularly within the GDR, are two
important arenas in which traditional patterns of obedience
by the East Germans to Soviet initiatives are of obvious importance. The first consideration, strikingly illustrated in the Soviet–
East German alliance, was reflected during the meeting of the
Communist and Worker parties in Europe, held in East Berlin
June 29–30, 1976.[16] In this vein the role of the GDR was pronounced not only because of East Germany's substantive preparations beginning twenty months before the conference was held

but in at least equal measure as a result of Soviet efforts to portray the SED as the preferred model for Western European counterpart organizations to emulate. And along with their Soviet colleagues, it was the East German insistence on the maintenance of "proletarian internationalism," in defensive response to the French, Italian, and Spanish positions emphasizing greater degrees of independence for European communists, that was one hallmark of this important meeting. At the same time, however, one should not lose sight of the reality that although the SED made a substantive effort to defend Soviet positions on the evolution of Eurocommunism within the framework of the international movement, the official SED daily *Neues Deutschland* dutifully printed the dissenting observations of Enrico Berlinguer, Georges Marchais, and of perhaps greatest significance, the most dissenting of all views articulated by the delegates, those delivered by the formerly orthodox Santiago Carrillo.

An analysis of the East Berlin meeting renders two specific conclusions: One, the westpolitik of the German Democratic Republic is strongly imbedded within the framework of East German–Soviet purposes in Europe as a whole. This by no means suggests an automatic and slavish imitation of Soviet policies by the GDR—although there were various instances in the past that suggest that such patterns of behavior are by no means foreign to the SED—but rather that a symbiotic alignment of ideological and political standpoints between the two systems now exists. In consequence, the German Democratic Republic has come to play an increasingly significant, albeit explicitly subordinate, role in the maintenance of orthodox communist hegemony in Europe. Two, and from the limited perspective supplied by domestic East German politics, this alignment of positions between the two countries will, if anything, become more pronounced in the event of a significant break—and this means primarily a public confrontation—in the European communist movement.

The subject of domestic political dissent within the Soviet

bloc cannot be separated from the dynamics at work in Western European Communist parties. Indeed, the two processes feed upon and condition each other. From the vantage point of East Germany's engagement with the West, several considerations seem especially important vis-à-vis the subject of domestic dissent. First, recent crackdowns on intellectuals in the GDR, triggered by the stripping of East German citizenship from the poet and folksinger Wolf Biermann, inevitably play havoc with the East German image in the West.[17] Indeed, the transnational dimension of East German society, which places the GDR within the framework of East–West dynamics, invariably places repressive actions on the part of security authorities in the harsh light of publicity. Second, although explicit cases of collusion between West and East German groups are hard (if not impossible) to document, there is little argument with the proposition that an "international effect" accompanies domestic political turmoil within the GDR. Witness the case of Robert Havemann, former member of the prewar German Communist party and the SED, who simultaneously performs the role of chief opposition spokesman within the GDR as well as being a widely recognized journalist in the Federal Republic and Western Europe more generally. As with the case of Wolf Biermann, Havemann's utterances on domestic politics in the GDR and within the Soviet bloc have transformed him into an international actor—and what Biermann and Havemann have to say elicits respect in the West. Three, the nature of authoritarian politics in the GDR produces a generalized and in general a negative impact on Western European communist organizations. Instead of serving as a developmental example for counterpart organizations in the West, the SED is viewed as an institution that could benefit from the democratic examples supplied by the Italian or the Spanish parties and their alternative orientations toward problems of civil liberties, dissent, and the general requirement of building an alignment of viewpoints between regimes and average citizens.[18] Finally, and as an initial introduction to the next section, the ongoing competition between East and West Germany on both the bilateral and multilateral levels supplies an important comparative dimension for a broader understanding of East–West relations.

III. Westpolitik and Intra-German Relations

The presence of a dynamic and relatively prosperous Federal Republic created problems for the German Democratic Republic almost from the instant the two competitive republics were formed in 1949. But as the cold war diminished and as the relationship between the Soviet Union and the United States continued to improve on issues relevant to detente in Europe, the relationship between the FRG and the GDR has changed correspondingly. My interest in this section is not in the realm of intra-German dynamics per se but in the implications that the relationship holds for the East German pursuit of a *westpolitik*. In this context some preliminary observations on the East German search for diplomatic and political legitimacy are appropriate.

The agent for resolving East Germany's struggle for international legitimacy outside the world communist movement has been the Federal Republic. The three Western allies responsible for the administration of West Berlin did not move to recognize the German Democratic Republic until the former government of Willy Brandt signaled its willingness to push aside, albeit temporarily, the pursuit of national reunification. This reality has now been translated into a more generalized aura of control in which the Federal Republic is able to maintain the advantage of policy initiatives, backed up by an imposing degree of political (it has very good relations with both the Soviet Union and the United States) and economic leverage in its dealings with the GDR. From the East German vantage point, several elements of its relationship with the Federal Republic are important for the waging of its westpolitik.

One, given the importance that East Germany assigns to an expansion of trade with the West, one should not underemphasize the real advantages that the GDR gains in its special trade relationship with the Federal Republic. Fully 10 percent of its trade is conducted with both the Federal Republic and West Berlin. Even allowing for the fact that economic and financial intercourse continued to occur during the height of the cold war, in view of the natural interests that each side had in the maintenance of such contacts, trade figures on both the import and export side since 1965 (through 1974) reflect dramatic jumps in commerce between the two systems. Further, despite the SED's contention that the GDR is an independent and "sovereign" socialist German nation, the regime has never renounced the privileged access that it gained into the European Economic Community via the 1951 protocols governing intra-German trade.[19] As a result East German commodities enjoy the same tariff preferences available to the other members of the EEC. And finally, West Germany's continuous interest in maintaining and extending economic relations with the GDR (for essential political reasons) has resulted in the extension of special "drawing credits." Since 1974 these credits have provided the East Germans with approximately 850,000,000 DM (West) worth of credit. This so-called swing arrangement theoretically allows either party to purchase products from the other, but given the GDR's rising import deficits (it purchases far more than it is currently able to sell on the West German market), the mechanism is almost exclusively used by the smaller partner.[20]

Two, as the Federal Republic conditions its assessment of the Soviet bloc with an eye toward its current relations with the GDR, so the East Germans condition their behavior within a similar frame of reference. This interlocking of perspectives is unavoidable given the proximity of the two systems in a geographic and cultural-historical sense. At the same time, however, the highly personalized nature of interactions between the two societies continuously threatens to distort each system's ability to see beyond the special exigencies that bind them. Viewed from the perspective of the East German mass media—especially newspapers and television—it is easy to lose sight of the fact that although the direct message conveyed of social alienation, rising inflation (it always is rising), unemployment, cynicism, distrust, and so on, involves a careful and highly biased portrayal of life in the Federal Republic and West Berlin, the larger image is based upon a more general perception of life in the West.

Three, and as an extension of the above observations, unlike other socialist systems in Europe, this double-image of East–West relations has tended to deepen the SED's awareness of how volatile the various issues are that divide the two parts of Europe, as they divide the Soviet Union from the United States. Further, and in contrast with the other societies of Western and Eastern Europe, the massive inflow of West Germans and Berliners into the GDR since the signing of the Basic Treaty has tended to personalize the differences that continue to exist between the two parts of Europe. And yet, given the areas of limited parallelism that now characterize the evolution of industrial societies in East and West Europe, perhaps the dynamic unloosened upon the East German system by the Federal Republic can be employed—eventually and somehow—to increase the level of understanding and the willingness to cooperate between East and West.

IV. Westpolitik and Survival

East Germany was created, as was its rival to the west, in the aftermath of World War II and allied disagreement about the future of postwar Germany. In sharp contrast with the history of the Federal Republic, however, the German Republic has only recently become a charter member of international society. One need not feel sorry for the GDR, despite the assessment of the late Ernst Richert that of all the nations that participated in World War II, only the East Germans came out the losers. Remembering the harsh reparation payments levied upon the then Soviet zone of occupation by the USSR, West Germany's highly successful diplomatic blockade of the fledgling socialist German state until the late 1960s (the Hallstein Doctrine), and the final humiliation of having the Soviet Union dictate the terms of a new policy of detente with the Federal Republic—one should at least understand why the German Democratic Republic approaches the West with such a pronounced mixture of suspicion and curiosity.

What about the future of the GDR vis-à-vis its newly developed relationship with the industrial democratic systems of the West? Prognosis is an extraordinarily difficult and in many cases a wholly unrewarding exercise. Nonetheless, certain general points should be kept in mind.

One, although emergence of the German Democratic Republic as an internationally recognized actor is a relatively new development, the SED has been preparing for that role for many years. No matter how attractive Western investment is to East Germany, and despite the continually increasing desire of its citizens to travel to the West now that the diplomatic blockade is over, the regime will make every effort to control the level of influence emanating from the West. But this understandable desire to control the tempo of change that the west—and especially West Germany and West Berlin—has stimulated in the GDR will not be easy to achieve given the exposed location of that society. Thus relatively new relations with the West, tempered by the SED's desire to control changes brought in their wake, introduce the possibility that East Germany may occasionally act in strange ways when the pressures created by these new relationships become too great.[21] Without excusing the regime for an unfortunate outbreak of shooting incidents that have erupted along the common German border, one should not lose sight of the possibility that overreactions of this nature are triggered by a sense of generalized nervousness about the future direction of international change and the regime's ability to control it.

Two, considering East Germany's strong and increasing desire for expanded economic relations with the West, there is every reason to assume that the GDR will push for a sharp increase in all forms of business—from encouraging direct foreign investment to the erection of as many foreign currency shops (*Intershops* as they are known in the GDR) as are necessary to absorb the increasing amounts of West German money. Further, it is highly realistic to expect that the growing economic dependency of this regime on the West will provide new incentives for it to employ all available means to find new ways of taxing foreign visitors. Such developments as the sudden imposition of a special 5 mark (West) visa charge for daily visits to East Berlin on January 1, 1977, are entirely understandable given the foreign exchange hunger of the GDR.

Finally, one should not forget the influence of the Soviet Union and the Federal Republic on the evolution of the 'GDR. For the Soviet Union, the East Germans continue to represent the most authoritative symbol of communist legitimacy in east central Europe, a status that the SED leadership has continuously worked to achieve. For the Federal Republic, the East German system represents an obstacle to the increasingly unrealistic goal of national reunification, but it also represents the potential for increased relaxation and communication between two societies that are providing Europe with alternative—and, in their separate ways, equally impressive—models of sociopolitical development.

In conclusion then there are abundant indications that the German Democratic Republic, despite its sense of geographic vulnerability and its long-term dependence on two larger systems (Moscow and Bonn), is an important actor in international affairs. Within the context of its special circumstances, one should expect an increasingly pronounced East German approach toward dealings with the West. And although it is nearly impossible to predict how its westpolitik will evolve, there is little argument with the general proposition that the participation of the German Democratic Republic in the affairs of the industrial West will be a fascinating one to observe.[22]

NOTES

1. For an earlier cut at this subject, see John Starrels, "East Germany's 'Westpolitik,'" *GPSA JOURNAL* (Fall 1975), pp. 31–52.

2. Some thoughtful views on this broad subject are supplied by Peter Christian Ludz, *Two Germanys in one World* (Paris: Saxon House, December, 1973), and Peter Christian Ludz, *Die DDR zwischen Ost und West* (Munich: C. H. Beck, 1977).

3. Two interpretations of this subject are found in Hermann Axen, *Zur Entwicklung der sozialistischen Nation in der DDR* and John Starrels, "Nationalism in the German Democratic Republic," *Canadian Review Of Studies in Nationalism* (Fall 1974), pp. 23–37.

4. There are few empirical studies on this subject, but two rather different contributions deserve consideration. On the level of mass perceptions in both German states, consult Gebhard L. Schweigler, *National Consciousness in Divided Germany* (London and Beverly Hills: Sage 1975); for a brilliant analysis of elite generational change, Peter Christian Ludz, *The Changing Party in East Germany* (Cambridge, Mass. and London: MIT Press, 1972).

5. For a brief discussion of the East German diplomatic struggle, see John Starrels and Anita M. Mallinckrodt, "Current Developments," in Starrels and Mallinckrodt, *Politics In the German Democratic Republic* (New York, Washington, London: Praeger, 1975), pp. 362–363.

6. *Address by Erich Honecker*, July 30, 1975, *Political Documents of the German Democratic Republic*, p. 12.

7. For a broad view of this dynamic, see (Bericht und Dokumentation) *Die Entwiklung der Beziehungen zwischen der Bundesrepublik Deutschland und der Deutschen Demokratischen Republic, 1969–1976* (Federal Ministry for intra-German Relations, April 1977).

8. Two articles on this subject are highly recommended: Karl Wilhelm Ericke, "Die SED und die europäische KP-Konferenz," *Deutschland-Archiv* (July 1976), pp. 674–77; Heinz Timmermann, "Eurokommunismus-eine Herausforderung für Ost und West," *Deutschland Archiv* (December 1976), pp. 1276–1298.

9. Manfred Steinkühler, "Die Beziehungen der DDR mit Rom und Paris," *Deutschland Archiv* (March 1973), p. 236.

10. See the late Ernst Richert's very fine article on this phenomenon, "Zur Wechselwirkung von Gesellschafts-und Aussenpolitik der DDR," *Deutschland Archiv* (September 1974), pp. 956–958.

11. Karl Wilhelm Fricke, "Die Militärs in der DDR-Führung," *Deutschland Archiv* (March 1974), pp. 231–234.

12. Dokumentation: "Europäische Sicherheitskonferenz aus der Sicht beider deutscher Staaten," *Deutschland Archiv* (January 1973), p. 86.

13. Consult *Statistical Pocketbook of the German Democratic Republic* (Berlin–East: State Publishing House, 1975), pp. 95–97.

14. Jürgen Nitz, "Europäische Sicherheit und ökonomische Zusammenarbeit," *IPW Berichte* (January 1973), p. 6.

15. Roy Macridis, "The French CP's Many Faces," *Problems of Communism* (May–June 1976), pp. 59–60.

16. See Peter Christian Ludz's brief discussion of this meeting in *Die DDR zwischen Ost und West* (Munich: C. H. Beck, 1977), pp. 263–275.

17. For a series of highly informative articles dealing with this complex subject, see Manfred Jäger "Das Ende einer Kulturpolitik," *Deutschland Archiv* (December 1976), pp. 1233–39; Erik Nohara, "Biermann-Reaktion und Gegenreaktion," *Deutschland Archiv* (January 1977), pp. 12–17; Dokumentation: "Der Fall Biermann," *Deutschland Archiv* (January 1977), pp. 69–105.

18. I put this forward as an opinion until hard evidence is available to support this position.

19. See John Starrels, "The Community's Silent Partner," *European Community* (April–May 1976); Peter Scharpf, "Die Bedeutung des inner-deutschen Handels für die Beziehungen der EWG zur DDR," *Deutschland Archiv* (March 1974), pp. 260–266; Also see Ludz's discussion of this subject in *Die DDR zwischen Ost und West*, *op. cit.*, pp. 312–318.

20. This point is taken directly from Ludz, *Ibid.*, p. 315.

21. For discussions on "border incidents," see Ilse Spittmann, "Heisse Tage im August," and Dokumentation: "Reaktionen auf Grenzzwischenfälle," in *Deutschland Archiv* (September 1976), pp. 897–899, and 982–989.

22. Although dated, I nonetheless recommend Robert G. Livingston's fine discussion on developmental opportunities for the GDR in its future dealings with the West in his "East Germany Between

Moscow and Bonn," *Foreign Affairs* (January 1972), pp. 297–309. For some analytical observations on East German political development, also see John Starrels, "Comparative and Elite Politics," *World Politics* (October 1976), pp. 139–142.

ECONOMIC
POWER AND
POLITICAL
RESPONSIBILITY*

Peter Hermes

1. The World's Economy as an Organism

"THE ECONOMY IS OUR DESTINY." This observation was made by Walter Rathenau, Germany's minister for foreign affairs in the early 1920s. What was then perhaps only a picture of things to come has now become reality. The observation applies not only to everyone of us but also to the whole range of our international relations.

The economic fortunes of a country like the Federal Republic of Germany in virtually every regard are linked with other states:

— We rely heavily on our foreign trade with all parts of the globe.
— We are deficient in raw materials—much more so than are other industrial states.

---

*This address was given during "German–American Week" (1977) of the Konrad Adenauer Foundation.

— Our economy is interlinked with that of other countries in investments and flow of capital, management and patents, labor and communications.
— Our prosperity rests on flourishing international economic relations and free world trade.

We can only prosper if our world economic partners also prosper. We are dependent on good relations with all states that participate in the international exchange of goods and services.

This interdependence, or "one world concept," in economic policy is the lesson that the turbulent 1970s have taught not only us but all industrialized states. We have learned to view the world's economy as an organism whose health as a whole rests on that of its integral parts. Synergism continues to be a task of the utmost political significance. It is also the reason why the seven heads of state and government of the major Western nations endorsed this proposition at their three "economic summit conferences."

II.   German Responsibilities

Every day we learn how much other countries expect of Germany. Although these expectations are not always the same, they nevertheless play a fairly big role—indeed one that is sometimes too big. We would prefer to think of our spectrum of opportunities as being more restricted. However, we accept our joint responsibilities in the light of the challenge of a changing world.

We are the second largest industrial state in the Western world (or, alternating with Japan, the third largest). We have one of the highest per capita levels of personal income, the largest foreign exchange reserves, and the second largest share of world trade.

We have something else that enhances our feeling of responsibility: a stable political, economic, and social society and constitution. This commitment imposes certain obligations upon us, especially in Europe.

Some time ago we learned of the death of Ludwig Erhard—the man who was quite rightly called the father of the social market economy. The economic system that he set up is endorsed and applied by all responsible political groups in Germany. It is surely no exaggeration to say that this is the best contribution that the Federal Republic of Germany has made to world economic cooperation since its foundation.

A few weeks ago the president of the German Trade Union Federation and the president of the German Employers Association met in public debate on neutral Swiss soil. According to press reports, the spontaneous comment of listeners was: "This is a convincing example of practical social partnership."

I am not trying to hide the fact that we have social conflicts and struggles. But these differences do not strike at the roots of our social order, which is based on autonomy in negotiating wage agreements, comanagement by worker directors, and a program of "concerted action" among the government, employers, and labor. Social consensus is not mere rhetoric: It is part of the reality of modern German life and a feature of our economic policy that deserves the highest praise

III. Basic German–American Consensus

In considering responsibility and challenge in a changing world, it is perhaps appropriate to give due prominence to the broad similarity of objectives pursued by the United States and Germany.

Both of us adhere to a policy based on:
- a sustained upturn in worldwide economic trends with a reduction in unemployment and inflation;
- the maintenance and development of a system of free world trade;
- the preservation of the international monetary system;

— an increasing integration of developing countries into the world's economy.

These were the main points expressed at the economic summit in London, and we accept them unreservedly.

Nevertheless, it is as important to define the special obligations incumbent upon each of our two economies in the world as it is to stress this basic German–American consensus.

On this account I would like to define these obligations with respect to our principal economic roles in

— Europe
— the Western industrialized world
— north–south relations
— German–American relations:

IV.   The German Economy in the European Framework

1.   *The European Community*

The EC is our most important market, accounting for slightly less than 50 percent of our foreign trade. Our major trading partners are France, the Netherlands, and Belgium.

Although we are the country with the strongest economy in the Community, we do not enjoy the highest per capita income; this record is held by Denmark.

Our economic strength means that we bear the lion's share of financing the EC. These burdens as well as the advantages that we derive from our membership in the Community are considerable. In the first place, there is our 33 percent share of the EC budget. Its volume of approximately 10,000 million dollars constitutes the largest international budget. Second, there is the balance of payments in which our guarantees and those of the Bundesbank represent the most important source of assistance within the Community. Among the achievements of our Community policy, firmly based on solidarity, mention should be made of the normally unrestricted functioning of the free interflow of goods within the EC despite all the fears and crises experienced.

2. *The European Countries outside the EC*

The next group in economic importance for us consists of those European states that are not members of the EC (Switzerland, Austria, Portugal, Sweden, Norway, and Iceland). With this group we effect 15 percent of our foreign trade, that is, three times our trade with the USA. The EC and these countries form a free-trade zone in which industrial tariffs were completely abolished this year. As a result, Europe has become a largely duty-free area.

3. *The EC in North–South Relations*

The role of the Community in north–south relations is marked by the Lomé association with 52 states in Africa, the Caribbean, and the Pacific. These links, too, fundamentally rest on the principle of free trade. An EC development fund of about 5,000 million dollars has been earmarked for a period of five years. The Convention of Lomé established the concept of stabilizing export earnings, and this concept was introduced by the Community into the north–south dialogue.

Today the wide network of EC trade and development aid spans the whole of the Mediterranean area as well as a number of developing countries in Latin America and Asia.

4. *German Trade with Eastern Europe*

Let me now turn to our economic ties with Eastern Europe.

The dynamic upswing recorded during the period 1972 to 1974 has slowed down since 1975. This development is by no means to our disadvantage, for the considerable expansion in trade (which in the case of the Soviet Union has nearly quadrupled in current prices since 1970) was accompanied by an equally substantial increase in the net indebtedness of the East European states.

For this reason, a period of consolidation would be advisable. However, I agree with the president of the German Association of Chambers of Industry and Commerce that the current level of East European debts gives no cause for alarm.

Unlike the practice adopted by many Western industrial states, German exports to the East are not promoted by grants of governmental credit or interest subsidies. The Federal government does not operate any financing machinery like the American Export–Import Bank. It confines itself to providing guarantees against the risks inherent in export business with the state-trading countries as well as with all other parts of the world In 1976 the state-trading countries accounted for only 20 percent of the total volume of these guarantees compared with 27 percent at the end of 1974.

The percentage of German foreign trade represented by East European countries in 1976 was 5.9 percent. It would be wrong to speak of an integration of the Eastern economy into the world economy. By the same token, it would be erroneous to assume that such countries do not play appropriate roles in north–south relations. For this reason, the wish voiced by the third world that these states should at long last provide adequate aid is perfectly understandable.

V.   Germany's Role Among Western Industrialized Countries

The three main aspects of the role played by the German economy and German economic policy in the Western industrialized world are:
— The management of the world economy
— International currency relations
— World trade

1.   *The Management of the World Economy*

The world economy is still faced with the problem of simultaneously realizing four goals—known in Germany as the "magic square"—that is, growth, full employment, stability in the value of money, and a balance of payments equilibrium.

It would appear as if we are farther away from achieving these goals than we were in the 1960's. The greatest problem at the present time is undoubtedly unemployment. On this question the London summit conference came to one important conclusion: Inflation does not reduce unemployment. On the contrary, it is one of its main causes. This recognition—which we Germans have espoused with a pertinacity that has often annoyed our partners—now seems certain of becoming generally accepted.

Another discovery was the impossibility of striving for economic growth as long as inflation continues undiminished.

This realization led in London to the idea of forming two groups of nations, a concept that had already been discussed at the second economic summit in Puerto Rico. One set of states would be expected to make systematic use of their non-inflationary scope for growth while the other would aim primarily at reattaining their internal and external stability.

Although Germany and the USA belong to the first group, there is one important difference between them. It now looks as if not only the rate of growth but also inflation and unemployment became greater in the USA than in Germany in 1977.

There was a lively German–American discussion at the beginning of this year as to whether the Germans ought to stimulate their economy more vigorously and thus perhaps relieve the burden on other countries. This discussion has subsided. In retrospect, I would point out the following:

The phase reached by the world economy has given rise to widespread misgivings about the usefulness of many of the cyclical measures hitherto adopted. This situation has been aggravated because opinions on the nature of the present crisis differ considerably. Is it cyclical rather than structural? Are its causes more economic or more sociopsychological? In view of the lack of convincing answers, should we perhaps base our policy on the principle of "who is doing better"?

It is interesting to note in this context that:
— the Federal Republic of Germany was the first major industrial state to take decisive steps to halt inflation (and it
did so as long ago as the end of 1973);
— It was also the first of these nations to overcome the recession (in the second half of 1975);
— It made an effective contribution toward improving conditions in other countries during the recession by substantially increasing its imports.

We are continuing to pursue the goals that were set at the
beginning of the year; an economic growth rate in real terms
of about 4–5 percent, an unemployment ratio of under 4 percent,
a ratio of inflation of under 4 percent, and a ratio of imports to
GNP of approximately 2 percent.

In the meantime the Federal government has made statutory
provisions for a DM 16,000 million program to safeguard growth,
increase employment aid, and cut the envisaged rise in the value-
added tax from 2 percent to 1 percent. In instituting these
measures the Federal Government was guided by the aim of
channeling budget surpluses back into the economy with a view
to promoting purchasing power and capital investment. The
Bundesbank has been backing this action with a comparatively
generous liquidity policy.

2.   *International Monetary Relations*

The international currency scene is one of both light and
shadow. However, there seems to be more light than shadow
if one compares the years 1976–77 with the agitation and turbu-
lence that followed the collapse of the system of inflexible
foreign exchange rates. The correctness of the decision to switch
to flexible parities may be deduced from the fact that such
dramatic adjustments as the appreciation of the German mark
by about 16 percent, the Swiss franc by 8 percent, and the
concurrent depreciation of the British pound by 14 percent, the

lira by 24 percent, and the French franc by 7 percent in one and a half years took place without the repercussions usually experienced in former times. Certainly there is no need for me to dwell on the fact that the unsatisfactory situation in the German labor market also stems from the conscious acceptance of such a substantial upward revaluation of the DM.

Among the deep shadows cast across the international currency scene, I would include the persistant, large disequilibria in the balances of payments. The OPEC surpluses of probably 40,000 million dollars in 1977 are matched by the 20,000 million dollar deficit of the developing countries that have no oil and the 25,000 million dollar deficit of the weaker industrial states. A sobering realization for everyone is that the elimination of these disequilibria will take much longer than originally assumed.

Whereas the view was still being expressed at the IMF annual meeting at Manila last autumn, that is, three years after the crisis over oil prices, that it would be possible to switch priority from "financing" to "adaptation," the main emphasis has again been placed on the creation of additional international lines of credit (IMF's Witteveen facility of DM 14,000 million SDRs, an increase in quotas).

There is, however, a limit to the extent to which foreign debts can accumulate. The indebtedness of the developing states without oil, for example, was in excess of the 200,000 million dollar mark in 1977. It is obvious that this entails grave problems. We regard the IMF as the most suitable and effective institution for overcoming the critical problems facing the world economy. It is reassuring to know in this situation that apart from the International Monetary Fund, we have strong, independent central banks in our two countries—central banks that are dedicated to maintaining the stability of the value of our money while recognizing their responsibilities for balance of payments aid.

It is largely because of the efforts of this trio comprised of the IMF, the Federal Reserve System, and the Deutsche Bundesbank, together with the economically judicious recycling carried out by responsible OPEC states, that methods of currency management have proved successful in the oil facility, the Jamaica resolutions, the IMF reforms, the major IMF credits for Britain and Italy, and the sale of gold for the benefit of the trust fund.

What we have not succeeded in doing is mastering international liquidity. As was quite rightly pointed out a short time ago, the situation is comparable with a national credit market lacking a central bank. The debts that we referred to largely arose on that money and capital market. Despite this fact, even the most heavily indebted industrial country (Italy in the amount of 17,000 million dollars) has only half as much debt as Brazil. This helps to explain the urgent appeal now being made by the commercial banks for a closer link between private deficit financing and IMF operations. The main focus of interest for the private sector banks seems to be the economic terms granted by the International Monetary Fund. We hold that credit aid can only fulfill its purpose when it is accompanied by convincing reform programs. On this account we agree with the USA that the new IMF special facility should also be made subject to certain appropriate conditions. Past experience has shown that the IMF keeps a close watch on what is politically feasible when it is negotiating specific terms.

3. The German Economy in World Trade

The USA has the largest volume of trade in the world while the Federal Republic of Germany takes second place. Together, our two countries account for 25 percent of international trade, which recently passed the 1,000 billion dollar mark. But whereas the USA's exports represent 6.8 percent of its gross national product, ours come to 22.8 percent of GNP. These figures by themselves explain the German attitude toward world trade that, for reasons of enlightened self-interest, must steer a careful course to avoid both protectionism and controls. Trade policy itself is a matter for the European Community in which we have always been the advocate of liberal policies compatible with a gradual process of adaptation devised to avoid sudden social hardship. As far as protectionism is concerned, we were pleased about its unequivocal rejection at the economic summit in London. It is hardly a coincidence that the statement issued on this subject was not merely clear but almost in the nature of an article of faith. After all, it is very tempting in times of economic uncertainty to turn to protectionism and even controls.

If we reiterate our belief in a system of free international commerce, we must be equally prepared for our achievements to be judged in terms of our own demands; and that includes a willingness to accept structural change. In principle, there is no disagreement about this in Germany, and none of the political parties thinks otherwise. Moreover, our trade unions are fully aware that any dwindling in world trade would exercise a fatal impact on employment and growth. Hence despite all the difficulties that we encounter, the watchword of the day must not be a contraction but an expansion of trade.

Let us now turn to our balance on current account and our balance of trade. Surpluses in the latter have now almost become a tradition in Germany, and they sometimes lead to a demand for a greater volume of imports or another upward revaluation. The Bundesbank recently pointed out by way of clarification that more than four-fifths of Germany's export surpluses were offset in 1976 by deficits in services and payment transfers. It recalled that no less than 3,700 million DM were remitted to the EC in net performances. As a result, the credit balance on current account for 1976 amounted to only 7,500 million DM (compared with 9,400 million in 1975 and 25,000 million in 1974). When viewed in this light, Germany was not very far from achieving an equilibrium in its balance of trade and payments in 1976.

4.   German Nuclear Energy Policy

Both in Germany and the USA this is a subject that arouses lively public debate. As in other countries, nuclear energy has become an important additional source of energy for us. The growing demand for energy and the inevitable decline of other sources indicate that after a careful consideration of all the advantages and disadvantages that we shall probably have no choice but to continue developing nuclear energy and to avail ourselves of it more and more in the production of electric energy. When the German Bundestag recently debated the government's energy program, it learned that 13 nuclear power stations produce 7 percent of the electricity used. There are plans to raise this figure to above 10 percent in the 1980s. (Currently the USA has 61 nuclear power stations with 42,000 MW, and there are plans to construct 148 stations producing 160,000 MW.)

The unavoidable increase in the use of nuclear energy in the world involves the increasing risk of an improper use of such nuclear power to manufacture nuclear weapons. It is imperative that we do our utmost to guard against this danger by taking counteraction. The government of the Federal Republic of Germany has always vigorously and systematically pursued policies based on this objective. All states possessing nuclear energy have been urged on the basis of the nonproliferation treaty to discover effective means and methods of excluding the possibility of improper use even if there is a substantial expansion in its utilization for peaceful purposes. However, this can only be achieved if all states interested in the peaceful use of nuclear power are integrated into a system of international cooperation and effective international control. As was demonstrated at the economic summit talks in London, the government of the Federal Republic of Germany is in complete agreement with the president of the United States on this matter. We are aware of our responsibilities and shall act accordingly.

The well-known agreement with Brazil on the peaceful use

of nuclear energy constitutes part of this policy. It makes full allowance for the goals of an effective nonproliferation policy as well as those of worldwide cooperation with threshold states in the third world. In political terms the agreement represents a systematic continuation of a policy introduced in 1953 by the United States in its "Atoms for Peace" program: cooperation instead of isolation, the inclusion of as many states as possible in an effective nonproliferation policy, and international controls. We are convinced that the agreement with Brazil will exercise a positive influence on a worldwide, nondiscriminatory, and efficient policy of nonproliferation.

Together with the USA and the participating countries at the London economic summit, we are continuing our joint efforts, in line with the American initiative, to develop effective methods of preventing the misuse of nuclear energy and simùltaneously promote the peaceful use of nuclear energy.

The Federal government issued a statement on June 17, 1977, to the effect that in view of this development it will not grant for the time being any permits for the export of reprocessing plants and technology. This decision does not affect existing agreements and their implementation. The Federal government assumes that agreements concluded in the past on the supply of nuclear fuels and other materials will continue to be observed irrespective of the progress of the talks on nuclear energy and nonproliferation begun at the London summit.

North–South Dialogue

I now turn to a subject that is universally recognized as a major item of international policy, that is, the north-south dialogue. There is no controversy about the goal. We must succeed in reducing the gap between rich and poor countries to a reasonable level if we are to maintain an economically stable and peaceful world.

We should judge the results of the north–south conference that ended in Paris on June 3, 1977, in the light of its contribution to this goal. The conference did not achieve a breakthrough, and in fact it was hardly to be expected that it would. If only one side had been completely satisfied and the other side disappointed, that would have been a poor result, for dialogue is based on continuity. As things stand, however, I would describe the outcome of the Paris conference as reasonably satisfactory. Despite the persistent differences between north and south, the dialogue has not been broken off and its continuation has been recommended.

One major step forward was achieved in Paris. The practice of conducting a sterile discussion on the basis of maximum demands that are often very remote from everyday feasibilities has been superseded by a much more realistic debate—however controversial it may also prove to be. Even though the two sides still agree to differ, they have at least begun to argue more in terms of real life.

The Federal government views with extreme distrust any theory of controls on world trade. It does so because experience has shown that regimented economic systems prove to be incapable of guaranteeing prosperity and freedom on the same scale as do market economy systems. We shall continue to adhere to the point of view that only a world economic order primarily founded on market requirements can attain a satisfactory solution to north–south problems.

Our advocacy of a free market system does not stem—as has sometimes been alleged—from excessive German dogmatism. We too have spheres of activity that do not rest entirely on the principle of a free market economy. Nevertheless, our fundamental adherence to the free market system is inspired by our own experience and, in equal measure, those of other countries. It may be objected that something which possesses validity at a national level need not necessarily apply internationally. It is, however, easy to turn the tables in this case. Anyone who asserts that an economic system that has hitherto invariably achieved less at a national level now constitutes an ideal solution internationally for a "new international economic order" will have to think up more plausible reasons and better arguments for his viewpoint than the champions of a regimented "new international economic order" have done to date.

There is, however, one principal objection to basing the world economy on free market principles. The argument is sometimes advanced that in international economic relations the social component should be brought to bear in a similar fashion to the way in which it takes effect in national economic policy. One might think of this as applying the "principle of fair distribution."

There are two objections to this point. The first can be discerned by merely glancing at the costs involved. Whichever world economic order that one supports, such a social component simply cannot be financed on a world scale either now or in the foreseeable future. As things stand at present, it already has involved us in enormous adjustment costs both nationally and within the framework of Europe. However, my second objection is more important. An "international social market economy," that is, the consistent realization of the social component in an otherwise free market economy would require worldwide recognition of the principle of fair distribution.

The countries of the third world would therefore be obliged, first, to realize certain principles at home before claiming them for themselves in the international sphere. Hence the idea of fair distribution presupposes a high degree of social integration such as exists only at a national level or such as is at present developing within the European Community. This would constitute a part of domestic policy and mean that everyone would have to allow others to have a say in his government. No one can believe that the third world is remotely prepared to do this. By the same token, the industrial nations are equally unwilling to permit this. The condition for an "international social market economy" would logically be an effective world government of one kind or another. And who would claim that this is a realistic outlook for the future?

However, I do not wish to be misunderstood: There are certain aspects of a "new international order" of which we approve and support. And this approval also applies to the "international social market economy" because our third world policy is, of course, influenced both by solidarity and a strong social component. My only objection is that I see no convincing or effective means of solving the north–south conflict within the framework of a new world economic order based on controls or in a global "international social market economy."

We must confess that we are at present unable to provide answers to all these questions and that this task is certain to occupy us for many years to come.

The principles of a free market economy to which we adhere also require us to regard developing countries as sovereign and responsible economic partners. Therefore, our aid to third world countries can only consist in helping them to help themselves.

We must therefore set out to remove the many obstacles still impeding the natural forces of the market, particularly by opening up our own markets. Within the framework of GATT the EC has granted unilateral tariff reductions on tropical produce, finished and semifinished goods, and agricultural products from developing countries. Moreover the Federal Republic has increased its imports from developing countries by 24.8 percent during the last few years, whereas our exports to these countries have only risen to 5.6 percent. We know that the indispensable structural changes in our economy can be brought about by means of an active adjustment policy. We are well aware that employment in our country will only be secured in the long term if we have solvent clients in the third world.

Whenever it was a matter of showing our solidarity in practice, we have played our part. I should like to mention just a few points:

—The EC's Lomé Convention.

—Development aid from both private and public sources

amounting in 1975 to 12,230 million DM (1.18 percent of GNP). Since 1950 more than 100,000 million DM have been given in development aid.

—Our participation in the various support schemes financed by the IMF to help improve the economic situation in third world countries.

Summing up, one could say that the north–south dialogue is both a necessary and a protracted process that calls for circumspection, discernment, and sacrifice.

The dialogue is much too important to justify any ostensibly quick solutions or "patent recipes." In this case, "patent" is often the opposite of "well-meant." The way toward a wrong policy is often paved with good intentions. In the end, what counts is not good intentions but the right policy, and this also implies that such a policy must be internationally feasible. Aid is not always what it seems to be. Our maxim must remain: cooperation, not confrontation; negotiate but do not dictate.

VII.   German–American Economic Relations

Nowadays the economies of Germany and the USA are more closely interlinked than are almost any other economies on both sides of the Atlantic. This fact, however, is not reflected in the exchange of goods for we are "only" the USA's third largest trading partner, and it is only our fifth largest. The United States supplies 7.6 percent of our imports and buys 5.7 percent of our exports. In 1976 our imports from the USA rose by approximately 11 percent. However, even our volume of trade with Belgium is larger than that.

Investment presents quite a different picture. The USA has been our most important partner in this sector for years. American assets in Germany (worth approximately 19,000 million DM, that is, 40 percent of all foreign investment in Germany) are still considerably larger than German investments in the United States (approximately 5,000 million DM); but since

1975 the growth rate has been reversed. We are now investing more in the USA than are Americans in Germany. This development has been primarily brought about by the changes in the rate of exchange. The building of a Volkswagen subsidiary plant in the USA—begun in 1976—provides a particularly good example of German investment activity.

On the other hand, we do, of course, welcome the large-scale investment plans drawn up by the Ford and Opel groups; they will help to promote our economic growth and domestic employment. This also applies to Esso, IBM, Dow Chemicals, and ITT—to mention but a few of the big American names on the German market.

In the course of such a survey, I cannot deny that there are developments now taking place in the American market that give us cause for concern. The serious problems are well-known—they can be quickly summed up in the following catchwords: "the Zenith case" (a lawsuit by a leading American color television firm against turnover tax refund claims on imports from Japan), the "United States Steel case" (dumping claims in respect of Japanese and European steel imports), "the International Banking Act" (exclusion of foreign banks holding shares in the capital of industrial firms in their mother countries). In particular, the two lawsuits worry us because they represent test cases on the basis of a law dating back to the protective tariff period (1890s) aimed at driving our exports out of the market. We know that the United States Government sees the matter in a similar light. We are confident that the proceedings will be fair and that Congress will pass fair legislation.

This survey has taken me from Europe via the world economic order and the north–south dialogue back to the relationship between the USA and ourselves. I hope that I did not go too far at the beginning of my analysis when I insisted on the basic consensus between Germany and the USA on international economic policy. This consensus forms the basis of cooperation between the two nations. During the next few years there must be especially close cooperation between our two countries in order to

- —strengthen confidence in stable world economic trends (in the OECD),
- —protect world trade from protectionism and economic regimentation (in GATT, UNCTAD, and the UN),
- —strengthen the international monetary and financial system (in the IMF and the World Bank group of nations),
- —continue the north-south dialogue by means of ad hoc cooperation (in the UN and UNCTAD), and
- —secure the supply of energy to the world economy (in the IEA and vis-à-vis OPEC).

6

EUROPE AND AMERICA: A REASSESSMENT*

Ralf Dahrendorf

I AM A EUROPEAN who has long believed that the American constitution and its practice are the greatest single achievement in human political history. What then would be more appropriate than to have another look at the relationship between the two pillars of the free world?

Two pillars, I said, but the word is deceptive. When you say that you are Americans, citizens of the United States of America, the term is ambiguous; it identifies you with this large subcontinent, its constitution, its dynamics, its much maligned culture, which has nevertheless given so many life chances to so many people. When I say that I am a European, this is quite different. I may in fact be referring to an area on our maps and even a total population that are comparable in dimension

---

*Commencement speech delivered at Wagner College, May 15, 1977, where Dr. Dahrendorf was given an honorary Doctor of Laws degree in recognition of his achievements.

116

to the United States, but that part of the story does not matter
much in practice. My own position is somewhat untypical; I
am in fact something of a European: a German who was once a
member of the Federal government and who is now responsible for a famous British institution in London, after having
spent over four years in the Belgian capital of Brussels as a European commissioner. Even so, I am acutely conscious of the
differences: Germany, the booming society that has taken over
many American values, notably, a sense of individual competition and achievement, with success often measured in material terms—and considerable success it is—but at the same time
a worried society, looking anxiously across the Elbe into East
Germany and further, wondering about its past and future. Britain, a society at one with its history—almost too much so in the
view of some—wallowing in tradition but above all bent on group
solidarity, on belonging to a club, a trade union, a class, seeking
happiness less in achievement than in a good life, even at a
fairly low level of economic attainment, stable political institutions under worrying socioeconomic conditions. And that, of
course, is only the beginning of European differences. There is
France, still torn between its glorious national tradition and the
modern world; there is Italy, the divided country; there is confident and independent Holland next to Belgium, which combines concern for the material welfare of its citizens with a
strange political impotence—in short, there is quite a story to tell
about every single country of Europe, and somehow these stories
do not add up to one constitution, one continent, one identifiable
unit to which people belong.

There are, of course, congruences, and as I proceed in these
remarks to explore the unfolding of the European–American
drama, I shall have more to say about them. But it is useful to
bear in mind the differences as well as the similarities of Europe
in order to understand why the story that I am going to tell is
in fact a drama.

A drama has five acts, I was told at school (from which statement you can see that at my time the teaching of literature had never advanced beyond the first half of the nineteenth century); let me try then to press the obvious complexities of European-American relations during the last ten years into this schema.

Act One: In the 1960s the scene of European-American relations was by and large one of bucolic harmony. To be sure, this depiction was not everybody's view on either side; also there were the first signs of coming changes, but they were few and far between. From a German point of view, it appeared that all relations fitted neatly into each other, like a Russian doll: Franco-German friendship, confirmed by a treaty and by the meeting of Adenauer and de Gaulle at Rheims cathedral, appeared to fit into the European Economic Community set up in 1957 to advance cooperation and perhaps integration in Europe; this in turn—at least from a German point of view—fitted equally neatly into the Atlantic alliance. I have presented the picture inside out, as it were, starting with the smallest doll and progressing to the all-inclusive one. In terms of importance, it was, of course, the other way around. I think it was probably assumed, at any rate in Germany and in many other European countries as well, that ultimately the American relationship had precedence; in case of doubt, the alliance prevailed over Europe, and Europe prevailed over bilateral friendship agreements.

But this idyllic relationship was not to last. Indeed *Act Two* started with a bang on August 15, 1971, a day on which, I still believe, ended an epoch of international relations. That was, of course, the day on which the United States government suspended the convertibility of the dollar into gold, that is, declared unilaterally that the dollar was not to be burdened with other people's economic sins forever, and introduced at the same time a number of measures designed to protect American commercial and economic independence. The United States, declared the then Secretary of the Treasury Connally, has the same right as everybody else to look after its own interest first.

In Japan the term Nixon shocks has become part of the political language used to describe these measures. In Europe memories may be rather less traumatic, but even so there is no doubt that the quality of United States–European relations changed as well. From August 15, 1971, onward there was at least an assumption that Europe and the United States are equals, perhaps twins, though not identical twins, indeed occasionally tied together in a rather tense relationship and at any rate two separate entities. Situations arose in which this new assumption became even physically visible. I remember representing the European Community at a GATT meeting on August 25, 1971, with the delegations of the then six members sitting behind me, their spokesman, and the delegation of the United States opposite, in the dock as it were, because we felt that we had reason to complain about the disruption of free trade brought about by the Connally measures. Elsewhere such unity was shown to be rather tenuous. On the monetary side, alliances were certainly more complex, and Germany for one was by no means unhappy about the new freedom gained by increasing universal floating, although, of course, this fact made the economic and monetary union of Europe a distant dream. Any description is bound to be a simplification. With that caveat, I would say that Act Two set the scene for the beginning of a new partnership, no longer the Russian doll of an inclusive relationship but a more complex and organized attempt to define common interests as well as in some respects agreement.

In many ways this is the theme of the remaining three acts. With varying degrees of tension or proximity, mutual understanding or mutual misunderstanding, Europe and America have tried and continue to try to work out a partnership that endures and produces common benefits. At first, this was extremely difficult. Indeed, *Act Three* was one of rather retrograde developments; it could also be called Kissinger One, or the Pentagonal Illusion. It is far too early to assess the historical role of the last American secretary of state, and when this is done, I have no doubt at all that the importance of his contribution will be vindicated. But his errors were as important as his achievements. I confess that I never liked the pentagonal notion of international relations that seemed to underly his early approaches: a world of five centers, Russia, China, Japan, Europe, and the United States, and world politics as an organized relationship among these five centers. I have always had a profound belief in the importance of *all* actors on the world scene, as on the scene of individual societies, and thus in the need to strengthen international arrangements and organizations that allow all to play their parts. Moreover, reliance on relations among the big powers is a tenuous concept, too personal to be comfortable, too cynical to be agreeable.

But in the context of my argument, the pentagonal concept had yet another disadvantage. Russia, China, Japan, and the United States exist—but where is Europe? Mr. Kissinger came to Brussels once in search of Europe. He was going to talk to the foreign ministers of the European Community. They were meeting in a room on the 22nd floor of a Brussels hotel to try to agree on the position that they would take with him; he was waiting in the main hall, and waiting, and waiting. It takes the Community many hours to agree on anything, and at the end of the day many agreements have little substance. This is in fact what happened on that unhappy occasion, and it is said that Mr. Kissinger then decided that one could really not deal with Europe at all. The consequences were almost predictable. Because one of the corners of the pentagon did not seem to exist it was quietly forgotten and ignored, except that one or two members of the disorganized Europe established their own close links with Washington. Act Three is a rather sad interlude in the definition of the partnership.

And while I am discussing this question of Europe, let me add a remark that you may find difficult to understand but that is of great importance for the relationship. It is quite true that the councils of the European Community do not belong to the most efficient decision-making bodies of the world. The attempt to discover congruences in the interests of nine countries takes a long time and often leads to decisions that reflect little more than the lowest common denominator. Also the nine are rather hesitant to accept any one spokesman; they prefer to have everybody or nobody speak for them. It is for that reason also that they find it difficult to accept one place as their common capital. Brussels, certainly, but the European Parliament meets in Luxemburg and Strasbourg, and the European Council of heads of government meets in the national capitals. Europe presents a picture of diffusion and disorganization. That is especially true in contrast with the United States, where all national decisions seem to be made in Washington, where the president at the White House seems to embody American power and where few questions are raised about where power lies and who has it.

Yet I want to argue that this picture is doubly deceptive. On the one hand, America is not as unified as it appears at first sight, especially to the outsider. The president is the visible symbol of power and of unity, and he is a very powerful man. Yet he is very far from being able to do what he wants. Indeed quite often, especially in international economic relations, the question must be asked: Can he deliver? Can he carry Congress? And as one shifts from the presidency to Congress, the picture becomes very diffuse indeed, if anything, more so than with the Council of Ministers of the European Community. Europe, on the other hand—and I am talking here of the organized Europe of the European Community, without overlooking the fact that not all the democratic countries of Europe are its members—may find it difficult to organize its decision-making process in a way that makes it possible to pinpoint the center of power. But there are profound common interests. Europe is more dependent on trade than is the United States; Europe traditionally has had a more intense relationship with developing countries than has the United States; Europe has learned to cope with mixed economies and welfare states, whereas the United States has not; Europe is much closer to the totalitarian threats of its own past and of the East European present than the United States has ever been. One could probably list a few more fundamental points of European interest, and whatever the difficulties in formulating them, they are there, and they inform the actions of European parliaments and governments. Indeed, if one likes paradoxical formulations and does not mind the overstatement that they invariably involve, one could well say: Europe has many common interests but no effective way of expressing them with one voice; the United States has highly effective ways of expressing its position, but underneath this there is a wide diffusion of interests and views. Less pointedly said, we both have our problems of defining and expressing interests.

This indeed is the underlying theme of *Act Four*, or Kissinger Two, if one wants to personalize the drama. The Atlantic Charter demanded or perhaps announced by Mr. Kissinger in 1973 never became very meaningful. The announcement was badly prepared; it came at the beginning rather than at the end of a period of redefining the relationship. But whatever the name, there is no doubt that the years from 1973 to 1976 brought a new awareness of the inevitable complexities of the European–American relationship. They also brought a new discovery of the interests that are common and can be spelled out, as the European interest can: There is, first, a common interest in defense, and in a defense alliance in which the American leadership is tempered by European concern and participation; then there is the overriding interest in maintaining the strength of the economic and political systems of free societies; this has specific consequences with respect to such organizations as GATT or the IMF; there is increasingly also a common interest in a more responsible organization of relations with the third and fourth worlds; and, of course, there is a common cultural heritage, indeed, it could well be said that the unity of Europe is nowhere more evident than in the peculiar mixture of nations and creeds that makes up American society (although I hasten to add that the American vocation is wider than that and includes African and Asian features as well).

Since 1974, therefore, numerous attempts have been made to give expression to these common interests. Some of the attempts are institutional. Regular joint meetings of United States government officials and the European Commission were started as the Samuels–Dahrendorf meetings and have been continued by my successors in Brussels, Sir Christopher Soames and Mr. Haferkamp and by Mr. Samuels's successors at the State Department. Private organizations stepped into the breach, notably the Trilateral Commission, which quite rightly included Japan in the new alliance. (One must not forget that Mr. Carter was a member of this commission and that Mr. Brzezinski was its secretary general). There was American recognition of the attempt of the European Community to speak with one voice on important occasions, such as the Helsinki Conference on Security and Cooperation in Europe, and the Nairobi conference on north–south relations. It would be wrong to say that Act Four was conclusive in defining the relationship; but I think that it was the beginning of a pattern that makes sense and will continue to make sense because it recognizes both the evident community of interest and the equally evident difficulties' in giving that interest appropriate expression.

This then takes us to *Act Five*, the one that you have been waiting for because it involves President Carter and the recent London summit. President Carter's policies are hardly formulated at this stage, and no one should blame him for that; in the first 120 days in office he has had an enormous impact on the style and the substance of international relations. But there is one theme about which fairly certain statements can be made. I have mentioned the fact that both the president and his national security adviser are members of the Trilateral Commission. This reference was no accident, for their membership has influenced their thought. It is probably true that, contrary to the last administration, neither President Carter nor Professor Brzezinski has ever been tempted by the kind of thinking that found its expression in the pentagonal illusion of Act Three. It is my impression at least that President Carter quite naturally thinks in terms of alliances and international organizations. He has sent an ambassador to the United Nations who is trying to give that organization meaning. He has attended a summit and a NATO meeting and presented himself as a member of these groups rather than as a cynic who believes that what ultimately matters is crude power. He sent Vice President Mondale to Brussels before he went to the capitals of Europe. The new style is one of multilateral cooperation rather than bilateral games, one of mutual recognition rather than of domination.

But, of course, Act Five is unfolding in a situation that is fraught with problems: and here I turn to recent events. At the London summit President Carter in fact found himself in a rather strange position. Looking around the table, he must have realized that he was about the only participant who could feel reasonably safe in his office. Prime Minister Fukuda of Japan has a more shaky majority than had any of his predecessors; Prime Minister Callaghan of Britain had just suffered a slashing defeat in local elections; Chancellor Schmidt of Germany was finding his own party in dire trouble; President Giscard of France had to reckon with a socialist–communist majority after the elections that would take place within a year; Prime Minister Trudeau, according to opinion research, had reached a rare low in popularity; and Prime Minister Andreotti of Italy was in power only because he had the dubious and precarious support of the Communist party.

As far as the process of European unification is concerned, the position is even more serious. I am not merely referring to the fact that European ministers and heads of government spent many hours trying to decide whether they wanted the president of the European Commission, Mr. Jenkins, to be present at the

summit, and in the end came up with the ridiculous compromise that he could attend the first dinner and the last morning
but not the discussion of economic affairs; this is merely a
symbol. What in fact happened is much more serious. After
many years of progress in European unification, this process
has now come to a halt. The accession of Britain, Ireland, and
Denmark was the last major step forward. I have alluded to the
reasons why economic and monetary union as an objective
faltered on the rocks of world monetary upheavals. The customs
union is still there, but, of course, it is precarious if there is
no progress; indeed all countries under pressure are liable
to be tempted by the virus of protectionism. There may be a
further enlargement of the European Community; the accession of Greece is under negotiation, and Spain and Portugal
have expressed interest; but enlargement is not internal progress. Nor is the direct election of a European Parliament
sufficient without any noticeable increase in its powers. Europe
needs a new definition of its purpose. These new objectives
must take account of the fact that the last few years have been
years of divergence rather than of convergence, years of difference rather than unity. It is time for somebody to interpret
the facts of life for Europeans, including both the European
interest and the interest in European–American relations.

Thus far this somebody has not emerged. And so we find a
rather paradoxical situation. The now president of the United
States is likely to be more patient with Europe and its difficulties in pulling itself together than were his predecessors because
he is a man of alliances who recognizes underlying strength and
significance as well as visible power. Rather than responding
to the encouraging challenge, Europe is further away than it
was from being a recognizable, organized, self-confident pillar
of the world of freedom, of human rights, and democracy. The
president will need a lot of patience to cope with his European
partners. And Europe will need a lot of initiative to pull itself
together. You will not have failed to notice that I hope that

these two virtues will prevail—American patience and European initiative—because I am quite sure that if they do, the world will be a better place. After five acts of drama, we can do with a little plain sailing and even with a few lighter touches of comedy.

The relationship between Europe and America takes a lot of understanding and mutual tolerance as well as respect. These attitudes have to be learned and taught.

PART II

THE SOCIAL
DIMENSION

1

INTERNATIONAL ASPECTS OF THE GERMAN RESISTANCE AGAINST HITLER

Werner Steltzer

NOBODY, NO GERMAN in his right mind, denies or belittles the terrible things that happened from 1933 to 1945. The six and one-half years before World War II and the more than five and one-half years of the war are recognized by the vast majority of Germans to have been the darkest phase in our history and a cause of deepest shame—especially for those who, like myself, were participants in and witnesses of the events in question.

And yet it seems that something extraordinary came into existence during that era; something unique developed perhaps as genuinely German as the dark aspect of the times, as though under the pressure and heat of dictatorship, inhumanity, terror, and brutality, a new understanding of human dignity in the sense of mutual responsibility was born. My thesis is that the victims of and the participants in the German resistance against Hitler showed that not only in theory but also in practice the national interest must be dethroned as the highest political value. They introduced an orientation toward politics and the evaluation of historical challenges.

Throughout history many German political efforts failed in the sense that their immediate goals were not accomplished: *Die Bauernkriege*, the farmers' upheavals and wars to free themselves of feudal despotism and exploitation in medieval times; the 1848 revolution for the realization of democratic values and guidelines in all fields of political life; the German resistance against Hitler; the 17th of June 1953, when the demonstrations by and the revolt of German workers for freedom and justice in East Germany were crushed by military force. Can the people who were engaged in these movements and fell victim to their oppressors be dismissed as irrelevant, or is it perhaps an obligation to learn from historical lessons?

The answer to this question is very important for the discussion of the topic: international aspects of the German resistance against Hitler. I consider three principles to be most relevant for the evaluation:

1. The principle of the nation-state as the highest political value and orientation for political action has been nullified.

2. The dignity of man is the ultimate consideration in politics.

3. People of different background, creed, and political affiliation can cooperate to achieve common goals.

Probably nobody would disagree with these principles in theory, although all of us know that they are not guidelines in practice. But as far as the German resistance is concerned, I shall submit evidence that

a) Some of the highest officials of the German government committed treason against their state in order to avoid world war;

b) People preferred concentration camps and death to obeying inhuman orders;

c) Junkers, trade unionists, conservatives, and socialists as well as representatives of the Catholic and Protestant churches cooperated in the German resistance against Hitler.

I understand quite well that many people who concede good-will and honest conviction to these statements may consider them personal opinions and subjective interpretations that lack proof. Let me therefore illustrate these points with a few quotations.

Gerhard Leibholz, for many years a judge on our supreme court, the *Bundesverfassungsgericht*, declared in reference to the fundamental political meaning of the German resistance against Hitler:

In the conflict between the principle of the nation–state on the one hand and—if I may say so—the ideological principle on the other, in this specific conflict which has to a great extent marked our century, the German resistance has given, for the first time in the history of mankind, priority to the principle of justice over the principle of the nation–state. Thus the German resistance has denied to the nation–state the supremacy (dignitas and autarchy) which it had acquired in past centuries. This, it seems to me, is an event of more than just European importance, an event, which National Socialism has produced against its own intentions and which has not yet been sufficiently recognized in the Western nations. The acknowledgement of the primacy of man—Humanitas—beyond the principle of the nation–state is in my view the most positive contribution Germany can contribute to the making of Europe. In reality we are witnesses to an event which has, if I see it correctly, opened a new age.

On another occasion Leibholz made a statement that, if valid, and I think that it is, reflects upon a primarily German but also an international aspect of the German resistance against Hitler:

The life of the German people will in the long run symbolically depend on the evaluation, rank and importance which we are prepared to allocate to the 20th of July 1944 in our history as all-German day.

In other words, Leibholz draws these conclusions in his analysis of the German resistance against Hitler:

1. The clear transcendence of the principal of the nation-state opens the possibility for a new age of international cooperation.

2. The German identity and the German understanding of their own history depend ultimately on their evaluation of the German resistance against Hitler.

These statements are made in full awareness of the fact that the German resistance failed completely, both militarily and politically. In retrospect, it is a fact that political and military developments and events would not have been different from what they actually were if there had not been any German resistance at all. It is also fair to say that the worst defeat that the German resistance ever suffered was the nomination of Adolf Hitler as chancellor of the German Reich by Reichspräsident Generalfeldmarschall Paul von Hindenburg on January 30, 1933. After this, there was practically no chance for a change without support from the outside. Thus another international aspect of the German resistance against Hitler becomes manifest: Once a dictatorship is established in a modern industrial state, the means at its command for surveillance, communications control, and policing exclude the possibilities of overthrow and change from the inside.

It is obvious that the German opposition against Hitler falls into the category of heroic political efforts that have failed. It remains to be seen whether it still carries a message of political meaning for our day and for the future. If the answer is no, we should leave the issue of the German resistance against Hitler to the historians. If the answer is yes, if there are important international aspects to the German resistance against Hitler, then we ought to try to interpret the principles behind these aspects.

Before I attempt to justify my positive answer to this question, I shall make two remarks, one personal, concerning the subject:

1. Theodor Steltzer, my father, was a well-known member of the German resistance against Hitler. As a member of the *Kreisauer Kreis*, he was sentenced to death but not executed because Scandinavian bishops intervened on his behalf at a time when for purely personal reasons Himmler wanted to avoid the further antagonism of leading Scandinavians. From these facts I derive no rights and no specific authority to deal with aspects of the German resistance. I was not a member of it. I was an officer of the reserve in the German army, and in spite of many apprehensions and strong criticism of the situation in Germany, I considered it my duty to be a good soldier in the service of my country. It was not until I became a prisoner of war and had access to the publication of the full truth about events behind the frontlines that I realized that by being an efficient soldier I was at the same time, although unknowingly and unwillingly, an outpost of German concentration camps. This kind of insight or understanding is not easy to deal with, and it will remain with many people of my generation to the end of our days.

2. Nothing of what I am going to say is meant to minimize, belittle, balance, or even exculpate our historic responsibility for what happened between 1933 and 1945. No remark about non-Germans or foreign countries is aimed at accusation or self-justification. All of these remarks, in my view, are essential to understanding the meaning of the implications of our topic.

I have chosen five questions concerning the German resistance against Hitler, questions that are understandably asked by many people:

1. Was there a genuine German opposition against Hitler after he was nominated chancellor?

2. Did the 20th of July 1944, the futile attempt to kill Hitler

after almost five years of war, embody all of the German resistance against Hitler?

3. What about numbers? Were there merely a few, or did many Germans try to change the course of events?

4. If any German opposition to speak of existed, why did it play such a small role compared with the resistance movements of other countries in national and international discussions after the war?

5. Why bother about the death of a few thousand when the war took the lives of more than 50 million people?

The answers to these questions may also furnish answers to the question of whether there were truly international aspects of the German resistance against Hitler. I shall not deal individually or systematically with these questions but rather discursively.

Nobody, not even the most skeptical critic, denies that the 20th of July was an act of resistance. But what went on before? When did the resistance actually start?

Let us pass briefly in reverse order through the years in question: Did it begin

in 1943, when Stalingrad fell, when Rommel was defeated in North Africa, when Italy changed fronts?

in 1942, when it became obvious that Germany had over-extended its means, resources, and capacities?

in 1941, when the Battle of Britain was lost and war was declared on the United States?

in 1940, when Denmark, Norway, Holland, Belgium, and France were overrun and occupied?

in 1939, when Poland was blitzed and humiliated, at the actual beginning of World War II?

in 1938, when Czechoslovakia and Austria fell and the "crystal night" of November 8 signaled to everyone the true face of Nazi terror within Germany?

in 1937, when theoretically the Enabling Act of 1933 ended and nothing happened?

in 1936, when the Olympic Games at Berlin seemed to justify Hitler's methods and successes?

in 1935, when the navy deal with Great Britain was settled and universal military training reintroduced?

in 1934, when Hitler liquidated his opponents in the so-called Röhm putsch?

in 1933, when Hitler was made chancellor, pushed the Enabling law through Parliament, and liquidated political parties?

For the moment, let us look at the years before the war only. They reveal two significant facts:

1. Beginning with January 30, 1933, the German opponents of Hitler were persecuted, illegally arrested, beaten, tortured, slain, murdered, or put into concentration camps whose inmates, for the first six years of National Socialist rule, were, for the most part, Germans only. As a matter of fact, the efficiency of the Gestapo and the whole terror machine of the Nazi system was developed by ruthless application against Hitler's political opponents.

2. All this happened, so to speak, in broad daylight as far as the international community was concerned. Foreign correspondents reported it in their newspapers and radio broadcasts. Willi Münzenberg wrote his famous *Brown Book of Hitler Terror* in 1933. It was published by Alfred A. Knopf in New York, making it available to a wide readership in the English-speaking world. Hans Rothfels,

a German emigrant and professor at the University of Chicago during the war, wrote in his book *The German Opposition to Hitler*:

It was well known, however, all over the world that, since early 1933, a wave of persecution had spread through Germany, and that the most energetic potential opponents were taken into so-called protective custody or had to flee the country. But as long as the inmates of concentration camps were Germans only, the horrors committed there were given little attention internationally. When the Brown Book of the Hitler Terror was published by Alfred Knopf in New York, it was reviewed in the New York Times of October 15, 1933, by Mr. James W. Gerard, former United States Ambassador to Germany. With this very book before him, Mr. Gerard saw fit to write: "Hitler is doing much for Germany, his unification of the Germans, his destruction of communism, his training of the young, his creation of a Spartan state, animated by patriotism, his curbing of parliamentary government, so unsuited to the German character, his protection of the rights of private property are all good." When people who had fled Germany told their English or American friends about their own or their friends' experiences in Buchenwald or Oranienburg or Dachau, they often met with a mild incredulity, certainly with regard to the numbers involved or the methods applied.

This quotation is not used for the purpose of blaming Mr. Gerard or any other foreign observer of the German scene. Its only purpose is to underline two facts:

1. German resistance was in existence and was engaged in a desperate battle.

2. The situation in Germany was well publicized in foreign countries.

But in foreign countries, as in Germany, the dangers of nazism were either ignored or underestimated. After carefully supervised visits to a few concentration camps, foreign delegations considered them tidy. In the view of many, law and order had returned to the politically restless scene of the Weimar Republic. The *National Geographic Magazine* had a long and quite flattering story about National Socialist Germany in its February issue of 1937.

The period of 1937–38 was perhaps the time of Hitler's greatest international recognition, the year after the Olympic Games of 1936 in Berlin, attended by practically all nations of the world—the Soviet Union had never participated in the Olympics and stayed away also in 1936—before Munich and the crystal night against the German Jews and Jewish property.

In November 1937 Hitler summoned leading officials of the armed forces and the foreign service to a special conference. He stated flatly that he intended to solve the problem of German space (Lebensraum) by force. When the foreign secretary, Herr von Neurath, and the chief of the General Staff, General Ludwig Beck, warned about the political implications and military dangers of such a step, Hitler declared that it was his "unchangeable decision" to take the Sudetenland, part of Czechoslovakia, by force on September 27, 1938—or shortly thereafter.

After this announcement, the chief of the General Staff and the permanent under-secretary in the Foreign Office, Ernst von Weizsäcker, decided to act. Their mental states and the philosophy behind their determination were best expressed in a memorandum from Beck to the commander of the army, General von Brauchitsch. At the end of this memorandum Beck concluded:

Final decisions about the continuity of the nation are at stake here. History will burden these leaders with a blood guilt if they fail to act according to their knowledge and their conscience both as experts and as members of the state. Their soldierly obedience has its limit at that point where their knowledge, their conscience and their responsibility forbid the execution of an order.

If in such a situation their advice and warnings fail to find a hearing, then they have the right and the duty to the people and to history to resign from their offices. If they act with a united will, execution of an action of war is impossible. Thereby they will have saved their fatherland from the worst, from ruin.

It is a lack of greatness and a lack of understanding of the task if at such times a soldier in the highest position sees his duties and obligations only in the limited frame of his military task, without becoming aware of his highest responsibility to the people as a whole. Exceptional times demand exceptional actions.

After careful preparations had been made and precautions had been taken, a trusted person, Herr Ewald von Kleist-Schmenzien, was delegated by Beck and von Weizsäcker to go to London to inform British leaders about the situation in Germany. On August 18, 1938, Herr von Kleist saw Churchill and Vansittart to whom he delivered this authorized message:

Hitler will wage war on Czechoslovakia shortly after September 27. The German High Command, ready for action against Hitler and his government, needs the encouragement of Great Britain to the extent that the British Government declares publicly it will not tolerate German military action against Czechoslovakia. If forthcoming, there would be a new Government in Germany within 48 hours.

Chamberlain, informed of the German message by Lord Vansittart, was convinced of Kleist's sincerity but recoiled from action—partly because he was disturbed by the "civil disobedience" behind the German activities.

Weizsäcker and Beck did not give up but initiated another most unusual action, which Rothfels described:

After several secret messages had already been conveyed to Chamberlain and Halifax, and after consultation with Beck, the Secretary of State in the German Foreign Office, Baron Ernst von Weizsäcker arranged for a rather unusual step. Through Erich Kordt, information and secret instructions were sent to his brother, Theodor, who at that time was Chargé d'Affaires in London. Having asked to be received in utmost secrecy, Theodor Kordt was invited to come to the backdoor of No. 10 Downing Street during the night of September 5. In his conversation with Lord Halifax he emphasized the necessity for the British government to take an unqualified stand against Hitler's plan to use force. In case a firm stand was adopted by the statesmen of the Western powers, the German army would refuse to fight against Czechoslovakia. This, at least by implication, meant a promise to overthrow the Hitler regime. The same communication was made to an influential conservative member of the House of Commons, Sir Horace Wilson, and, as will be shown later, it reached Winston Churchill too.

The message was transmitted by a cousin of the Kordts. She was not allowed to carry anything written with her but had to learn the text by heart. It was an urgent message.

Von Weizsäcker declared that he notified the British foreign secretary in the name of "political and military circles in Berlin that desired to prevent war by all means." The backing of the British government was considered essential to stop Hitler's warmongering. If Hitler's policy of force were given free rein, a return to decency and honor among European nations would definitely be blocked. If, on the other hand, a British statement were issued, Hitler's regime could very well crack because it would not be able to survive such a diplomatic defeat. Solemnly and even dramatically the message ended by saying that if Hitler proceeded according to his original plans, the political and military circles for which the message spoke would "take up arms against a sea of troubles and by opposing end them." According to Rothfels,

While awaiting British action, Beck was prepared to press the button. A setback, of course, occurred when Chamberlain decided to fly to Berchtesgaden. But in the critical days at Godesberg, with Hitler increasing his demands, and during the ensuing deadlock, there still seemed to be reason for hope. Beck, however, had meanwhile been dismissed, and the plan of making his resignation the signal did not come off. But his successor, General Halder, was prepared to go ahead, and orders were about to be issued for the action to take place on the morning of the twenty-ninth. All was ready, the Foreign Office was informed by the War Ministry. But then, at midday on September 28, word came that Chamberlain and Daladier had accepted the invitation for a conference at Munich. This sensational news ran like an electric shock through government circles, and the whole scheme collapsed.

A period full of tension ensued. The leading officials of the German Foreign Office and of the German military high command felt this tension more than did anybody else. There was no chance of avoiding action. The only choice seemed to be an impossible alternative. On the one hand, there was Hitler, supreme commander of the armed forces and head of state of the German *Reich*, to whom all had been obliged to swear oaths of allegiance. Hitler wanted military action against Czechoslovakia, action that the officers of his Foreign Office wanted to forestall. Insurrection, although intended, planned, and well prepared, would be most difficult at a time when foreign respect for Germany—after the Olympic Games of 1936 and before the next series of criminal acts against Germans and foreign countries was perpetrated—was high, and the German people were aware of this respect. For political as well as psychological reasons Germans who wanted to change the clearly foreseeable course of events needed the support requested in the German under-secretary's message to Lord Halifax: The public declaration by the British government that unprovoked German military action against Czechoslovakia would not be tolerated.

However, during this period, unbeknown to the German plotters, preparations for the fatal meetings at Berchtesgaden and Munich were already under way. The agreements at Munich spoiled everything. It was not possible to overthrow Hitler after he had achieved by negotiation an international agreement that had not only been signed by himself and Mussolini but also by Chamberlain and Daladier.

Let me insert a premature remark: After the war it was said by many foreign observers—in stunning accordance with what German Nazis and Hitler himself had said—that the people who stood behind the attempt to kill Hitler on July 20, 1944, constituted merely a small clique of overambitious officers who wanted to save themselves and their interests in view of a clearly lost war. The implications of these observations were—

and are—that all members of the 20th of July movement had supported Hitler in times of his successes and had only forsaken him when his failure became obvious; by implication, these people in particular and the German resistance against Hitler in general were discredited. It is true that some early supporters of Hitler needed the experiences of disappointment and the war losses before they realized the full danger of Hitler and joined the resistance. But it may be worth remembering that those who were first executed after the coup that failed were also those who had tried to avoid World War II before it started: Beck, Goerdeler, Witzleben, Hoepner, and Oster, to name a few.

After Munich, the Foreign Office and the military high command—as a matter of fact, German resistance as such—did not give up their quest for support from foreign countries. Adam von Trott zu Solz traveled to Great Britain and the United States in 1939 for that purpose but with negative results. Louis P. Lochner, for 20 years Associated Press correspondent in Berlin who had personal ties to members of the German resistance, tried in vain to deliver similar messages to President Roosevelt after his return to the United States. Roosevelt refused to see Mr. Lochner. Two German pastors, Bonhoeffer and Schönfeld, saw Bishop Bell of Chichester—the meetings took place in Stockholm—and delivered a memorandum about the German resistance, explaining its aims and the need for support. Bishop Bell forwarded this information to the British Foreign Secretary Anthony Eden. The bishop received this answer:

Personal and confidential   Foreign Office, S.W.1
                                                        17th July 1942
My dear Bishop,
When you visited me on 30th June you were kind enough to let me have a memorandum on your talk with two German pastors whom you had met in Stockholm at the end of May, together with a report on a statement by one of the pastors.

These interesting documents have by now been carefully examined. Without challenging the honest convictions of your informers in the least, I have no doubt that it would be contrary to the interest of our nation to provide them with any answer whatever. I know well that this decision will be somewhat disappointing to you, but in view of the delicate circumstances connected with it I cannot do other than ask to accept it, something that you will surely understand.

Sincerely yours,

Anthony Eden

"Contrary to the interest of our nation" is, in our context anyway, the crucial formula of that letter. The interest of the nation did not allow the British government to give support to the German resistance or at least the assurance that it needed for successful action. This was not a casual but a historic misunderstanding between two sides that had identical aims: the end of Hitler's rule, the end of National Socialist rule in Germany. The predominance of national interest in the British deliberations is clearly stated in Eden's letter to Bishop Bell. For many people it is perhaps unbelievable that for the German resistance the motivation was precisely the opposite. Therefore, to support that statement and to dig a little deeper into the problem, I shall quote a few prominent people:

1. Carl Friedrich Goerdeler, former mayor of Leipzig and thereafter head of the conservative group in the resistance against Hitler, wrote to an American friend shortly after the failures in 1938:

... the German people did not want war; the army was ready to do everything to prevent it. ... the world had been warned and informed in time. If these warnings had been heeded, and if one had acted accordingly, Germany would be free of her dictator today and could turn against Mussolini. In a few weeks we could begin to shape a lasting peace which would be based on justice, reason and decency. Germany with a government of decent men would have been prepared to solve the Spanish problem together with France and

England, to remove Mussolini and to create peace in the Far East
in cooperation with the United States. The way might have been
open for good cooperation in the economic and social fields and for
pacification between labor, capital and the state, for an elevation
of moral concepts, and for a new effort to raise the general standard
of living. . . .

2. Hans Rothfels, the late historian, remarked shortly after
the war in a book about the German resistance:

The different resistance movements which developed during the last
war in the occupied areas, were all part of international politics. In
different ways and with different weight they all contributed to the
great alliance against Hitler and were supported by this alliance.
Some of them had considerable influence on the outcome of the
fighting. It seems dubious whether this point of view is applicable
to the German opposition. Certainly not, if one only looks at the
support from outside, or the scope of the actual and practical cooperation. And yet it might be argued—and is perhaps even of utmost
importance—that the resistance movement in Germany was in a very
significant way much more international than any other resistance
movement inasmuch as it broke through and overcame—in a way
that had never been done before—the conventional categories of
political and social thinking, interests of nations and classes. Thus the
German resistance movement pointed into the future of our present
situation in which the humanitarian or human but anyway international fronts cut through the borders of states, power-blocks or
social systems which exclude each other.

On another occasion, Rothfels commented:

As they had to strive for a negative goal—defeat of their own country—they needed a positive ideal that transcended the obvious one,
to get rid of the dictator or abolish tyranny in one particular country. On the whole the opposition had won (politically) a conciliatory
but firm position between the principles of East and West—a very
progressive position which should be worth considering in face of
our present crisis of ideology and social systems.

3. Golo Mann, the son of Thomas Mann and now a retired
professor of political science, who also lived in the United
States during the war, had this to say:

It, the conspiracy, did not come late. It was of a very early origin, and its goal then was not to avoid the utmost consequences of military defeat for Germany but war itself. We did not know it then, did not know it in 1944 but members of the British Government knew it then; and it was neither nice nor intelligent of them to conceal it and to put the men of the twentieth of July off as hardened militarists, who only now, by far too late, wanted to save their own skin—at best their army—because they knew that the war was lost. This is one of the disgraces (Schandflecken) in the history of allied policy and warfare. Winston Churchill knew that in 1938 the Generals Beck, Halder, Witzleben, Hoepner, Oster had prepared nothing less than a coup d'état, that they had planned to overthrow Hitler, to arrest him at the very moment he actually waged war and to prove his crimes before a German court. A bold enterprise for which chances of success were incomparably better then than 6 years later. He, Churchill, had personally seen their emissary Ewald von Kleist, had disapproved of the cold, suspicious attitude of the Prime Minister, Chamberlain, towards the German opposition. He knew why Beck and Halder had failed. Not because of themselves but because of the Munich agreement; because of the capitulation of the western powers who gave to the German dictator the greatest bloodless triumph, which in return silenced all criticism.

4. Winston Churchill is quoted as having said in 1946:

In Germany there lived an opposition which grew weaker and weaker through its sacrifices and an unnerving international policy, but which belongs to the noblest and greatest that has ever been produced in the political history of any people. These men fought without help from within or without—driven only by the restlessness of their consciences. As long as they lived they were invisible and unrecognizable to us because they had to hide. But in their dead the resistance became visible. These dead do not have it in their power to justify everything that happened in Germany. But their deeds and sacrifices are the foundation of the reconstruction. We hope for the time in which this heroic chapter of German domestic history will find its just evaluation.

Again, this survey of the resistance is no attempt to vindicate Germany of its responsibility for the crimes of 1933 to 1945 or to accuse other people and countries. But the presentation of these facts seems unavoidable if we want to understand the incompatibility of mentalities that frustrated cooperation between the German resistance on the one hand and allied authorities on the other. It involved, in my view, no mistake, or failure, or guilt on either side but the clash or divergence of the overruling principles invoked by the two sides: an understandable but obsolete one, the principle of the nation-state on the allied side and on the side of the German resistance, the principle of international cooperation beyond the limits of national sovereignty that perhaps had been theoretically postulated but never really practiced before.

On the German side, the highest officials of the supposedly most nationalist branches of the German government—the military branch and the diplomatic branch—knew that their national resources against catastrophes were completely exhausted, and circumstances compelled them to seek international assistance in an attempt to avoid catastrophe. The often quoted slogan "right or wrong, my country" had taken on an absurd and cynical meaning for those Germans because the "wrongs" had developed in directions that were totally unacceptable. In both internal and foreign affairs, nationalist arbitrariness and extremism had forced the leading people of the German resistance to reach beyond nationalism in order to ensure the return of human values to the domestic and international scenes. Against this background one has to consider the fact that German patriots in the highest positions broke their oaths of allegiance and committed high treason in order to stop Hitler. By informing the British government—a potential military enemy—of Hitler's plans to invade Czechoslovakia and of their plans to overthrow the Nationalist Socialist government, their actions constituted clear cases of treason, the ultimate offense against the nation-state.

On the other side, specifically the British, there was a democratic government, instituted by free national elections and controlled by a freely elected parliament. Yet there was no doubt expressed in the principle of nationalism, especially as there seemed to be very little reason to leave the solution of important questions to international institutions. On the contrary, the clear dangers, even threats to the nation, activated and intensified national thinking and feeling, and the expression "right or wrong, my country" received new and actual meaning for a people who had a great national history. It was understandable, almost logical, that they could not see any sense in thoughts and motivations other than those based on nationalism, that they were suspicious of people who seemingly acted against their own country. Seen in proper perspective, the remark of Mr. Chamberlain about "civil disobedience" with which he dismissed the message of the German resistance to the British government is pardonable.

To me, this fundamental difference in mentality is the only convincing explanation for the fact that before the war, during the war, and—in a way—even after the war, understanding and cooperation between the German resistance on the one hand and allied authorities and resistance groups in the occupied countries on the other were not achieved. Allied war aims and those of the national resistance groups in occupied countries were clear and easy to describe: peace, the restoration of national integrity, punishment, and defeating the enemy. The aims of the German resistance were fundamentally different. In the first place, the resisters had to work, pray, and fight for the defeat of their own fatherland. They knew—or sensed— that there would be no status quo ante, not for their country, not for the rest of Europe, nor even for the world. They knew also that Germany—as a nation and as a people—would have to suffer, to pay, and to sacrifice once the goals for which most members of the German resistance fought so conscientiously were achieved.

In my remarks about the international aspects of the German resistance against Hitler, I have limited myself to military and diplomatic resistance activities before the war and by no means to all of them. There is, of course, much more to be said if the task involves drawing a comprehensive picture of the German resistance. I do not say this in order to boast or to blow up a neglected historical episode but in order to apologize to those persons whose activities I have not mentioned.

There were numerous groups other than the military and the diplomatic ones. Let me mention very briefly a few of them. Before the question arises of why there were so many resistance groups instead of one efficient group, let me try to develop an explanation that perhaps will help to illuminate both the fatal political schism of Germany at the end of the Weimar Republic and the diversification of the German resistance against Hitler. The political situation reflected in the many political parties fighting each other passionately although acknowledging the democratic principle, froze and was petrified into some kind of immobility, once democratic freedoms were abolished. To a certain extent, the different resistance groups mirrored the party situation that existed when Hitler came to power. Hitler, his party organization, and the machinery of administration under his command took great care, if this is not too polite an expression, to ensure that there was as little communication as possible between and among adversaries of the Nationalist Socialist government.

Not surprisingly, the strongest resistance group consisted of those who are normally called "left": the Social Democrats, the trade unions, and the Communist party. Perhaps it is misleading to mention the Communist party and the Social Democratic party in the same breath because until the end of the Weimar Republic the Communists considered the Social Democrats their worst enemies and called them "Sociofascists."

The Communists were the most experienced in subversive activities, the best organized for that purpose, and the most vulnerable when confronted with a ruthless opponent in power. They maintained extensive files that the Nazis seized immediately. After the Reichstag fire of February 1933, 4,000 functionaries of the Communist party were arrested. The Communist party also suffered from other problems because of the Stalin-Hitler Pact of 1939. Their losses were extremely high.

The trade unions and the Social Democratic party also suffered serious disadvantages from the fact that they were better organized than were other opponents of Hitler. Their property was seized and their members were brought under immediate control. Socialist opposition to Hitler was the strongest in Germany. Accordingly, their losses were high and, as many later felt, tragically high.

My father, who was one of the founders of the postwar Christian Democratic Union, told me in our first conversation after the war that apart from the tragedy of the death of so many millions of people all over the world, the heaviest loss for Germany was not in material destruction but in the death of such Social Democrats as Julius Leber, Theo Haubach, and Adolf Reichwein.

It has been argued—and not wrongly—that millions of German Christians supported or followed Hitler. However, the very strong and brave resistance groups in both denominations cannot be overlooked. Two names, Martin Niemöller for the Confessing church and Bishop Graf Galen for the Catholic church, may stand for the many who lived, fought, and suffered in the Christian resistance groups against Hitler.

The "Red Band" (Rote Kapelle) was perhaps the best organized and most efficient German resistance group of all. It was clearly communist and worked with the Soviet Secret Service. After the discovery of this group, all of its members were liquidated. There is little doubt that this group acted out of idealism and for human values and not as obedient tools of the Soviet Union.

The conservative resistance centered around Carl Goerdeler, former lord mayor of Leipzig. Its political aims differed from those of other groups, but its members shared with all other resistance groups the conviction that future policies, whatever they would eventually be, would have to be worked out on a democratic basis and with democratic procedures both internationally and at home.

The *Kreisau* Circle received its name from the estate Kreisau that belonged to the central figure in this group, Count Helmuth von Moltke. It was especially in this circle that men of all (democratic) political convictions and from all social backgrounds integrated their efforts to plan new European cooperation based on the central value of human dignity. Because of their preoccupations with postwar plans and conceptions, this group became after the war the most interesting one for intellectuals all over the world—including those in the Soviet Union.

The National Committee for a Free Germany consisted of German emigrants and soldiers in the Soviet Union who wanted to fight and stop Hitler by all available means. In this very large group people from all backgrounds and positions cooperated. Perhaps it should be borne in mind that when the Western allies talked about the fragmentation of Germany, the Russians emphasized that the continuation of a whole Germany was one of the dominant points of their postwar plans for Europe. All German resistance groups pursued independently three identical goals:

1. The abolishment of the regime;

2. The democratic establishment of a humane political system;

3. The institutionalization of international cooperation.

We have no accurate figures on the number of victims who were members of the German resistance against Hitler. In the last relatively free election, on March 5, 1933, although held under Hitler's government and after the Reichstagsbrand, the National Socialist party did not win a majority. At least more than 50 percent of Germans were against him. According to estimates, 1.5 million Germans were inmates of concentration camps, approximately one million of them for political reasons. At the beginning of World War II, 25,000 Germans were in concentration camps. After the war and the enormous losses incurred among the members of the resistance, 250,000 were officially acknowledged as active opponents of the Nazi regime in Germany. These figures do not include those who became opponents by behaving decently, even if they acted in violation of the legal statutes of the time. For instance, 5,000 Berliners took German Jews into their homes, hid them there, and shared their ration cards with them, knowing that discovery would mean capital punishment for guest and host.

Two things usually come to mind when people hear this report:

1. Why are no accurate figures available?

2. Why is so little known about what these impressive, although only estimated figures, represent?

There are many reasons.

a) Nazi authorities took great care to obscure the differences between crime and political offenses.

b) The regional authorities of the regime could act arbitrarily against political opponents and were free of bureaucratic routine in this field at least.

c) No systematic research was conducted after the war under allied authority, because facts about another Germany were not only unwanted but suppressed. Even American journalists who did research about the German resistance on their own initiative were forbidden to proceed.

d) When the captured archives and files were finally given to German authorities, the German government was not interested in research into and publication of information about the German resistance in general. It was the time when the Federal Republic of Germany was being integrated into the Western alliances. It was also the time of the East-West conflict, the cold war, and presentations about German resistance would have had to include favorable reports about communist participation in the resistance.

e) Because there was no systematic research after the war, the records, data, and material were so scattered that central documentation and evaluation were later impossible.

I shall close with a quotation from our first President Theodor Heuss. On the tenth anniversary of July 20, 1944, he challenged each and every German by saying:

The shame, to which Hitler had subjected the Germans has been wiped off the befouled German name. The legacy is still efficacious; the obligation not yet discharged.

2

THE CHURCHES
AND THE
RECONSTRUCTION
OF GERMANY*

Frederick Spotts

RELIGION AND POLITICS can be separated analytically by historians and schoolteachers, Leopold von Ranke observed, but in fact they are intertwined. This epiphenominalism in the evolution of church and state in Europe is nowhere truer than in Germany, where the Reformation and its political consequences mark the face of society to this day.

The churches—the Lutheran, the Reformed churches, and the Catholic church, comprised of almost all German Christians—have greater continuity than has any other institution in Germany. In a country whose history falls into a series of rough temporal fragments—from the Treaty of Westphalia to the Napoleonic invasions, from the dissolution of the Holy Roman Empire to unification, from 1871 to 1918, from 1918 to 1933, from 1933 to 1945, from 1945 to 1949, and so on—the

*This paper is based on the writer's book, *The Churches and Politics in Germany*, Wesleyan University Press, 1973.

churches have been the only institution to traverse these convulsions. Consequently, they have been a central element of whatever stability German society has known over the centuries.

In 1945 the churches were the only institution that survived the Third Reich, the war, and the capitulation. Despite their blemished record in the Weimar Republic and the Third Reich, they alone had maintained their autonomy from the Nazi state and alone at times had openly opposed it. Neither church had been a friend of the Weimar Republic. Many, perhaps most, Protestant churchmen at first welcomed Hitler's accession to power, anticipating that the Third Reich would restore all the virtues of the Second. The signature of the *Reichskonkordat* in July 1933, which the Vatican intended as a way of protecting German catholicism, was under the circumstances a step forward in the National Socialists' consolidation of power. Far from strengthening the Catholics will to resist, the treaty appeared to many of the faithful to signify the regime's acceptability and the church's desire for a modus vivendi with it. It was this independence that raised a continuous challenge to the Nazi system. At the war's end they enjoyed a status and influence, both among Germans and among the occupation powers, that was unique at the time and virtually unprecedented in modern German history. Therefore even though the German state itself passed into the control of four foreign powers, the churches—and only the churches—were permitted to retain their independence from occupation controls and to carry on their activities virtually unimpeded.

The churches' tremendous authority had two important results. On the one hand the occupation armies, including the Russian, turned to church leaders—pastors and priests in villages and towns, and bishops in large cities—for advice on the entire range of civil affairs: Who should be given important positions in civil government; who should be dismissed from positions in important public and private institutions; who should be allowed to teach in schools and universities. American and British authorities went so far as to ask two bishops—a Protestant in the former case and a Catholic in the latter—to be regional civil governors. The Russians appointed a clergyman from each church to the Berlin city council.

At the same time the churches became the de facto political representatives of the German people, filling the void left by the collapse of the German government. In the simplest sense they were the only bodies that could address communications to the military government, were permitted to maintain foreign contacts, could hold meetings, and whose officials were allowed to travel freely throughout Germany. In a larger sense they became the defenders of the interests of the German people vis-à-vis the occupation powers, striving to influence the decisions of the military governments and to ameliorate their punitive policies. In this capacity it was inevitable that they would come into conflict with the three Western military governments over a broad range of political and social issues.

At the Potsdam conference the four powers agreed that Germany should be democratized, denazified, and demilitarized —objectives that the churches supported in principle—but had no clear idea of what such broad aims meant in practical terms. When they began to interpret these aims as requiring German society to be radically reshaped and the German people to be—in the Orwellian terms of the day—"reeducated" and "reoriented," church leaders began to view occupation policies with the deepest skepticism. Most religious leaders were convinced that Germany was on the threshold of an economic and social misery so profound that the middle class would be wiped out and only the extreme left would survive. They feared that the Western powers did not understand the risks and were inviting social revolution. The Catholic bishops in particular were obsessed by the fear that with the widespread destitution of the country and the Russians at the Elbe, all Germany would easily be engulfed by communism.

In the churches' view rehabilitation and reconstruction were the most obvious needs of the German people. Consequently, when the occupiers made industrial dismantlement and denazification their overriding political aims, the churches fought them with moral and social conviction. Many factories were saved from dismantling through the intervention of church leaders in support of political figures until the policy was finally recognized by the allies to be a grave mistake.

An even more bitter dispute arose over denazification, particularly in the American zone where it was a paramount aim of occupation policy. As most Catholic and Protestant bishops saw it, national socialism had been imposed on the German people by a group of political thugs and had been accepted by most of the population at first for innocent reasons and later because there was no choice. Because there were few, if any, convinced Nazis left by 1945 denazification would be a relatively simple task that must not cause social or political turmoil. They insisted that the broad approach of trying to "denazify" the whole adult population by imposing arbitrary and mechanical criteria was not only doomed to failure but would make it difficult to distinguish the innocent from serious offenders. Church leaders were also aware that a purge based on a person's membership in a Nazi organization would leave virtually only Social Democrats and Communists eligible for positions in public life.

Ecclesiastical officials fought the denazification program—privately, through their contacts with military leaders, and publicly, from the pulpit and in pastoral letters as well as in criticism printed in the press. When they made no headway by argument, they took to sabotaging the program through influencing the denazification tribunals that were in German hands and by persuading German lawyers who were engaged in the program to withdraw from it. By the end of 1947, the program was clearly failing and for the reasons that the churches had foreseen. The steady pressure by the churches—joined in their opposition by trade unionists, Social Democrats, and even

Communists—finally forced American authorities to alter the program in many of the ways that the churches had called for. By the fall of 1948, denazification was finished.

The churches' reservations had proved sound; it was they who had been largely guided by cold empiricism, whereas occupation policy had been too much based on fuzzy-minded idealism. Experience demonstrated that the aims of denazification were ambiguous and that its procedures were largely unworkable. Ecclesiastical leaders anticipated sooner and more clearly than had the occupiers, that individual injustice and social revolution could result if the policy were carried through. It is true that the churches failed to make clear that in opposing the denazification program they were not opposed to denazification as such. But by being more right than the military, they not only had the force of logic on their side but the great majority of the public as well. Against the churches' determined opposition, the program was almost certainly doomed to failure. The churches enjoyed greater public confidence than did the military government. During the whole of the occupation period there was no clearer example of how the occupation authorities ignored a basic fact of German society and as a result largely failed to achieve their most important objective.

※   ※   ※

The churches' role in the political and social reconstruction of Germany was of considerably greater and more lasting importance than were their interventions, successful and unsuccessful, with the occupation powers. It is probably not going too far to say that the Federal Republic would not exist in its present form today had it not been for the political stance taken by the churches at the end of the war along with the continuing importance of the religious element in German political life. This ecclesiastical influence made itself felt in a variety of ways: in some cases through a direct political decision that set in train a vital course of events; in other cases through giving the government the support indispensable for its most important policies; and in still others through powerful though indirect influence in favor of certain political concepts and practices. These influences helped to mold the Germany of today: a country with a two-and-a-half party system, pragmatic, nonideological politics, conservative economic policies, and a foreign policy based on the Atlantic alliance and the European Community. What is taken for granted today was anything but predestined in 1945, when every political question was open and when the only organized political forces—those of the left—had entirely different goals.

This is not to suggest that at the end of the war the churches had a grand political strategy or that they worked together on behalf of common political objectives. None of this was the case; the two churches, although maintaining unprecedentedly good relations after 1945, worked in opposite political directions and employed divergent means to advance their objectives. However, the political approach adopted by the two churches was in direct reaction to what each regarded, with differing degrees of candor, as its mistaken political behavior in the Weimar Republic that had contributed to the National Socialist accession to power.

On the Protestant side this volte-face required admitting that the churches' traditional erastian, authoritarian, strongly conservative character, and its inculcation of a submissive political temper in its adherents had perverted the church's political mission and had helped to lead Germany to disaster. At their first meeting a few months after the war, Protestant leaders—whether of Lutheran or Calvinist background, whether personally conservative or liberal—made this acknowledgment. They declared that the church dare not any longer consider politics and religion separate spheres but must recognize a responsibility to itself and society for bringing Christian principles to bear in public life. The church would seek to play a role in the country's political life and would encourage its laity to recognize public service as a duty. However, church leaders cautioned that there could be no "Christian party" or "Christian policies" and that the church dare not associate itself with any political party but must work with all democratic forces in society. These views marked a radical break with the past.

The pledge was far from the accomplishment. In succeeding years there were still some clergy and laity who could not grasp as Karl Barth once put it, that "there is not a single problem harassing the state by which the church is not affected in some way or another." But there was no turning back. The occupation had drawn the church into direct political engagement. Then because the Evangelical church was split in half by the East-West frontier, every aspect of the cold war had a clear impact on the life of the church. Consequently, all of the great issues that faced the Federal Republic at its outset—reunification, the Western alliance, rearmament—were matters of both political and ecclesiastical concern to everyone in the church. By the end of the 1960s the church's annual report could note as a matter of course that when church leaders met they had "been frequently and sometimes continuously occupied during each of their sessions with the major domestic and foreign policy questions and controversies."

More often than not there were passionate disputes within the church over both the substance of the issues and what the church should do about them politically. There were some, such as Martin Niemöller and Gustav Heinemann, who at one point wanted the church to form an alliance with the Social Democrats to combat Adenauer's policies. Others wanted the church to remain silent. But under the able leadership of such men as Otto Dibelius, Kurt Scharf, and Hanns Lilje, the church took a stand on every issue of domestic and foreign significance, at times supporting and at times differing from Adenauer's objectives but without ever compromising its political neutrality.

Although these disputes at times tested ecclesiastical unity, they served in themselves to fulfill one of the major aims that the church set for itself in 1945—to encourage the Protestant laity to face difficult political issues, to debate them, and to find solutions compatible with their own convictions. Far from trying to disguise these disagreements, church leaders always argued them frankly and publicly. At times the average Protestant might have been as much confused as inspired, and for many years the spectacle of an argumentative, divided church contrasted starkly with the outward serenity of German catholicism. But the Evangelical church was one of the few institutions in the early postwar years in which dissenters, even violent dissenters, were as much a part of the institution as anyone else. The toleration of dissent put pluralist democracy into practice. It also spared the Evangelical church the grave crisis of confidence that afflicted the Catholic church in the late 1960s.

There were other and more deliberate ways in which the Protestant church worked to encourage strong democratic institutions. For its own part it cultivated good relations with all the political parties and exhorted its laity to enter politics and government service and to be active in the work of other institutions such as the trade unions. When a group of Catholics, nudged by several members of the hierarchy, organized a Catholic-Protestant secession from the German Trade Union Federation to form a Christian Trade Union, Protestant leaders intervened to preserve the federation's unity. It was central to the church's whole approach to public and political affairs that there should be no confrontation between Christians and non-Christians.

The church also used its various lay activities as a means of encouraging Protestant involvement in public life and of bringing churchmen into contact with groups outside the church. One of the most successful of these activities was the Evangelical academies. The spontaneity of their development and the fact that they originated with the laity were signs of the new mood in postwar German protestantism. The academies were established as places for a free exchange of views on the entire range of political and social problems. Novel and daring as they were under postwar conditions, the academies were exactly what Germans wanted politically and psychologically after thirteen years of national socialism. The fourteen academies held about a thousand meetings a year; probably a half million persons attended them between 1945 and 1970. The sessions, completely nonreligious in tone, dealt with an extraordinary range of topics, a catholicity that was matched by the variety of persons who participated—presidents and chancellors, industrialists and housewives, workers, students, and politicians, both German and foreign.

The Evangelical church fell short in determining what role it should play in the day-to-day political process. Given the nature of protestantism and the confederal structure of the Evangelical church, there was little possibility that the church would speak with a strong, single voice, much less be a decisive influence on the government. Torn between certain old-fashioned Lutherans who thought that the church should not be involved in specific political issues and the disciples of Karl Barth who wanted it to be an active and partisan force the church was never able to move beyond a vague consensus that it had a role to play, without ever being able to decide how much of a role or how to play it.

The Evangelical church's contribution to the Federal Republic lay therefore not in its having achieved certain concrete goals but in its broad role in inculcating general democratic principles and practices. Such an evaluation may sound trivial at this distance from the Third Reich. But learning how to govern themselves in a liberal and democratic way was the most important need of the German people after 1945. And although it is impossible to measure the extent of general influences on communal psychology, the Evangelical church deserves tremendous credit for its role as the largest institution in Germany dedicated to social conciliation, compromise, and tolerance— traits for which German political life had traditionally not been well-known but that were indispensable if parliamentary democracy were to work.

*   *   *

In the case of the Catholic church everything was the reverse. Its historic problem had not been political inactivity but an excess of involvement through the Center party in politics at every level of government. Consequently, in 1933 it had been an unwitting accessory to the destruction of the Weimar Republic. For this reason ecclesiastical leaders resolved at the end of the war that because the church had been so badly compromised it must avoid any direct participation in politics. This decision had one immediate consequence of profound significance.

The church's fateful act, its most important in the postwar period, was its decision that the Center party should not be reestablished but that Catholics should instead join Protestants in a new and secular interconfessional party. In this resolve most bishops were in agreement with most Catholic laymen. The knowledge that Catholics alone would not be strong enough to maintain the political center against the anticipated power of Communists and Social Democrats swept away all doubts. Yet giving up the Center party for the Christian Democratic Union was a tremendous gamble on the part of Catholic politicians no less than on the part of the Catholic hierarchy. And in subsequent years Catholic members of the CDU had to make important concessions in party doctrine and policy to gain Protestant support. By the time that the Federal Republic was established in 1949 a modus vivendi between the two had evolved, giving social policy and foreign affairs to Catholics and leaving economic policy in the hands of Protestants. Adenauer and Erhard were the compromise made flesh. And the gamble paid off brilliantly. The Christian Democrats won every federal election from 1949 to 1969. They became in consequence the architects of the Federal Republic and of all the policies, domestic and foreign, that it has since followed. Such was the end result of the course of events set in motion by the Catholic bishops and laity when they decided in 1945 to sacrifice the Center for an interconfessional party.

Yet in their decision to abstain from open political activity, the bishops had no intention of giving up their political influence or of disclaiming a central role for the church in public affairs. Politics would rest in the hands of the Catholic laity, but those hands would have ecclesiastical guidance—no more and no less. The bishops therefore saw it as indispensable to maintain the psychological and political unity that Catholics had developed during the Kulturkampf and had expressed through the Center party.

Strength through unity was the obsession of the bishops throughout the postwar period. They wanted Catholic secondary schools, a comprehensive range of Catholic professional and lay organizations, a Catholic press and radio station, and a Catholic university along with a trade union and a political party effectively in control of Catholics—in other words, an organizational infrastructure that would encompass Catholics from the cradle to the grave. The establishment of an inter-confessional, secular party in place of the old Centrum made Catholic cohesion even more essential if Catholics were to be dominant in the party and have a powerful voice in the state. As a result the ideal of Catholic solidarity became indistinguishable from a policy of keeping Catholics in the CDU and the CDU in power.

The sociological and political consequences of this attitude were drastic. Compromise, dissent, and pluralism had no place in the hierarchy's scheme of things. Catholic lay organizations, activities, and the press were so organized as to prevent non-conformists from having a voice or a position of authority. When a number of Catholic splinter parties, including a small revived Center, grew up after the war, the bishops and clergy bent every effort to destroy them.

Obviously, such political engagement conflicted with the church's principle of staying out of politics. In its effort to square this circle the church was drawn into its most questionable tactic of all: to legitimize its political involvement, it depicted German politics as an ideological struggle, a clash between spiritual values rather than political viewpoints. Disagreements between the parties and disputes in the Bundestag were portrayed not as matters about which persons could honorably differ but as a struggle over ultimate values and divine mandates—a position even carried over into defense and foreign affairs. On the rearmament issue, for instance, the church was not only well ahead of any other group in German society in supporting Adenauer's policy but even declared that it was a Christian duty to support such a policy. When an equally passionate controversy broke out some years later over equipping the German armed forces with nuclear weapons, the Catholic bishops once again produced a moral and a political justification for Adenauer's policy. These are only two examples of how the whole weight of the church was brought to bear upon the laity to adopt this point of view and to act politically as Catholics rather than following personal political preferences, political ideals, or material aspirations.

For about twenty years the bishops succeeded. Assisted by the lay organizations, they herded the majority of Catholics into a political bloc, tied this bloc to the CDU, muzzled their own dissidents, and conducted an ideological war against the Social Democrats who were depicted as morally unfit for political office. It would be difficult to exaggerate the political consequences of the bishops' stance. At the critical moment in the Federal Republic's history, the Catholic church gave the Adenauer government the support that it needed to carry through its policies. As one prominent Catholic politician and lay leader said, "Without the political conformity of German Catholics, the Adenauer era as it was would not have been conceivable." And it is in fact difficult to see how Adenauer could have pursued his foreign and defense policies against the formidable opposition that existed in non-Catholic circles had it not been for what the Catholic official characterized as the "automatic and unquestioning" support of Catholics. Here again, whatever is to be said about the cost to the church and the laity and to democratic principles, the bishops' position had a formidable impact on Germany—and on Europe.

There was another way in which the Catholic bishops had a substantial and lasting influence on German political life— by forcing the Social Democrats to try to come to terms with the Catholic church. For almost fifteen years after the war the Social Democrats had lost every federal election, had been defeated on every key issue of defense and foreign policy, and had made no appreciable gain among the electorate. By the mid-1950s party leaders recognized that the SPD would have to play politics on the terms set by the Christian Democrats. This tactic would require adopting the CDU's foreign and defense policies, which the Social Democrats unabashedly did. It would also require getting a sizable number of Catholic votes. But here the Social Democrats confronted one of the basic facts of postwar German political life—the interrelation between religious affiliation and voting behavior. Stated in its baldest form, the Social Democrats could count on roughly 50 percent of the Protestant vote but received at best 25 percent of the Catholic vote. Party leaders realized that in such a situation the SPD would never receive much more than one-third of the total vote in a federal election and would therefore be permanently in the opposition. The only way to make electoral headway would be to destroy the Catholic bloc vote for the CDU. To accomplish this the party would have to renounce its formal but long meaningless Marxist heritage and seek ecclesiastical acceptance. These were the central points of the Bad Godesberg program of 1959, which was in essence a ratification of the accumulated changes that had occurred in the party since the war.

The reaction in Catholic circles varied from cool to intensely hostile, with general agreement that the program was fraudulent. In the bishops' view the program was a cynical tactic of seducing Catholic votes for a party ideologically opposed to the Catholic church, as demonstrated by the party's positions on foreign affairs and public support for Catholic schools. But even when the Social Democrats altered their policy on these points a short time later, the hierarchy continued to maintain its distance. What was unacceptable to the German bishops, however, was evidently satisfactory to Pope Paul VI who in 1964 received a Social Democratic delegation, suggesting that he had no sympathy for the German hierarchy's adamancy or its one-sided commitment to the Christian Democrats.

Rome influenced the situation in another way as well. As a result of the Second Vatican Council, along with sweeping sociological changes in Germany after the mid-1960s, the old psychological and political unity of Catholics began to break down. By 1969 the Social Democrats had gained enough support from Catholic voters to form the first Social Democratic government since 1930.

      ✽   ✽   ✽

In these ways and often with effects drastically different from those intended, the Catholic and Protestant churches produced important and lasting effects on the West German state. Had Catholics founded their own party in 1945, it undoubtedly would have enjoyed the backing of a great majority of Catholics. Because Catholics constituted half of the Federal Republic's population, this situation would have left the political spectrum sharply fragmented. Protestants would have been scattered throughout a variety of other parties. The Social Democrats, without an incentive to change, might have remained fixated in their early twentieth-century brand of anti-clerical Marxism. The probable result could have been a society and a political system deeply riven by ideological and practical differences, an unstable political balance, and weak govern-ments based on shifting coalitions. Bonn would have been a repeat of Weimar. But because the Catholic church abandoned the Centrum and the Protestant church encouraged its laity to become active in both the CDU and the SPD, these two parties developed into political institutions that had never before existed in Germany—nonideological coalitions dedicated to the politics of moderation. The two parties together pro-moted the social and political circumstances under which the Federal Republic has become the most stable, pragmatic, and successful political system on the Continent.

3

THE STATUS OF
WOMEN IN A
CHANGING SOCIETY

Wendelgard von Staden

You will seldom find a German who does not start a subject away back in history or develop a complicated philosophy about it. I, too, find it best to point out chronologically the main factors that during the past century influenced the fundamental changes that we are witnessing today in our society. For what we have now is something entirely new.

One must remember that society in Europe remained static for a long time. From Charlemagne to the latter part of the nineteenth century, it was an agrarian, patriarchal civilization. The big family—three or four generations living under one roof, each member important as a helping hand, autarchic to a large degree—was the center of education and the conservator of tradition. This family was the foundation of European culture.

From childbirth to death, everything vital happened within the family. The place of the woman was clearly defined. The

167

nature of her situation required her to be responsible for the inhouse administration of the family's economy. Actually, the three K's (*Kinder, Küche, Kirche*) made sense. In addition to children and kitchen, the church provided the field for community activities. Only later, when the substance of women's traditional responsibilities began to dwindle with the rise of the bourgeois class and with the industrial age, did it become an empty cliché.

Roughly speaking, society had for a long time been divided into three main strata: the rural population, the middle class in towns and trade centers, and the aristocracy. The economic base for the ruling class was land ownership and service to the king—the one connected with the other from the time of the Franconian knights. This structure began to change only with the industrial age and finally broke down at the end of World War I. It is understandable, therefore, that we still have a strong traditional element in our mentality, only reluctantly giving in to modern times, that tempts us to regard these changes as clear signs of the end of the Western world.

Later than in Great Britian, where industrialization started, the struggle for equal rights for women began in Germany with the liberal uprising of 1848. In the constitution drafted by the assembly of the *Paulskirche* the liberals demanded equal rights for everyone as well as the right to form associations. As is well known, events in America influenced developments in Germany a great deal. But the revolution of 1848 failed, and many of our best people came to the shores of this country in the aftermath of 1848. The governments of the various German states tried to suppress political movements, forbade "women apprentices and pupils" to join discussion groups, and denied them participation in political meetings. When, in the first women's gazette, edited by Louise Otto-Peters in 1848, equal rights for men and women were demanded, the German public reacted with alarm. But the process had begun. Despite all prohibitions, groups and associations were formed to advocate the opening of job opportunities for women and their access to better education and training.

The systematic fight for equal rights was taken up by the Social Democratic party—the party of the growing working class. August Bebel, its founder, published a book entitled *Women and Socialism* that furnished the main arguments for the debates. In 1891 the Social Democrats demanded the abolition of all regulations discriminating against women. By that time German industry had absorbed many women as cheap labor, and because they formed a reservoir of potential voters women could not be overlooked any longer. But when the Social Democrats, even with the backing of middle-class groups, submitted a bill to the Reichstag granting women the right to vote, it was defeated. No other party voted for its passage.

The system of values prevailing in a given society is, I think, quite well reflected in its laws. The changes that our civil law has undergone since the turn of the century show various phases on the road to emancipation:

The Starting Point.

Before 1919 the code of law limited women's rights in the most vital spheres:

They had no right to vote.

The husband determined all matters concerning marriage and children.

He managed the family property, including his wife's, and all income from her property was his. (Hence the elaborate marriage contracts.)

Women had no right to receive pensions.

Marriage was, by law, reason for dismissing a woman from her job.

It was evident that the main struggle for equality would be concentrated on altering these legal restrictions.

At the end of World War I, after the Kaiser had fled to

Holland and the defeated German army streamed back into an impoverished country, the revolutionary government called upon all Germans—men and women—to vote for a national assembly. In 1919 the first government of the Weimar Republic granted women the right to vote and the right to hold public office, thus laying the foundation for all developments in this field. Ten percent of the representatives in the Weimar parliament were women. Universities were opened to female students (there were few before). The right to study law and to be admitted to law practice and to the courts was granted. Preparations were made for changing those stipulations of the civil law that were discriminatory.

But the economic crisis, the mounting avalanche of unemployment, and the ensuing political unrest that eventually led to Hitler's victory suffocated all efforts in this respect.

Second Phase: 1933–1945

It is rather difficult today to explain the role of women during the Third Reich. The ideology—called "the Myth of the Twentieth Century"—tried to revive old values in a strange and phony way and created the image of the "German woman" as the beautiful blond bride, the mother of many children—mothers of more than four children received the decoration of the mother's cross. Her place was at home, in the house, and in the garden. The man was the master, the warrior, the hero.

The Nazi government did away with the eligibility of women for election to parliament (which was completely powerless anyhow), and it closed the legal profession to women, an action that was even more ominous. While the censored press and all party indoctrination painted this image of the German woman, reality was totally different.

The war began and took its course. Fathers and sons joined the army and more and more often did not return from the front. Women had to take over all family affairs, the farms, the businesses. Thousands upon thousands worked as nurses in military hospitals, millions were drafted for war services, and the demand of war industry for female workers was insatiable. The beautiful bride-mother-housewife image melted into the ruins of our cities, where the rubble had to be cleared by women. In endless daily efforts they tried to collect food for the family, to save whatever was possible to save. At the end of the war it was said that the only men left in Germany were the women. However that might have been, it seems that women emerged from that terrible war with an awakened self-confidence.

Third Phase: Since 1949

After the end of World War II German society changed fundamentally. Eleven and a half million refugees from the predominantly agrarian eastern territories arrived in the Federal Republic with only the belongings that they could carry. They had to be integrated into the economy. The enormous problem that faced the first Bonn government of Dr. Adenauer involved the loss of private property suffered by the entire population, the masses of war invalids, of war widows, the plight of old people who had lost their sons, and the rebuilding of the cities. There was no choice but to embark on the road to a welfare state based, however, on the concept of a free economy.

Reconstruction with the aid of the Marshall Plan led in an amazingly short time to gigantic industrial growth, an economic boom, the "German economic miracle." German society changed into a technical, industrial civilization. Cities grew beyond all boundaries, villages died. The impact of technology on agriculture transformed rural life that had lasted so long without much change. Mobility grew to previously unknown "American" dimensions. The gross national product grew tenfold between 1950 and 1970. Soon the labor market experienced acute shortages. More than three million guest workers from southern Europe, Yugoslavia, Greece, and Turkey moved into the lower echelon of the labor pyramid while German workers advanced into the middle class as highly paid specialists. The work week—at the same time—was reduced from 48 to 44, and then to 40 hours. There were ample opportunities for women in each and every field—limited only by their training and qualifications. Between 1961 and 1971, 65 percent more women with children under 15 years of age took on jobs.

Article 3 of the Basic Law, adopted in 1949, was decisive in establishing equality. This article states that: "all persons are equal before the law, no one shall be discriminated against because of sex, race or religion...." The Basic Law gave a mandate to the Federal government to alter existing laws according to that article.

At the center of our government's consideration stood the family that had to be protected against the onslaught of "anti-family forces." With the rapid spread of technology in all spheres of life, the big family ceased to exist. The small family became the model. Family size dropped from four to two children. Now the one-parent family is on the rise, reflecting a divorce rate of close to 25 percent in some areas. In the FRG, much as it is here, the family is no longer the center of education. There are too many influences exerted on children that escape parental control.

In 1949 the Bundestag created a special department, the *Familienministerium*, headed by a woman who became a minister with cabinet rank. This department periodically submits reports on the situation of the family and on the status of women in the Federal Republic. It has made many suggestions, in particular for improving the situation of the working mother. The first bill passed by the Bundestag in this area was the *Mutterschutzgesetz*, the law for the protection of mothers. This law, among other things, obligates the employer to pay sick leave for six weeks before and eight weeks after childbirth. Much effort is directed toward improving education and job training for women.

In spite of all the progress made, the equality promised by the Basic Law is still not attained. Therefore, in 1973 a commission was created by the Bundestag to suggest further measures that would provide for the social and legal equality of women. The findings of this commission, which were published in 1974, not only provide a rather candid picture of contemporary society in West Germany but also reflect modern and balanced attitudes toward existing problems.

What then is the situation today?

In 1976 there were 29 million men and 32 million women in the Federal Republic. Just under half of these 32 million women are married. Forty percent of the married women have jobs, fifteen percent of them part-time jobs. This means that 37 percent of the German labor force consists of women.

But their earnings are 50 percent less than those of men. A rather high percentage of women is still employed in so-called light-wage jobs; two-thirds of the assembly lines are "manned" by women.

The reasons for this phenomenon are at least twofold: Among the working class there still prevails the feeling that girls do not need as much education or job training as boys because they will get married anyway. Of the 17 million youngsters who received no training after finishing school, 72 percent were girls.

The other reason is the so-called double burden. It is customary for women to do the housework in addition to their jobs. Often seeking jobs is postponed until children reach school age and then it is difficult to find suitable employment after a long absence from the job market. Because they have families at home women seldom take on overtime work. For these reasons they are harder hit by unemployment when layoffs occur.

The double burden is also, I think, one of the main reasons why women move up to highly qualified positions at a rather slow pace. However, we do have many outstanding women in high positions. There are 38 women representatives in the

Bundestag, 2 are heads of departments. Until recently Mrs. Renger was president of the Bundestag, the second highest position in the state. Mrs. Hamm-Brücher is a state secretary in the Foreign Office. We have journalists, architects, doctors, scientists, and others, but there still could be more.

However, a definite change has been taking place. In 1957, 22 percent of our university students were female. By 1975 their number had reached 36 percent. Marriage is not their only goal any more. On the contrary, young women are striving toward a profession, and they want to practice it when they marry.

In the light of this development it is evident that the question of the double burden and of how the marriage of two working persons should be arranged became a most important issue in Germany. Only if men would accept the idea of sharing the tasks that traditionally were the wives' domain—only if they would treat women as equal partners—would there be a chance of adapting the woman's situation to the technological age.

In July 1977 a new family law came into force. It effects a significant change. Our code of civil law dates to the year 1900. Legislation regarding marriage and divorce was based on the concept of the so-called housewife's marriage. For instance, in case of a controversy the woman had to prove that her job did not impair her ability to perform her duties as a housewife. The new law treats marriage as a private arrangement between husband and wife as equal partners. Between themselves they can determine who does the dishes and who does not. Both have equal responsibilities toward each other and toward their children. Legally the husband ceases to be the finance minister of the family.

As long as one can remember, it was the husband's name that was given to the wife and the family. Now it can be his name, hers, or a combination of both.

German citizenship can be retained by the woman if she

marries a foreigner. Children of a German mother acquire German citizenship automatically.

In order to get a divorce one had—until now—to prove the guilt of the other party. Now divorce will be granted when marriage fails; the reason for the failure is immaterial. If both parties agree, divorce becomes effective after one year of separation. If only one seeks the divorce, the period of separation extends to three years. The financial aspect of this new law is very complicated. Here, too, the principle of equal partnership is applied: If one partner cannot earn his or her livelihood, the other has to assist him or her financially. The partner has to pay until job training is completed. And he or she has to provide help in case of illness or old age. The one who takes care of the children can claim financial aid from the other. An old-age pension has to be shared. Work as a housewife during the years of marriage is taken into account in divorce settlements.

There has been much debate about this new law. It certainly does not make divorce easier. How it will affect the statistics remains to be seen. Among the younger generation that grew up in an environment far removed from traditional moral standards, quite a few find the whole business of marriage too complicated. Only the old-fashioned parents mind if they live together without so many legal strings attached. It is very important for the younger generation to earn as much as possible in order to maintain the high standard of living that we enjoy today. And there is the image of the chic, professional woman striving toward self-fulfillment who looks at us from TV screens and magazine covers.

Off the record I am tempted to make a personal observation: In the eyes of the young, independent thinking professional woman, the Foreign Service looks like a very unfortunate career. A few years ago, when a young woman married a young and ambitious attaché, she dropped everything to follow him wherever the government sent him. She found it not an easy but certainly a worthwhile duty to be the hostess, to take care of family matters in adverse and difficult surroundings, to help him in any possible way. She felt herself a needed and important partner in his professional life. Now 99 percent of the wives of our attachés either have rewarding jobs or are about to enter professions. They are becoming quite reluctant to abandon the rights and the opportunities that they have acquired. They resent the government's having two trained persons on the job for the price of one. Some women let their husbands go abroad and continue with their own careers, trusting that they will be back. They may be right. I do not know. They seem very confident and think that self-fulfillment for women must be found in independent jobs and hope that these commitments will not get in their husbands' way.

During the past 25 years we in the Federal Republic have experienced an unprecedented economic stability and affluence. A whole generation grew up with a feeling of almost total security, with no worries about finding jobs. Our system of health insurance, public welfare, and social security is most advanced and elaborate. Schools and universities are free. Our society is open. With sufficient qualifications or with success in business everybody can move up the ladder.

But it is possible that we are now heading toward more difficult times. As it turns out, we have far too few openings in positions requiring academic training for the number of students that graduate from our universities. The system of social welfare is getting more and more expensive, requiring an economy in top shape. Competition for jobs is becoming very serious. How all this will affect equal rights I do not know.

I have tried to give a broad outline of the developmnt of equal rights, the legal framework created for them, and of some of the problems as we see them today. Whatever the future may bring, the German mentality has changed drastically, and things will be shaped accordingly. It is left for us now, it seems, to continue on our way toward the twenty-first century, freed of many prejudices, possessing considerable self-confidence, proceeding with care and circumspection in order to avoid treading on values that could prove vital for human society because, as the poet says,

> Die Geduld der Welt ist klug und kühl...
> Clever is the world's patience, and detached!

4

ISSUES IN
GERMAN
EDUCATION

Charles R. Foster

THE GERMAN EDUCATIONAL SYSTEM can best be described as a tunnel system. All children begin their education in a four-year elementary school after which, at the age of 10, they are distributed among three types of schools. The nine-year *Gymnasium* is the elitist college-preparatory school that involves nine years of secondary schooling and culminates in the *Abitur* that gives a 19-year old access to the universities—provided that the universities have space. The two other kinds of schools, the six-year *Realschule* and the five-year *Hauptschule,* educate the bulk of students. It is possible to move from these schools to the upper sections of the *Gymnasium,* but this method of entry is becoming increasingly difficult. These schools permit access to vocational institutions, some of which can be classified as post-secondary.

The German school system is still a class system, but the large increase in the number of *Gymnasium* students indicates a broadening of the upper classes. As late as 1967 only 8 percent of the appropriate age group graduated from the *Gymnasium*. The number of graduates rose to over 26 percent in 1975. Nevertheless, any society that makes judgments about children at the age of 10 takes into account not only the talents of individual children but also the social and the financial status of their parents.[1]

The educational system is reinforced by a career (*Laufbahn*) system that depends upon university degrees. Not only the civil service but also other occupations depend largely on a selection process based on paper degrees rather than on competence tested on the job. As a 1972 OECD report[2] noted, the essential task facing education in Germany is one of modernization. The adoption of new educational goals and their implementation have only begun in Germany.

In this essay the focus will be on three major areas of concern. First, we will examine the key issue of equality of educational opportunity as indicated by the struggle for the comprehensive high school (*Gesamtschule*). Second, we will focus on the system of access to German universities that is under attack as a result of the drive toward mass higher education. Third, we will examine the teaching of civic education in the Federal Republic.

The Politics of Educational Reform and the Comprehensive School

There is more to educational reform in West Germany than the comprehensive school issue. A good deal of energy has been devoted to such concerns as preschool education, vocational training, curriculum reform, and teacher training. However, the comprehensive school issue has assumed a central and contentious role in the entire debate about reform. The issue is connected with normative assumptions about social stratification. The existing tripartite system reinforces and reproduces the status hierarchy of West German society. Hans Weiler, in a report to the National Academy of Education,[3] indicated that the chances of a child whose father earns less than eight hundred DM per month of going to the *Gymnasium* are around 8 percent, whereas his or her peer whose father is in the over DM 2000 income bracket has a 67 percent chance of entering. Moreover, the pattern of attrition and retention in secondary education is very much a function of social background. In the *Gymnasium* a lower class student is three times as likely to drop out at some point between grade 5 and grade 13 as is his or her peer from an upper class background. A differential selection process operates both at the crucial distribution point between grades 4 and 5 and in the retention pattern of the high prestige *Gymnasium*.

The major elements of the distribution pattern at age 10 are parental motivations for their children's educational mobility, achievement differentials based on different home learning environments as well as aptitude, and patterns of physical access to different schools. Much of the debate about the comprehensive school has been polarized around the notions of "equality" (*Chancengleichheit*) and "achievement" (*Leistung*). The key value in this debate is the maximum development of each student's talents. Ultimately the issue involves not only the organization of German secondary schools but also what kind of a society West Germany will become in the future.

In order to understand present reform issues, we need to examine West German educational politics in the 1950s and 1960s. Although in the late 1960s German education was characterized as "two decades of nonreform,"[4] some qualitative and structural changes have been adopted in all of the *Länder* that sought to improve opportunities for the individual and produce greater efficiency for the system as a whole. These educational policy developments were appropriately characterized in an OECD report as "two decades of small initiatives without comprehensive planning." What reforms were accomplished were determined largely by the nature of political support and by the ideological characteristics of the state governments. The great increase in the establishment of comprehensive schools in the late 1960s emanated from the changed political situation at the national level and a 1969 constitutional change that allowed Federal government subsidies for experiments in education. Indeed, had this constitutional change not permitted experimentation, it is unlikely that more than a fraction of the present 100 comprehensive high schools would have been built.

Neither the Social Democratic party nor key interest groups were willing to try to take the "fortress *Gymnasium*" by political means. The powerful German *Gymnasium* teachers' association, the *Philologenverband*, was able to safeguard all the advantages that its members traditionally enjoyed over the elementary teachers, for example, those covering salaries, working conditions, and social prestige. As an affiliate of the Civil Servants Federation, the *Philologenverband* had an influential ally throughout the bureaucracy, and its contacts with middle-class parents' associations allowed it to form powerful coalitions against SPD *Landesministers'* proposed reforms of the tripartite secondary school structure. Even the more progressive elementary school teachers' union (GEW) has remained ambivalent toward comprehensive reform. The GEW's school reform programs scarcely kept ahead of conservative official commissions, and its endorsement of a diluted "differentiated" comprehensive school did not occur until 1966. The SPD did not really wish to risk alienating large segments of white-collar and professional voting groups. Furthermore, reformers in the SPD were held back by the examples of several innovative *Land* education ministers whose political careers were set back when the electorate or their party colleagues refused to extend necessary political and budgetary support for the comprehensive school.

In February 1969 the *Bildungsrat*, a prestigious educational commission, issued a report calling for a large-scale experimental program of comprehensive schools.[5] This report was approved by the Permanent Conference of State Ministers of Education but with an amendment that cut back integration within the school. In the following year the new SPD Federal Ministry of Education endorsed this report. A national debate ensued despite an increasing conservative climate brought about by attention given to radicals in the universities. In a June 9, 1971, *Bundestag* debate conservative parliamentarians advocated rejection of the report by linking it with student radicalism. Even CDU moderates stressed in television debates some recent studies that indicated that working-class students had become more numerous in the *Gymnasien*.

The government then embarked on a maximalist strategy and called for a program to restructure the educational system by beginning a vast expansion of investment in education from DM 20 billion in 1969 to DM 100 billion in 1980. The latter figure alarmed finance ministers and gave the CDU a target against which vested interests could be mobilized.

Educational reformers fought a losing struggle during the 1972 general election campaign. At the federal level the SPD did not want to emphasize divisive campaign issues. Furthermore, the education report's stress on the FRG's backwardness in providing educational opportunities clashed with the SPD theme that West Germans could again be proud of their country. With the decline of Federal leadership, the main initiative returned to the *Land* education ministers, most of whom tried to handle the issue gingerly. In Hesse, where there are more comprehensive schools than there are in other *Länder*, parents complained that the parallel existence of the *Gymnasien*, attended by a majority of upper secondary pupils, could lead to the final failure of the comprehensive school.

Today, with only 3.2 percent of secondary school pupils in comprehensive schools, reform of the tripartite secondary school system in Germany seems to have reached a standstill. The fact that there has been experimentation, however, has opened the door for a tangible manifestation of alternatives to the existing system. There are choices now where there were none before. The existing comprehensive schools have tended to attract a group of imaginative and socially committed teachers. The existence of the few experimental comprehensive schools has provided a cooling-off period during which tolerance can develop in the debate between two conflicting educational philosophies.

Access to Higher Education

One of the most controversial areas in the German educational system today concerns the process of admissions to the university. As is the case throughout the German educational system, the universities are all publicly controlled and administered. This means that all disagreements, controversies, and attempts at reform are automatically issues of political contention. The admissions process to university study and the reform of the system have accordingly become subjects of heated political controversy.

The basis of the problem concerns the rapidly increasing number of young people who want to study at the universities and take advantage of the right to higher education that was affirmed in a 1972 Federal Constitutional Court decision. The number of university students increased from 270,647 in 1965 to about 450,000 in 1970 and to almost 700,000 in 1975. It is estimated that by 1979 the number will have risen to about 820,000.

The process of allocating students to the various fields of study has become the center of the controversy and of reform attempts as well. Naturally, it has been easier to expand the volume of students in the social sciences and humanities than it has been to increase their number in the areas of natural science and medicine, leading to increased pressure and competition for acceptance in areas least able to expand. Until now the selection process for admission to the most competitive areas of study (the so-called *numerus clausus* fields, including human and veterinary medicine, dentistry, biology, psychology, and pharmacy) has been based on the grade point average from high school (*Gymnasium*) and the length of time that the applicant has waited for admission for which he or she reapplies each semester. The administration of entrance acceptances has been performed centrally by computer in Dortmund (the ZVS-*Zentralstelle für die Vergabe von Studienplätzen*).

With the increasing number of university students in the 1970s, more and more fields of study were threatened by *numerus clausus* procedures, as faculties and facilities became overburdened.

It became apparent that the *numerus clausus* procedure was an unfair and arbitrary means of coping with the problem. First, the procedure was based in part on the high school grade point average, clearly less than an impartial criterion because of differences among various high schools. Second, the selection criteria, especially the waiting period, tended to favor the more affluent who were better able to afford to wait a year or two. In addition, the waiting period was generally spent studying in a non*numerus clausus* field, which meant increased burdens for faculties and facilities in these fields, greater competition and depersonalization of teaching for those already in such areas, and greater costs for the state. Finally, the system favored those already studying at the universities which tended to encourage the changing of fields, the extension of the number of years spent at the university, and higher costs.

Since 1969 the admissions procedure has been the subject of much study and controversy and has generated numerous reform proposals. In its 1976–80 program the Social Democratic party even declared that the *numerus clausus* procedure could and should be replaced in almost all fields of study.

The most significant recent development was a decision by the Federal Constitutional Court in Karlsruhe on February 8, 1977. The court declared that the present system was clearly unconstitutional and that the state must speedily adopt an improved system, at least for the most restricted fields of study. The court suggested that a new system based on either standardized tests or a lottery in conjunction with letters of recommendation could conceivably meet constitutional requirements.

The court's recommendations included a more thorough use of the already existing facilities and faculty in order to expand the capacity of the educational system to absorb more applicants. A number of studies has shown that even in the very tight field of medicine, more students could be accommodated by a more intensive use of present capacity.

The exact direction of the reform ordered by the court still remains unclear, but the decision will force the government to devise new methods of access as well as a more efficient determination of capacities in the various fields.

Civic Education

Recent political developments in the Federal Republic of Germany have stimulated a discussion of civic education in that country. Sparked by the introduction of the *Rahmenrichtlinien* by the Ministry of Culture of the state of Hesse as well as by the efforts of the SPD to institute educational reforms, the highly politicized German educational system has witnessed not only a polarization of social educators but also a debate on the issue that has national significance and impact. The methodology and the purpose of civic education are being questioned, as are in some instances the very premises on which such education is based.

Civic education has a broad educational function that is vital to the social life of the nation. It is derived directly from the prevailing political culture, and its role in society is to inculcate in the population those norms, values, and authoritative standards inherent in the national political culture. Thus the differences in opinion over curricula, teaching methods, results, and the ultimate purposes of civic education may be traced to the very nature of the German political culture.

The roots of much of the discontent with the present system of civic education in the FRG lie in the system's difficulty in achieving the goal of providing young people with an adequate appreciation of a pluralistic political democracy. The broad goals of civic education—preparing responsible citizens and promoting democratic citizenship—in no way ensure agreement on the specific objectives and procedures considered necessary for attaining them.

In Germany civic education is not especially conducive to the development of political self-awareness—an awareness that one participates in politics, is affected by the political environment, and influences that environment.

Because of the structure of the German educational system and the political heritage of the Federal Republic, German civic educators face problems. There is an element of historical irony in German civic education that dates to the days of the empire. As Minssen has noted, one observes in Germany a strange relationship between cause and effect, between intended political formation and its results.

The Empire created liberal republicans; the Weimar Republic National Socialists; the experience with Nazism consolidated the sympathies of the free, democratic and social state based on constitutional rights which is represented by the Federal Republic of Germany. Within the past few years the schools of this state produced an increasing number of young intellectuals who, influenced by Marxism or neo-Marxism of various colorings, endeavor to overcome the "system" of the Federal Republic.[6]

This quotation touches on a multi-faceted problem critical to the field of civic education—the relative passivity and cynicism with which many Germans tend to view the political process. The orientation of many citizens toward the Federal Republic is more that of subject than that of participant. A fundamental problem is the demonstrable incapacity of the present system to elicit widespread active participation in German democracy. Voting frequency is high, for example; but there is little formal involvement in the political process.

The school system, from primary school to the university, has also become politicized. This process limits the freedom of the teacher, for in the FRG it is the teacher who makes the ultimate decision about how state prescribed material is to be presented in the classroom. Given the present class and economic structure in the FRG, it is much easier for conservative views to legitimate themselves. The pressure of public opinion is felt most by teachers, who are civil servants, and by textbook authors. The criteria used in hiring teachers now include an examination of their political affiliations and fidelity to the constitution.

The Federal government has no direct influence on civic education. Despite laws requiring the *Bundeszentrale für Politische Bildung* and the *Landeszentralen* to be "above the parties," they are sometimes influenced by the views of the party in power. Political influence tends to be greatest in the universities since they have lost most of their autonomy and are subject to the supervision of the various state ministries of education. They have developed along political lines, and appointments to chairs often reflect political pressure. In many cases industry will not hire graduates from universities that are viewed as "leftist," namely, the universities of Berlin, Marburg, Bremen, and Frankfurt. Given the fact that the ideological goals and lines of conflict among political parties are quite pronounced in Germany and given the inherently political nature of the German education system, it is encouraging to observe that questions bearing on the nature of civic education are becoming the subject of statewide and national debate.

Germans concerned with the promotion of better civic education must also attempt to change the process by working within a bureaucratized school system in which conditions are less than supportive of either reform or of effective civic education. The status of teachers as civil servants tends to reduce the local influence of parents. Textbook selection and curriculum development are the responsibilities of the state Ministries of Education, not local school boards. The absence of community influence in the school system is coupled with a school bureaucracy that manages to stifle parental interest in curricular matters. This lack of community and parental influence exemplifies and reinforces the political nature of the German school system. Parents may not like the ideas presented to their children in school; but because no direct procedure for community input exists, they cannot become involved in the issue. Because of the centralized nature of the system change must be brought about by exerting pressure on the state Ministry of Education. At the level of the state government, school issues inevitably become intertwined with politics, and the resolution of local disputes takes place at the state rather than at the community level. Nowhere is this process more clearly illustrated than in the dispute over the introduction of the *Rahmenrichtlinien* by the state of Hesse and in the current movement to include as a criterion of employment the political records of those seeking teaching positions. One can easily see how the entanglement of educational and political questions contributes to the slowness of educational reform.

The lack of local input, the centralized and politicized nature of the educational system, and the relative newness of civic education as a separate and recognizable discipline have all contributed to what may ultimately prove to be the greatest obstacle to more effective civic education, the institutional resistance to change.

Although the introduction of new methodologies will bring about certain improvements in civic education, it will also create problems. The universal problem of civic education disregards the student's ability to grasp the subject and the type of educational institution in which it will be taught. The unified, interdisciplinary approach of the *Rahmen* plan would require the critical examination of social, political, and economic institutions. It has already been subject to criticism from both political and professional circles.

The primary concern in examining political education is its observed inability to transmit to the young an understanding of the national political culture in its entirety. The results of the first cross-national study of civic education are significant.[7] The findings for the Federal Republic indicate a very high score in democratic values among young people, a reasonably high cognitive understanding of the system, a low nationalism/patriotism support, but also a low interest in participation and a certain degree of skepticism about the efficacy of such participation.

Given the recent history of Germany, it is ironic that by focusing almost exclusively on the curriculum, civic educators in that nation have failed to instill widespread support for liberal democratic life styles. In the last analysis the German political culture itself may also be considered a source of difficulty. The traumatic course of German history in this century has had an impact on the political culture. Whereas in the United States civic education serves to promote pride in the national heritage, national unity, and self-respect, all of these ideas are overshadowed in Germany by the events of the recent past. Both time and a concerted effort are needed to implant more firmly the democratic tradition in young people.

Conclusion

In many ways the adoption of new educational goals and their implementation have only begun in West Germany, and the difficulties that the first few steps have encountered are indicative of the magnitude of the task. This task is essentially a political one. A team of OECD examiners expressed this point in another 1972 report.

We have emphasized throughout this report our conviction that the task facing education in Germany is, in general terms, one of modernization. The economic, social, and political realities in Germany have changed fundamentally since the 1920's. Yet, in most important respects, the educational system has remained as it was recast after the Hitler period in the mould of those earlier times. Bringing education into closer congruence with the new social and political facts of German life is one of the great tasks facing the people in Germany in the 1970's. An essential step in this reformation is the recognition that schools and teachers do not operate in a social and political vacuum. They have social obligations that should be recognized and, in many cases, even welcomed. The "pure" pedagogical ground has too often been employed as a cloak for doing nothing, or for doing too little, too late. The need to spread opportunities more widely, to open new types of opportunities, to remake curricula, to restructure educational governance and to retrain teachers are all exceptionally pressing. The shape that such changes must eventually take should certainly be influenced by considerations put forward by professional educators and, of course, many teachers are among the more forward-looking of thinkers about education in Germany. But they can have no claim to an exclusive voice in determining the structure, content, and style of Germany's educational system. These matters must, in the end, be political decisions made with an eye to a democratic nation's social needs.[8]

Can society be changed through educational reform? Recent studies by David Conradt[9] and others suggest a remaking of the German political culture as well as changes in German life styles. If education is a mirror of the society, then the long-term prospects for educational reform in Germany are bright.

NOTES

1 For the school year 1975–76, 44 percent attended the *Hauptschule,* 22.5 percent the *Realschule,* 26.7 percent the Gymnasium, 3.2 percent the comprehensive school (*Gesamtschule*) and 3.6 percent the *Orientierungsstufe,* an integrated class 5 and 6 to determine where the child will go from form 7–10. See *Bildung und Wissenschaft,* no. 16, 1976, a newsletter of *Inter Nationes,* Bonn.

2. OECD, *Educational Policy and Planning: Germany,* (Paris, 1972).

3. Hans Weiler, *The Politics of Educational Innovation*—A Report to the National Academy of Education (mimeographed, October 1973).

4. Saul Robinsohn and Caspar Kuhlmann, "Two decades of non-Reform in German Education," *Comparative Education Review*, vol. XI, (1967), pp. 311–330.

5. Bildungsrat, *Einrichtung von Schulversuchen mit Gesamtschulen*, (Bonn: Deutscher Bildungsrat, 1969).

6. Friedrich Minssen, "Framework of Conditions Determining Political Education in the Schools of the FRG," unpublished paper prepared for a conference on political education at Bloomington, Indiana, September 1975.

7. J. Torney, A. N. Oppenheim, R. Farnen, *Civic Education in Ten Nations* (New York: Wiley–Halsted, 1976).

8. OECD, *Reviews of National Policies for Education: Germany* (Paris, 1972).

9. David Conradt, *The Germany Polity*, (New York: Longmans, 1978).

5

THE
MARSHALL PLAN
REMEMBERED

Robert G. Livingston

NO EPISODE IN THE United States postwar relations with Europe shines more brightly through the years than does the Marshall Plan. Britain's Foreign Secretary Ernest Bevin called it "the most unsordid act of history." A Frenchman closely involved with it, Robert Marjolin, has recently recalled "its extraordinary effectiveness." Within the three short years between 1948 and 1952, the European Recovery Program (ERP), as the plan was known at the time, completely revived Western Europe's productive capacities, generated new and unprecedented political and economic dynamism, and induced the victors and the vanquished of World War II to work together as never before in a common endeavor. The $14 billion of Marshall Plan aid to Europe ($1.3 billion of it to defeated Germany) set in motion the main currents that have formed the United States-European and particularly United States-German relations for the past thirty years.

The thirtieth anniversary of the Marshall Plan in 1977 passed virtually unremarked in the United States and was only modestly commemorated in Europe. Governments on both sides of the Atlantic are concerned nowadays to resist frequent and often carelessly voiced calls for "new Marshall Plans" for this or that purpose—to rescue the cities, for instance, to shore up dying industries, or most often to render assistance to the developing world and redress historic injustices dating back to the colonial era. Pressed fiscally from all sides, governments reject what they assert is a false parallelism between a needy Europe and a self-sacrificing America of 1947 and the needy third world and the less than generous industrial countries of 1977.

As conquered enemies of the United States, the Germans had particular cause to welcome the magnanimity and foresight that included them in the Marshall Plan. Participation in the ERP presented them with an opportunity not only to restore a devastated country but also to cooperate first economically and then politically with their recent adversaries and thus work their way back to a position of trust on a completely new basis. The ERP rekindled Germany's industrial vitality, producing a thirty-year economic miracle, and it reinstated the country's political credentials as well, leading it over these past three decades gradually to assume a role among the industrial democracies second only to that of the United States.

Remembering the centrality of the Marshall Plan to the entire direction of its postwar economic and political development, the Federal Republic has always taken special note of ERP anniversaries. One such commemorative act, on the twenty-fifth anniversary in 1972, stands out as unique in generosity, concept, and purpose. This was the establishment of a private foundation to memorialize the Marshall Plan and what it stood for: the *German Marshall Fund of the United States.*

On June 5, 1972, twenty-five years to the day after General George Marshall, then secretary of state, delivered his speech heralding the European Recovery Program, Chancellor Willy Brandt announced a gift that established the fund. Brandt's remarks, delivered, like Marshall's, at Harvard University, pointed out that Europe's real return gift for ERP assistance was the restored ability of European countries to be partners of the United States and "... to assume our share of responsibility in the world at large." Noting that the gratitude of Europeans had remained alive, he announced that as a token of this gratitude his government would for the next decade and a half provide each year on the June 5 anniversary of Marshall's speech a grant of 10 million Deutschemarks—150 in all—to establish a United States foundation devoted to seeking solutions to the problems common to industrial societies, particularly to Europe and North America.

Behind the chancellor's announcement lay more than a year's planning in which the chief figures on the German side had been Alex Möller, Federal minister of finance, 1969–1971, and Horst Ehmke, secretary of state in the chancellery, and on the American side, Professor Guido Goldman of Harvard's West European Studies Center. All four parties voted unanimous approval of the annual allocation for the German Marshall Fund (GMF). The money has since been included, quite appropriately, as part of a special budget proposal, known as the *ERP–Sondervermögen*, which is submitted to the parliament separately from the regular budget each year and has its origin in the United States-German counterpart fund of the Marshall Plan years.

The establishment of the GMF as a way of remembering the Marshall Plan was an imaginative and unprecedented action between nations—one that other foreign governments have subsequently taken as a model. And it was an act of trust that remains unique, for the Fund was set up as a completely independent United States institution. Most important, the GMF's charter provided that the money was to be administered "without any influence by the German authorities"—a commitment that the writer can testify from personal experience has been meticulously observed. Responsibility was vested in a board of trustees composed entirely of Americans who were selected by Americans. The fund's staff, initially headed by Benjamin H. Read, is also all American.*

A key phrase in the fund's charter directs its activities toward "common problems of industrial societies." Clearly these societies have much to learn from one another in both domestic and international affairs. Despite obvious political, social, historic, and cultural differences among them, which sometimes make difficult the transfer or adaptation of knowledge and practice across national frontiers, many of their most pressing problems are similar. And yet there are few governmental, international, or private resources or institutions designed explicitly to facilitate the systematic transfer and sharing of experience and information. And so solutions for dealing with social, economic, and administrative problems found satisfactory in one country are often unknown in another. Such considerations were uppermost in the minds of the fund's trustees in deciding during 1973 how to interpret the fund's charter and how best to apply the funds placed at the disposal of the GMF.

The trustees' decision was to concentrate these resources on a few selected problems facing contemporary industrial societies. Since early 1974, when the fund began full-scale operations, priority has been given to support for projects in urban affairs; employment and labor market problems, including those of worker participation and of employed women; land use and environment; administration of criminal justice, including pretrial services, bail reform, and the postsentencing employment of convicted offenders; international economic, trade, monetary, and resource issues; and European-American studies, including

---

*Detailed information on the fund and its programs can be obtained by writing or telephoning the German Marshall Fund, 11 Dupont Circle, N.W., Washington, D.C. 20036 (telephone 202–797–6430).

an annual fellowship competition open to advanced American and European scholars. To increase awareness among Americans of the similarities of problems facing citizens in all modern industrial societies, the GMF has also funded numerous media projects: the International Writers' Service, which distributes twice weekly articles to almost 100 newspapers and magazines across the United States; a weekly 30-minute radio program, "Atlantic Dateline," now broadcast by over 120 stations; and several public (noncommercial) television network series and special public affairs programs.

The fund is expending its annual gift at a rate of about $3 million at present. (A portion of each installment is invested in order to accumulate assets sufficient to permit the continuance of activities at a meaningful level after the final installment in 1987.) Since beginning operations in early 1974, the GMF has funded more than 100 projects. All of them have involved both Americans and Europeans in one way or another and were designed to promote an exchange of practical experience across the Atlantic in the fields selected by the trustees.

The fund's operating policy of including both Europeans and Americans in its projects is in keeping with the spirit of the Marshall Plan that the fund exists to memorialize, as is a second operating policy: to bring together and when feasible to develop working relationships between practitioners and experts, between those from the world of action and those from the world of thought.

Although people, goods, and ideas now cross national boundaries with an ease and frequency unimagined thirty years ago, this flow is highly uneven. In the basic sciences there exists a worldwide community in which national boundaries are fading. The growth of transnational corporations has accelerated this process in the world of industry and finance. But much practical knowledge and experience, usually related to the day-to-day conduct of domestic affairs, hardly move from their points of origin. Much of this knowledge is highly localized in application.

The fund focuses its efforts on promoting the exchange of these kinds of information and experience. It finds fields in which private initiatives and carefully targeted applications of relatively small amounts of money can help Americans and Europeans first to understand the commonalities (and the differences) in their social, economic, and administrative problems and then to learn from each other how to manage and perhaps solve them.

McGeorge Bundy, president of the Ford Foundation, observed that "the greatest shortage of useful thought is in transnational applications of knowledge." In deciding what socioeconomic problems to put first nowadays, Americans must "ask not only what is best for ourselves ... but also what is best for the world." The German Marshall Fund, a small foundation by American standards but one of the few in this country that has an exclusively transnational orientation, focuses on this question and seeks Europeans and Americans to try to answer it.

This approach also corresponds to the operational spirit and indeed to the operational procedures of the Marshall Plan. The plan was predicated on an American assumption about the solvability of problems. And this assumption, as Brandt put it in his 1972 speech, gave birth to the ERP as a "constructive answer [expected by Europeans] from the United States to the challenge of despair, helplessness and distress...." The European Recovery Program was in many ways a uniquely American amalgam of concern for others in the world, of idealism and certitude carried over from wartime successes, and of that congenital conviction that all problems, social, economic, and political, can, like scientific, technical, managerial, and military problems, be solved if only attacked energetically, cooperatively, and with dedication. Of course, political self-interest, the anticipation of commercial profit, and strategic and military considerations were ingredients of the blend also. But idealism and generosity predominated.

Typical of American attitudes too was the Marshall Plan's

concentration on the problems of the day and a willingness to put the past aside. Hence the decision to include Germany in the plan. During the Marshall Plan years the first of today's many links between the Federal Republic and the United States were forged—at the government level. Since then they have proliferated at all levels, private as well as governmental. Delivering the Marshall Plan Memorial Lecture in Bonn in June 1977, Roy Jenkins, president of the European Community, pointed out the continuing need for a variety of vehicles "for the type of international contacts and studies which are the lifeblood of mobile societies like those of the Western World ... [which] needs to organize and encourage the flow of information, techniques, and approaches to common problems in order to stimulate the renewal of their inventiveness."

It was during the Marshall Plan years that Europeans and Americans first became used to working together on an extraordinarily wide range of complex economic, social, and administrative problems. They discovered then not only how similar the problems were but the similarity of their past experiences in dealing with them at home. They discovered too that the character of the problems cut deeply into domestic structures and at the same time affected relations between national governments. Since those years, more than a quarter century ago, the issues facing Americans and Europeans have changed. But these characteristics have not. In fact they are more widely recognized than ever before.

The Marshall Plan spirit of a common European-American effort directed toward analyzing, understanding, and coping with such problems is worth sustaining. The projects of the German Marshall Fund may help in a modest way to sustain it—a spirit that brightened the dark postwar years and illuminated the paths of cooperation that Germany and the United States have since followed. And so should the Marshall Plan be remembered.

PART III

THE LITERARY
DIMENSION

1

COMMITMENT AND PROVOCATION— RETURN TO REALITY: AN ASSESSMENT OF THE NEW LITERATURE

Viola Herms Drath

TRADITIONALLY GERMAN WRITERS and intellectuals have been accused of a lack of political astuteness, of hiding in proverbial ivory towers, of elitism, and a flight from reality that permitted nazism and related blights of inhumanity to gain a foothold in their society. But a close look at the German literature of the recent past-exploring 1950s, the politically activist 1960s, and the more introspective seventies, with its sharpened sense of awareness, suggests a profoundly different situation.

Contemporary writers along the Danube, the Main, Lake Geneva, and the Rhine react with surprising aggressiveness to social and political pressures, injustice, unresponsive institutions, and a morality and a jurisprudence lagging behind changed social attitudes and human conditions. They are quick and blunt in spotting and revealing existential contradictions emerging in a social order unable or unwilling to keep up with the

developments imposed by the unfolding technetronic era.[1] Young
and middle aged, the majority of these writers are concerned
about the here and now. They are morally committed. No
matter what their literary style, what school they represent,
whether they are practitioners of the new realism, *Beschreibungs-
literatur,* trivial or documentary literature, the expression of
perception (*Wahrnehmungsliteratur*) or the absurd, concrete
or serial poetry, they are involved in a struggle to get a firm
grip on reality.

In these consciousness-raising writings elements of a new
realism in flight from unworldly prose, estheticism, and formalism
are readily discerned. Mysticism, the romantization of nature,
glorified sunsets, and resounding evening bells—once so dear
to the German writer's heart—are shunned. The lament about
the powerlessness of the individual, a popular theme in early
postwar literature, has given way to a quiet rebellion against
the decline of man's individuality and his loss of identity.

To be sure, there is no "mainstream" in contemporary German literature. As in the fine arts, its many faceted development
progresses in multilinear patterns. What is shared by most
of the younger writers, however, is the notion that the communication of the immediacy of reality is preferable to the
theory of alienation. Peter Hamm, a literary critic, has called
this generation of writers, now in their thirties and forties, the
sober, prepared-for-anything generation.[2] Because many of them
have concluded that literature has indeed influenced and even
changed their thinking, they mean to change others by means
of a literature engaged in breaking up all absolute concepts.

"I have never been educated by official educators. But I have
always been changed by literature," comments Peter Handke.
"I felt challenged by it and trapped when it showed me the
facts of which I had not been conscious before. The reality
of literature has made me attentive and critical for the real
reality."[3] Long before Peter Weiss turned into a socialist
propagandist, he observed: "Each word I write for publication

is political, that is, it aims at a contact with larger groups of population in order to attain a certain effect."

Many writers of the sixties, especially the younger ones, no longer thought of themselves as being mere analysts of social processes and mechanisms of suppression but as initiators (*Inbewegungsetzer*) of resistance against unacceptable human conditions, from the absurdity of wars to inscrutable hierarchical structures and bureaucratic stupidities. Swiss author Peter Bichsel (born in 1935), seconded by Max Frisch (born in 1911), promised to make difficulties for the establishment and its self-serving management where democracy is gathering dust like a "forgotten museum piece."[4] At a convention of the *Verband Deutscher Schriftsteller,* Heinrich Böll called for "energetic" involvement in political affairs. From the basic assumption that art is an element of man's nature that is part of free man, many writers of the sixties proposed to explore literature as a vital carrier of values. Because survival is inexorably linked with culture, culture figures as an important instrument for survival.

Neither content with the interpretation of the world around them nor with their own positions in society, this generation of writers hoped to bring about a change. To achieve this end experience had to be filtered through an expanded critical consciousness and conceptualized through a totally new approach to language. Like wide-awake watchmen, they were on the lookout for danger signals. Hans Magnus Enzensberger set the tone in the late fifties when he urged his colleagues not to "wallow in powerlessness" but to multiply the anguish of the world by "a grain." In persistent attempts to stimulate public exchanges about the individual and the collective, the dangers of ideology, consumerism, and false progress, the readers were to be sensitized, if necessary, by means of provocation. A case in point was Enzensberger's incentive poem "for a senior college textbook" with its rousing challenge to the defenseless to "blow the deadly powder into the lungs of power."

None of these literary guardians overestimated his role.

Like Martin Walser, they looked upon the effectiveness of their activities with considerable skepticism. "This relative sadness which the author [Walser] experiences when he realizes all his words are spoken into the wind," is well-known to all of them. Perversely, this despair becomes, as Walser maintains, precisely the reason for writing. The poet Nicolas Born (born in 1937) displays a similar ambivalence toward the impact of his craft. "No poem can affect a measurable change in society," he muses. "But poems can be subversive, if they adhere to the truth. A man who reproaches poetry for being inconsequential is mistaken about the poems. A man who reproaches his own poetry for being without consequences—overestimates his capabilities." For writers like Gabriele Wohmann, writing becomes a daily challenge as well as an opportunity to articulate "taking offense."

Littérature engagée, a French import, became the focal point of many heated controversies. Although it has a politically activist, leftist ring in the ears of some writers, others interpret it as a bland sort of humanist commitment, always part and parcel of the writing profession, hence superfluous. The wild discussions about whether *engagiert sein* mean active participation in party politics, including electioneering for political personalities and immersion in *demokratischen Kleinkram,* as Günter Grass interprets it, or an overall commitment that "provokes nothing but writing" and finds its sole expression in the author's work, as Walser advocated,[5] were reminiscent of the spectacular public discourses between Sartre and Camus in the postwar years. Walser, of course, from time to time engaged in gathering petitions and staging protests against the war in Vietnam, the emergency laws, and other issues jeopardizing the constitution of liberty had not always practiced what he preached. When he founded the "Vietnam Büro" in 1966, the war in Vietnam had neither been condemned by the German press nor by any of the major parties. In a scathing attack against writers like Grass who looked upon their campaign activities for the Social Democrats as a sort of civic duty for intellectuals, Walser sarcastically argues: "Too bad, when the political interest of a writer is judged less by his literary output than his political appearances. What good is a signature supplier or a writer, seized by campaign fever every four years, when he conjugates an unworldly prose containing no trace of the incisive conflicts in our world the rest of the time."[6]

Of special interest is the posture of the skeptics and cultural pessimists, influenced in some ways by Marcuse's principle of negation. These angry writers with their clipped speech conveying inhumanity and their shrewd manipulation of logic and dialectics, ever ready for contradiction, critique, and reprimand even when they were in favor of a regime or a cause, aligned themselves with the heretics. To a degree this attitude of not necessarily passive defiance is at times also noticeable among writers in the GDR. Wolf Biermann, Peter Hacks, Karl Mickel, Robert Havemann, and others—all of them loyal communists—were not afraid to accentuate the negative. The daily escape from forced adjustment, duty, resistance to institutionalized compulsions, necessity, *das grosse Muss*, as Peter Härtling[7] calls it, exerted by family, society, the state, and other freedom curbing controls, becomes an inexhaustible topic. This kind of engagement, a far cry from party politics and global resolutions, promises no solutions, no utopias, but a consciousness of what *really is*.

In the GDR this approach tended to embolden the voice of the individual vis-à-vis the officially prescribed themes of public virtue. In their novels *Die neuen Leiden des jungen W.* and *Nachdenken über Christa T.*, Ulrich Plenzdorf and Christa Wolf make strong statements on behalf of private life and personal integrity. In the West, on the other hand, where the predominance of public virtue does not prevail, the recognition that in order to survive freedom must be based on a critical awareness, which never loses sight of the permanently threatening possibilities of enslavement by others and the self, resulted in a defensive and therefore aggressive stance.

Attempting to assess this new literature, one is struck by the fact that its representatives define it neither as an institution nor as a myth. The concept of normative esthetics has been bypassed so far by polemic inquiries and a stream of critical commentary issued by the writers themselves. Because of their provocative reflections and a lack of fixed criteria, much of the Germanic note giving habit of literary criticism has withered away. These developments, perhaps, may not seem overly impressive to the American reader. But in the context of traditional *Literaturwissenschaft*, they signal pivotal changes in attitudes, amounting almost to a cultural revolution.

Were current German literature to be judged by the literary criteria and social values in the tradition of *Weimar Klassizismus* or by bourgeois literature of the nineteenth century, one would have to accept the verdict of certain critics that it is too politicized, too trivial, too precious, too experimental, too derivative—in a word, that it is dead. Yet with the momentous existential upheavals, the concept of literature was bound to change and new, not fully developed criteria take precedence. As painting has been pronounced dead a thousand times since the invention of impressionism, not to mention Dada, minimal, op, pop, or body art, the death of literature—itself a literary metaphor—is often celebrated in times of great transition.

At this point German literature, produced by writers of both Germanys, Austria, and Switzerland, constitutes a most vigorous, sprightly, sometimes witty and oftentimes gutsy antiauthoritarian body of work. With the exception of Peter Handke, whose *Wunschloses Unglück* was chosen by the editors of the *New York Times Book Review* as one of ten outstanding books in 1975, few of the younger German writers have made their presence felt on the international scene. Although Günther Lothar Buchheim's compelling submarine story *The Boat*, Joachim C. Fest's *Hitler*, and Max Frisch's *Montauk*—none of them young men—enjoyed respectable successes in recent years, the popularity of Grass's *Tin Drum* is still unsurpassed in this country. Although the sale of millions of Böll's novels tops everything written by other foreign novelists in the Soviet Union and in Scandinavia, his work (or is it his personality) has not caught the fancy of America's literary elite. Theatrical hits such as Friedrich Dürrenmatt's *Visit of the Old Lady*, Peter Weiss's *Marat/Sade*, and Rolf Hochhuth's *Deputy* have faded from memory. Grass's *Wicked Cooks* and *Uptight (Davor)* have mercifully been forgotten. In view of the flood of translated American literature eagerly consumed by the German-speaking public, the balance of literary exchange is marked by glaring disparities. Notwithstanding the Australian *Thorn Birds*, a convincing argument can be made that literary imports from France, Britain, Italy, and Latin America have been equally underrepresented on American best-seller lists.

With Grass's panoramic *Tin Drum* the past as a topic came virtually to an end. The writers of the sixties and seventies preferred to probe the fluidity of individual and social reality, the complex interdependencies, structures, and the widening gap between the individual and his fellow man in an alienated environment against the background of historic authoritarian and remembered psychological patterns. The manifold reactions to these experiences often were articulated and communicated in strictly personal terms. A society glued to the corruptive conventions of yesteryear, conventions curbing human potential and the integrity of human life, was relentlessly attacked as a breeding ground for the "virus of inhumanity."[8]

To ensure full expression of these experiences, the extension of literary boundaries—actually their breakdown—seemed a logical step. The result was the release of a tumultuous burst of energies, a confusing simultaneity of directions, the heterogeneous and the contradictory happening at the same time. This pluralism attains a strange cohesiveness through a sense of anxiety, unrest, and self-doubt. Uncertainty concerning the essence and function of contemporary literature runs deep. It is expressed in the multitude of experimental efforts with material and form in which the nineteenth-century concept of *Gehalt* and *Gestalt* no longer plays a norm-setting part.[9]

Forceful avant-garde gestures, misbegotten starts as well as brilliant beginnings—all of them reflecting "pure experience" as a medium for getting a handle on the elusive reality—would seem like an end station to many a reader were it not for their irreverent freshness, their precocious naïveté and wit. Actually these many leveled, sometimes frantic attempts at writing were certain to blow away the clinging cobwebs of past literary myths. They are mind openers in the discovery of new impulses, vibrations, and assessments of a quantitatively and qualitatively altered society. For example, social injustice was no longer to be regarded as only a moral problem but a technical mistake that can be remedied by calling it to the attention of the collective community and its managers. Documentary literature, such as Erika Runge's tape-recorded protocol of a housewife whose miner husband lost his job because of a mine shutdown or Günter Wallraff's controversial on-the-scene reports on dehumanizing processes, social and political *Missstände*[10] have undeniably accomplished their objective, that is, a moral demand for societal action. Nevertheless, the question has been raised, and not without justification, as to whether the compilation of selected facts can create anything more pertinent than the "illusion of reality."

Obviously, highly organized mass societies breed different sets of problems. Even if the old politicians, hung up on ideologies, were to be replaced by managers in charge of strategic planning of human coexistence inside the nation's borders and in foreign affairs, even if the individual were granted maximal amounts of personal freedom, the insidious danger of manipulation will always be present, warns Peter Handke in *Kaspar*. In this chilling play the manipulated unexpectedly turn into the manipulators. Other writers detect an inevitable loss of self, of personality, once praised by Goethe as mortal's *höchstes Glück.*

Helga Novak is convinced that the individual in the old sense no longer exists in "our time of uniforms." She maintains that a literature that still reveals itself as style or as a special—apparently, individualistic—form perpetuates the biggest lie, namely, the lie that the traditional individual still exists today. Barbara König writes wistfully of the exchangeability of places and persons. Thomas Bernhard's world, peopled by emotional and physical cripples, is inundated with perversity. The feeling of terror is rampant. Deformation of personality becomes the leitmotiv, loneliness the norm. In his tense portrayals of a potentially self-destructive society only superficial human contacts remain possible. Each existence resembles an end phase of a situation in which the major avenues of mobility are closing down.[11]

The crisis of consciousness experienced by these writers in their confrontations with reality sharpened their sensibilities to awareness. Like Günter Kunert, they want to be ahead of life at least by an hour.

Next to their myth-smashing activities, the young writers, supported by the old vanguard, are furiously at work knocking the props from ideologies, the dogmatizing of error, the escapist idealization of history, personalities in nostalgic allegories, and conventional fables in modern dress. The noble lie, glossing over past and present horrors, is intolerable to them even as an "act of kindness." The traditional, the time proved, is as suspect as the *Naturmystik* that cropped up in the fifties with its flights of fancy into timelessness, the universal, images of clouds, and the cathedral of the woods. They also have little use for the "slice of world" writers of the early sixties, the seismographs, content with the faithful registration of social and psychological data. They refuse to offer illusions, opinions, theses, *Lebenshilfe*, or lofty interpretations of *das Ganze*. Words like *Weltanschauung* or *Vaterland* are as tabu as is "timeless poetry."

In contrast to the illustrious *Gruppe 47*, that fraternity of engaged literati that tried to help democracy to its feet after the ravages of war by functioning as the "conscience of the nation," scant interest in functioning as a group is displayed now. Linking themselves squarely to reality by shunning artificial stories and plots, they try to avoid their predecessors' pitfalls: preoccupation with the German past and esthetic theory, while authoritarian structures quietly reappeared in real life. They remember well the harsh words of Peter Weiss when he reminded the *Gruppe* of its moral and political responsibilities during its much publicized meeting at Princeton in 1966.

The problem of how to remain anchored in reality as the means for gaining access to cognition became the focal point for the new realism. Its immediate response was *Wahrnehmung*, the interpretative perception of everyday experience, the obvious and the hidden. When Wolf Wondratschek (born in 1943) strings together his seemingly value-free perceptions, the impact is anything but bland. Together with the rediscovery of the "documentary character of the language," as critic Heinrich Vormweg[12] formulates it, these two elements constitute a common denominator from which the identifiable impulses of the new literature originate to a large extent.

Language itself becomes the subject matter for most of the writers of experimental prose and concrete poetry, among them Jürgen Becker, Helmut Heissenbüttel, Franz Mon, Eugen Gomringer, and the avant-gardists of the *Wiener Gruppe*, midwifed into existence by Hans Carl Artmann in 1946. The rediscovery of language as material, helped by Wittgenstein's *Sprachphilosophie* and the French structuralists, left a profound impression on the realists as well. Although they are not inclined to "play" with language like the *Sprachbastler*, notably, Ernst Jandl or Bazon Brock, they recognize language as a form of reality rather than as a tool.

Asserting that literature does not consist of images, feelings, opinions, spiritual everyday objects (*geistige Gebrauchsgegenstände*) but of language and language only, Heissenbüttel offered the philosophical underpinnings of the intriguing search for the identity of language and reality. "A literature, which today wants to call itself realistic, could not, I believe, newly activate language (perhaps by the invention of new combinations) in order to describe a world changed in fact as well as in consciousness," he maintained.[13] Through language as the medium in which the "I" and the world have a chance to meet and make experience possible, Heissenbüttel proposes to make accessible a world that is slowly slipping away from us. The liberation of words from the stranglehold of conventional and ideological prejudices is achieved by breaking up stultified language patterns, questioning the most hidden meanings and relationships of language, penetrating its core, the destruction of syntax, the testing of substance, the elimination of all traditional metaphors, pictures and formulas inserting themselves between language and experience, thereby corrupting and distorting it.

Wittgenstein had referred to the logic of language. Heissenbüttel assumes the identity of language and reality, the word and the object. However, the actual thrust of the attack on conventional language is aimed at conventional thinking. Presumedly, thinking patterns can be broken by breaking up language patterns. In order to exorcise the lingering past, the last scraps of obsessive Fascist jargon had to be demolished. Because language determines that form of experience that can be summed up as knowledge, judgment, sensibility, a new way of thinking is envisioned by the pursuit of the reform of language. By bombarding the reader with masses of clichés, stereotypic expressions, idioms arranged in collages, disrupting rhythms of sound, and endless repetitions—often highly entertaining—that mean nothing, language experimenters like Michael Scharang intend to expose hidden social and private attitudes. For Franz

Mon the cliché becomes an irritant, a medium to convey unrest, a means of sensitizing the reader, making him allergic to prevailing social conditions. As Wolfgang Hermann Körner (born in 1941) demonstrates in his "Texte," the cliché, the empty phrase, is indeed capable of betraying certain truths about the morals and values of a society. In his *Krautgärten* the choice of language turns into damaging evidence, into an indictment of the mentality of the speaker.

Handke, who first dared to call attention to the impotence of descriptive literature, concludes that all speech forms are determined by society. Consequently, sentences are interpreted as "mechanisms of oppression" in his "texts." Because reality is most strikingly revealed by words, his plays are without plots, action, gestures, and the usual actors' parts. Using clichés from reality, he attempts to extract from them new findings about reality. Acoustic effects become creative elements in his radio and stage plays. Sound serves as a carrier of information. Language montages and verbal exercises are effective instruments in the exposure of the endangered and dangerous society. The manipulators and the manipulated reveal themselves. Their roles are interchangeable. Handke expects literature "to break up all images of the world that appear absolute."[14]

None of these experimental efforts was lost on the practitioners of pop literature, inspired by Frank O'Hara and his New York circle, and of *Trivialliteratur*. Shifting from one mode of experience to another, they blend the trivial and the sublime with baubles of slang, slogans, tongue-in-cheek comic-strip comments into incredibly complex assemblages, every step accelerating the other until our object choked consumer's world begins to take on a surrealist Boschlike quality.

In Ror Wolf's writings the whole compositional structure rests on language rather than on action. Every sentence is as important as the next. They are tightly knitted into a volatile, open-ended prose without beginning and end. Present mixes with past and future, reflection, platitudes, remnants of dreams.

Every item is tested for its usefulness and preserved no matter how banal or irrelevant, how fleeting or minute the experienced encounter. In her candid defense of banality, Barbara König pronounces it as "vital" to the kind of literature in which "essence is hidden behind the story."[15] Writing in this case has the "function of a window," König explains. "One could paint on it beautifully, but then nobody could see through it. The writer who wants to make thought visible should make use of banality—for the simple reason that it is more transparent."

The influence of the concrete writers on descriptive literature, informed by structuralism in general and by Alain Robbe-Grillet's *roman nouveau*, the theories of Claude Lévi-Strauss, and the theater of the absurd in particular, can be detected in the works of a number of younger writers. Their fascination with surface often finds expression in a cool, precise prose that exudes an overall sense of powerlessness, of inescapable gloom and paranoia. Persons and objects become equivalents, notably so in the stories of Günter Herburger and Rolf Dieter Brinkmann. The pressure on the private sphere in our theoretically open society permeates everything. Herburger's works picture a bourgeois landscape of genteel, deadly boredom. But hidden behind this innocuous surface the reader discovers another layer of reality that Herburger describes as a "cottoned hell."

As expected, the representatives of *Dokumentationsliteratur* are subject to much the same influences in their inquiries into the nature of life. The updated *Arbeiterliteratur* of the twenties, invested with new life by the *Dortmunder Gruppe 61*, is devoted to the reportage of *konkrete* experience. Language is treated by this group, which includes Günter Wallraff and Max von der Grün, as an autonomous force, as a powerful medium for the liberation of human potential instead of as a passive vehicle.

The variegated new realism—as opposed to neoromantic subjectivism, mannerism, and the grotesque—certainly constitutes no revival of the milieu-happy *Neue Sachlichkeit* of the twenties, nor can it be related to the socialist realism fostered by GDR officialdom. The deliberate effort to impress the human will on societal developments, foreshadowed by the revolutionary advances of the technetronic age, imbued this genre of writing with an unparalleled urgency and a sense of the proportion and nuances of contemporary experience that are plainly its own. Dieter Wellershoff astutely defined new realism as the "permanently changing articulation of the principally inexhaustible reality."

It has been suggested that the obsessive preoccupation with linguistic details, analysis, and the cultivation of novel forms during the highly experimental sixties was bound to lead down the narrowing doctrinaire path into the dead end of effete modishness. But anybody who samples the massive, multi-structured literary output of that dynamic decade of restless quest will no doubt be stunned by the quality of ingenuity and the exhilarating freshness of this particular body of fiction and verse. Surely, without this sound, other directed foundation the notes of subjectivity and introspective navel gazing that were to reassert themselves in the seventies would have degenerated into pure sentimentalism.

In retrospect the sixties were anything but confining. On the contrary, far from limiting human consciousness, they helped to emancipate it. In their portrayal of the complexities of contemporary life, these writers attempted to mirror the baffling uncertainties and ambiguities inherent in the *condition humaine,* thereby unlocking a German reality otherwise unknowable.

Notwithstanding these reflections, it must be emphasized that overlapping trends and movements that may or may not necessarily exist except as events spotlighted at the popular level by the mass media keep emerging and disappearing, complementing and contradicting each other and continue in varying disguises in the new *deutschsprachige Literatur.*

Notes

1. Viola Herms Drath, *Engagement und Provokation*, Texte zeitgenössischer deutschsprachiger Autoren, (New York: Macmillan, 1973).

2. Peter Hamm, *Aussichten* junge lyriker des deutschen sprachraums vorgestellt von peter hamm, (Munich: Biederstein, 1966), pp. 335–336.

3. Peter Handke, Prosa, Gedichte, Theaterstücke, Hörspiel, (Frankfurt: Suhrkamp, 1969), p. 263.

4. Peter Bichsel, speech delivered at the bestowal of the Prize of the Canton Solothurn in 1969, reprinted in *Tintenfisch 2*, (Berlin: Verlag Klaus Wagenbach, 1969), pp. 13–16.

5. Martin Walser, *Engagement als Pflichtfach für Schriftsteller* (Commitment as obligatory subject for writers), radio lecture broadcast in 1968 in rebuttal to Günter Grass's address at Princeton during a meeting of the *Gruppe 47* in April 1966: "About the lack of self-confidence of writing court jesters taking into account nonexistent courts."

6. *Ibid.*, published in *Heimatkunde*, (Frankfurt: Suhrkamp, 1968), p. 109.

7. Peter Härtling, *An den Studienrat Dr. S.*, essay written before the elections of 1969, published in *Engagement und Provokation*, pp. 240–246.

8. Ralf Dahrendorf devotes a chapter (Humanistic Theory and Practical Inhumanity) to the discussion of this theme in *Society and Democracy in Germany* (Garden City, N. Y.: Anchor Books, 1969), p. 328 ff.

9. Heinrich Vormweg, see "Material und Form," in *Die Wörter und die Welt* (Darmstadt: Luchterhand, 1968), p. 8 ff.

10. Günter Wallraff, *13 unerwünschte Reportagen* (Cologne: Kiepenheuer & Witsch, 1969). Wallraff's unconventional methods were not without consequences: legal charges for impersonating public officials and the withholding of the money for the literary "Förderungspreis" of Nordrhein–Westfalen after official reprimand.

11. Renate Matthaei, *Grenzverschiebung*, Neue Tendenzen in der deutschen Literatur der 60er Jahre (Cologne: Kiepenheuer & Witsch, 1970), see pp. 34–35 ff.

12. Heinrich Vormweg, *op. cit.*, p. 112.

13. Helmut Heissenbüttel, see *Über Literatur*, Luchterhand, Neuwied, 1966.

216 Germany in World Politics

14. Peter Handke, *op. cit.*, p. 264.

15. Barbara König, *Eine Lanze fürs Banale*, essay written in 1971, see *Engagement und Provokation*, p. 206.

SOCIAL CRITICISM IN THE GERMAN NOVEL OF THE TWENTIETH CENTURY

Hugo Mueller

SOCIAL CRITICISM IN LITERATURE is a term so frequently used that it does not seem to call for renewed definition. As a first reaction, one usually thinks that an author's political attitude and ideology lead him to expose the shortcomings of contemporary society and possibly to offer his own ideas about how to improve it. But this definition of social criticism is too narrow. Not all writers whose works we view as critical of society will agree that they are trying to show what is wrong and how society should function. Some even claim that although they are themselves painfully aware of the misery by which they are surrounded, literature, like any other form of art, should be kept free from politics. This is the opinion of some writers in other parts of the world also. As recently as 1976, the great Argentine writer Jorge Luis Borges said in an interview: "Many writers are getting into politics. I try to keep my own political beliefs out of my writing. I have always spoken out very freely.... [But] poetry should be something more intimate than political beliefs.... I have never written of contemporary politics." German writers, for example, Hermann Broch and Martin Walser, expressed similar opinions when they said that literature and politics do not belong together. And still they are known to have been politically quite outspoken.

Then there are writers who comment on society without being negative about it. It is quite conceivable that social criticism can take the form of justification and defense, of ideological support. This kind of literary criticism can be found in any society but predominantly in an environment that enhances or even expects ideological support from its intellectuals. In a totalitarian society any other kind of literary comment on the society would be suppressed in any case. German literature of the present century has known examples of this kind of criticism.

Finally, not all writers who deal with social conditions are critical of the society as a whole but possibly of a segment of society, a certain aspect of it. This observation allows us to distinguish writers according to the range of their perspectives, their horizons. The outlook of the author may be cosmic, that is, it may extend over mankind as a whole, including past and future epochs of history, and at the other end of the spectrum his view may be restricted to his own personal relationship to the people around him. In between we find authors who comment on smaller or larger sections of society or who have had experiences that make them aware of particular events in their lives. Family problems, community issues, school experience, life in the military, working conditions, the life of the artist, the judicial system—all evoke the critical reaction of the writer. Social scientists may well receive a clue about the nature of a particular society if its literature presents an uncommon amount of critical reaction from writers, for example, regarding the military establishment or the school system. One may be led to ask how far literature reflects actual sociological conditions, not merely an individual writer's idiosyncracies.

This question leads to another dimension in which the author's position toward society may be investigated, namely, the degree and the nature of his emotional involvement. He may be an aloof, scholarly observer or an objective judge of the world in which he lives, or he may be experiencing strong emotional reactions to the conditions in which he participates. He may be indignant and hateful; he may be doubtful and reserved; he may react with cynicism, sarcasm, or irony; and he may have given up all hope and have withdrawn into resignation. He may be fearful of the future and search for a way to escape, or he may attempt to arouse his readers to action. Conceivably also his attitude toward society may be understanding and forgiving, even displaying a positive endorsement and a sense of humor. In some instances, the literary artist may be a religious person whose relationship with his fellow human beings is founded on love and faith.

These are the rather complex variations and possibilities that may emerge when we explore the general theme of social criticism in literature. It is obvious that literary criticism as it is practiced today concentrates on social criteria and on the effects that a literary work may have in changing social conditions. It is no longer the biography of the author, not the artistic form and the style of the work, not the place of the work in the history of its genre, and not the intellectual atmosphere of the period but the social and political relevance that mostly interests contemporary literary critics. This aspect of literature does in many instances contribute essential insights into the significance of a literary work. At the same time it may not do justice to other elements that are part of the work of art, for example, the personality of the writer, the circumstances under which he writes, or even the technical perfection of his art. It seems that we need to remind ourselves of the dangers of an overly restricted approach to literature and that in dealing specifically with the element of social criticism in a literary work of art, we may unjustly downgrade facets of aesthetic individuality.

It is with this reservation in mind that we will approach the mass of narrative literature that has come out of the German-speaking countries in recent decades. We will try to avoid an oversimplified categorization by labeling a particular author as being representative of this or that group. Rather we will focus on individual novels because writers, like anybody else, are liable to change their attitudes and opinions over the years. We will try to recognize in each case what the author's state of mind was and what his reactions to society and the world around him were while he wrote his book. In doing this we will find that we have chosen an approach that yields some intriguing clues to the evaluation of the literature of the twentieth century. We will find ourselves naming authors side by side whose names are usually not grouped together. And we will also find that for some varieties of emotional reaction to society we have an abundance of examples, whereas for others there are only very few instances. There happens to be a considerable number of novels that clearly reflect the authors' disgust with the state of humanity; there is also an abundance of novels that betray the authors' despair and doubt about man's future. On the other hand, there are only a few instances of a harmonious relationship between the author and his society. The smiling observer of the world, the philosopher who is able to laugh in the face of human weakness, is rare indeed among the novelists of this century.

The overall picture—this can be said at the outset—indicates awareness of a sick society, even expectations on the part of the writers of a terminal phase of the European tradition and of the world as we have known it. In a retrospective analysis of the year 1976, the German weekly newspaper *Die Zeit* published a summary of events and an evaluation of the current intellectual climate. It was noted that a trend in literature was clearly discernible in which problems of personal concern—sex, death, psychological conflicts—have replaced society and political ideology. Why is this? The writer who was interviewed for that article—an author from East Germany, Günter Kunert—thought that the reasons for this phenomenon were to be found in the growing awareness that the end is near—not simply because a military or ecological catastrophe was imminent but because the people of our cultural tradition have accepted the inevitable. "The end is near, because man, in fact, wants it."

Kunert vermutete die Gründe tiefer. Nämlich in einem nach aussen hin zwar noch immer verdrängten, in den Innenwelten sich aber um so unabweislicher Bahn brechenden Bewusstsein, dass das Ende kommt—nicht einfach darum, weil eine militärische oder ökologische Katastrophe hereinbrechen wird, sondern vielmehr, weil sich der Mensch unseres Kulturkreises mit ihrem Hereinbrechen längst abgefunden hat. Das Ende sei nahe, weil der Mensch es im Grunde will. (*Die Zeit*, Jan. 7, 1977)

We will try to demonstrate in detail what has been; stated so far in general terms.

1. Novels of hate and indignation, that is to say, novels in which the authors reveal their extreme opposition to the society in which they live, have been part of the German literary scene from the beginning of our century. The foremost critic and accuser of the society of the German Empire before World War I was Heinrich Mann (1871–1950). The picture of the typical German bourgeois in his novel *Der Untertan* (The Subject), 1916, is not so much a true description of actual conditions in Germany as a scornful caricature of a tense situation. His own brother Thomas Mann spoke at that time of the author as a "Zivilisationsliterat," a term that bears a connotation of decadence. He said that Heinrich Mann described entrepreneurs that do not exist, laborers that do not exist, social conditions that may have existed in England around 1850 but not in Germany at the time in which the novel takes place. He characterized this kind of social satire as calumny and nonsense.

Heinrich Mann wrote other novels in which he also voiced his hatred of the German society of that period. *Der Untertan* is part of a trilogy called *Das Kaiserreich* (The Empire). The other two parts are *Die Armen* (The Poor) and *Der Kopf* (The Head). The three novels were published between 1916 and 1925 and were somewhat less than sensational successes. Among the better known works of the author is *Professor Unrat,* 1905, which was made into the classic movie *Der Blaue Engel* (The Blue Angel). In it Heinrich Mann gave vent to his utter contempt for the German schoolteacher of his time. Again, undisguised hatred dictated the work, and the result was a rather crass exaggeration of a society whose realities were already strained.

Heinrich Mann was not exactly a maverick. He was not the only writer who hated the society that he perceived. He had famous company. The empire and the First World War resulted in social conditions that justly enraged the idealists among the writers. The war itself, incidentally, spawned a series of novels that dealt with the misery of warfare, but it would be hard to find examples of blunt hatred toward those responsible for the misery. More often than not, the critical exposure of militarism was softened by pity and sympathy for the suffering victims. This is the case with Remarque's famous novel *Im Westen nichts Neues* (All Quiet on the Western Front), 1929, and with Arnold Zweig's *Der Streit um den Sergeanten Grischa* (The Case of Sergeant Grischa), 1927, in which the authors' disapproval of society never degenerated into such grotesque exaggerations as appear in some of Heinrich Mann's novels.

In 1918, Leonhard Frank (1882–1961) wrote the collected pacifist novellas *Der Mensch ist gut* (Man is Good). There, too, we have criticism of the war in unmistakable terms, but the author is not burning with fury; he is pleading for peace, reason, and fraternity. Frank himself understood the book as a manifesto against the war mentality. Leonhard Frank had been one of the most outspoken critics of the society around the turn of the century. His literary fame was established with his first novel in 1914 called *Die Räuberbande* (The Gang). What appears to be a novel for adolescents is in reality an autobiographical protest of the nonconformist author against the authoritarian structure of a small town society. Würzburg is Frank's home town, and his early years there left an imprint on his views of society that he never forgot. Family, school, and church combine to break the individual's desire for freedom until he either becomes a docile member of society or he is crushed and perishes.

Frank is quite outspoken in his hatred for the tyranny of the school system, but he feels pity and understanding for the authoritarian fathers and mothers who are themselves products of the system. The pity and understanding that he shows here are facets of his nature that become even more evident in later novels in which he also criticizes society but with the firm conviction that man is basically good. Frank became a Marxist, although his idealism suffered setbacks and his initial activism and hopeful outlook on the future of mankind later gave way to resignation and escapism into the world of fantasy and fairy tale. He was an eternal nonconformist and a critic of society who was never quite at ease in his relationships with the world around him.

Ludwig Renn wrote his autobiographical novels *Krieg* (War) in 1928 and *Nachkrieg* (Post War) in 1930. Both books are clearly antimilitaristic, but rather than blaming the ruling class for what happened, the author reflects on the impact that the war had on his own personality and on the development of his political opinions through the war experience. Eventually Ludwig Renn (whose real name was Arnold Friedrich Vieth von Golssenau) became an active member of the Communist party. Yet his novels are not inflammatory or shrill; rather, they are documents of the author's search for truth.

The fury that is reminiscent of Heinrich Mann's style was revealed again in the postwar period, in the twenties and early thirties, when social conditions degenerated from bad to worse.

A demagogic writer comparable to Heinrich Mann was Hans Fallada (1893–1947). He wrote several novels in which he relentlessly directed his attacks against the society of the Weimar Republic. *Bauern, Bonzen, Bomben* (Peasants, Bosses, and Bombs) was published in 1931. It deals with the plight of farmers who are forced to demonstrate against overtaxation and who run up against the bureaucracy and the interests of party politics. Violence leads to confrontation with the police and to court action in which the underdogs are the losers. Best known is Fallada's novel *Kleiner Mann—Was nun?* (Little man—what now?), 1932, which deals with the misery of the unemployed during the depression in Germany. But not only the pathetic life of the honest, lower middle class white-collar worker is impressively described, the focus is also on the corrupt ways of the Berlin underworld and the hopeless situation of the little man when he gets into the clutches of organized crime. The author's hostility against a society that fails to deal with the poor man's needs is revealed in no uncertain terms. Fallada's third novel *Wer einmal aus dem Blechnapf frisst* (If you ate out of the tinbowl) was published in 1934. It is the story of a young man who gets into trouble with the law, first as an innocent victim and then as a first offender, and never makes his way back into society because he is stigmatized for life. He finally becomes a real criminal and welcomes his return to the orderly routine of prison where he can feel safe and quiet. The novel was an indictment of the judicial system, and the author seems to have hit some sensitive spots in the social structure of his time. The German reading public made Fallada's novels resounding successes.

Similarly successful was Erich Kästner (1899–1974) whose children's books *Emil und die Detektive* (Emil and the detectives) and *Das doppelte Lottchen* (Double Charlotte) are probably better known than is his adult novel *Fabian*, 1931. This novel has been described as a venomous satire and, indeed, at first sight it looks like an infuriated condemnation of the Weimar

Republic in the nineteen twenties. But one gets a little suspicious about whether the rotten characters and the dingy bars and brothels in the story were really so detestable in the eyes of the writer or whether he loved this decadent society. The indignation of the accusing author Erich Kästner rings somewhat hollow in this novel.

Hostility among the intellectuals was aroused again when the National Socialists came to power in 1933. Obviously, a writer cannot freely express his disapproval of the society in an authoritarian state, and thus some of the best literary minds emigrated; whereas some writers waited until the situation had changed—until the war was over in 1945—to say what they thought about the Third Reich; and some who stayed in Germany expressed their criticisms in disguise by creating fictitious situations, the real significance of which, however, was obvious to the intelligent reader.

There is no doubt that Thomas Mann (1875–1955), while in exile in California, hated the Third Reich with all his heart, and yet the picture of German society in *Doktor Faustus*, 1947, is not painted in blind hatred but is mellowed by sadness and a sense of tragedy. There was a deliberate effort on the part of the artist to create an inner distance between himself and his topic. The story is told by an intermediary, a narrator, and it is brought into perspective by linking it with historical parallels. The symbolism that pervades the novel blurs the edges of direct representation of the present time. Hatred, yes, but spread over a larger target area and put into words from the vantage point of a distant watchtower.

Hostility against the conditions in the Third Reich is also the underlying message of the novel *Der Grosstryann und das Gericht* (Matter of Conscience), 1935, by Werner Bergengruen (1892–1964), one of the literary persons of rank who stayed in the country. The message had to be encoded because a direct indictment of the absolute power of a ruler would have blocked the publication of the novel. But the messages comes through nevertheless. It shows the temptation of the tyrant to abuse his power and the readiness of the powerless to be deceived. Although the author was opposed to this form of society, his hostility was mitigated by his religious background and his philosophical humanism.

It was said that some writers waited to give their comments on the Third Reich until it was all over. This statement should not be understood as a blemish on their characters, for the power of the state would easily have silenced any direct attack made by them. And moreover, many of the post–1945 writers were too young to be writers before the war. This includes such well-known German writers of today as Böll, Grass, Walser, Siegfried Lenz, Alfred Andersch, and Arno Schmidt.

The post-World War II literature is overwhelmingly characterized by its social criticism, sometimes blunt, sometimes sophisticated, satirical or philosophical, resigned and passive, or encouraging and active. But when the recent past, meaning National Socialist society, is mentioned, the reaction is quite uniform: an unqualified condemnation. In several instances we find an author who is writing a novel with a contemporary postwar setting that depicts complex characters with modern problems introducing in grotesque distortion a surviving specimen of the Fascist era, thus rendering the whole story somewhat less convincing. This is the case in novels like *Die Rote* (The Redhead), 1960, by Alfred Andersch (b. 1914), and *Der Tod in Rom* (Death in Rome), 1954, by Wolfgang Koeppen (b. 1906).

Among the writers of today the best known by far is Heinrich Böll (b. 1917), according to a recent poll in the Federal Republic. Not only through his novels but also through his public statements made during political controversies and through essays and newspaper interviews, his reputation as a critic of society is well established. Initially, he pointed his accusing finger at the militarists and at the wartime mentality. In 1951 he published his first novel *Wo warst du, Adam?* (Adam, where were you?), a set of scenes from the war as experienced by the underdog, the little man. When German society was slowly recovering during the fifties, he took the side of the poor employee who succumbs to the stress of life in the ruined city and who tries to save his marriage in spite of his catastrophic living conditions. The novel is called *Und sagte kein einziges Wort* (And Did not Say a Word), 1953. Society was again taken to task in *Haus ohne Hüter* (The Unguarded House), 1954, for allowing the destruction of the family as a moral institution. A more demanding novel followed in 1959, *Billard um halbzehn* (Billiards at Half Past Nine), which reached into previous generations and showed the unchanging traits of narrow-mindedness, stubbornness, and petit bourgeois insensitivity that Böll sees as typically Prussian. Incidentally, he likes to think of himself as not belonging to that type of person, his native Rhineland being of a different ethnic origin. But the Roman Catholic Rhenish society also has its defects, and in 1963 Böll exposed the hypocrisy and egotism of the representatives of the church in the novel *Ansichten eines Clowns* (The Clown). In 1971 a novel followed that dealt with a new social problem that had developed in Germany in recent years. It is the problem of integrating the foreign workers, and the novel is *Gruppenbild mit Dame* (Group Portrait with a Lady). And in 1974 he took on the press and the judicial system in West Germany when he publicly condemned the handling of the Baader–Meinhof group, the left-wing radicals who had been prosecuted for their terrorist activities. The novel, which was also made into a controversial movie, is called *Die verlorene Ehre der Katharina Blum oder Wie Gewalt entsteht und wohin sie führen kann* (The Lost Honor of Katharina Blum or How Power Originates and Where it Can Lead).

After listing all these critical novels of Heinrich Böll and after stressing his disillusion with and contempt for society, it must be said in fairness that Böll is not a fatalist. He has never given up fighting against the defects and the perversions of society because he envisions a better world, a more perfect society that is closer to his ideals of love and humanity. In the meantime, for the world as it is, he cannot feel much more than disgust and animosity.

2. Negative and radical criticism of society appears to be a fitting characterization of the writers mentioned so far, but it is necessary to point out that their aggressiveness and continuous protest assume that something can be done about the sick society.

Not every writer shares this assumption. There are several who doubt that literature can achieve anything in politics, who would prefer a clear separation of the writer from political opinion making. In fact some writers who began as propagandists for a cause grew tired as the years went by and finally reached a state of resignation. This is a phenomenon to be observed in a surprising number of novelists in recent years, for example, Wolfgang Koeppen, Martin Walser, and Günter Grass. Others never tried to influence society directly through their writings, although they write about problems that society created for them. They, too, are critical of the prevailing social conditions, but their reactions involve withdrawal, escapism, and flight rather than protest. The typical novel of escapism is one that describes the bewildered human being of our modern world who is longing to get away from it all, like Ernst Wiechert's *Das einfache Leben* (The Simple Life), 1939. Better known is the Nobel prizewinner Hermann Hesse (1877–1962) and his utopian novel *Das Glasperlenspiel* (Magister Ludi: The Glass Bead Game), 1943. Hesse was an escapist all his life. He ran away from school and from his family. He left Germany during the First World War and stayed in virtual seclusion in Switzerland until his death. Whether in *Siddharta*, 1925, *Steppenwolf*, 1927, or the *Glasperlenspiel*, Hesse was eager to escape into himself, away from the dangers of the world. Symbolically, the Magister Ludi, Josef Knecht, perishes as soon as he leaves the monkish community of the glass bead players and enters the ordinary world.

Another writer-philosopher who reached the conclusion that active participation in the problems of society is not the task of the literary artist was Hermann Broch (1886–1951). In his novel *Der Tod des Vergil* (Death of Virgil), 1945, the central issue of the relationship between art and the worldly power is discussed during the long confrontation of the emperor with the poet. In the great dialogue between Augustus and the dying Virgil, the poet tries to explain to the emperor, who can only think in terms of politics, that the task of the artist is different.

I recognize that everybody has his duties because man alone is the bearer of duty, but I also know that art cannot be so burdened. It cannot be forced to serve the state or anybody else. All one would achieve would be to turn it into nonart. And when the duties of men are outside the realm of art, as nowadays, man has no choice but to drop art, even out of respect for it.

(Ich anerkenne jede Pflicht für den Menschen, denn er allein ist Träger der Pflicht, aber ich weiss, dass man der Kunst keinerlei Pflichten aufbürden kann, weder ztaatsdienende noch sonstwelche; man würde sie dadurch nur zur Unkunst machen, und wenn die Pflichten des Menschen, wie eben heutzutage, anderswo als in der Kunst liegen, so hat er gar keine andere Wahl, er muss die Kunst, und nicht zuletzt aus Achtung vor ihr, fallen lassen.)

This is a surprising thought coming from an author who had previously written the trilogy *Die Schlafwandler* (The Sleepwalkers), 1931–32, which is full of bitter criticism of Austrian society before World War I, and who published another critical novel, *Die Schuldlosen* (The Guiltless), 1950, after the *Death of Virgil*. But this last novel was a collection of earlier stories held together by a few new chapters, and Broch found it necessary to add an explanation of its genesis. In it he confirmed once more what the poet had said to the emperor: Art cannot be burdened with social problems; in fact, art is not an effective tool for bringing about social changes. "Never has a work of art 'converted' anybody to anything." (Noch niemals hat ein Kunstwerk irgendjemanden zu irgend etwas 'bekehrt'.)

As Hesse created a utopian world for himself in order to avoid the burning problems of society, so did Ernst Jünger (b. 1895), one of the most remarkable writers of the twentieth century. Originally an enthusiastic activist prepared to sacrifice himself in the service of his country, highly decorated as a soldier in the First World War, a protagonist of the warrior spirit in his novel *In Stahlgewittern* (In Storms of Steel), 1920, he later developed his own ideas about the society of the future in *Der Arbeiter* (The Worker), 1932, and eventually found himself in an irreconcilable conflict with the authorities during the Third Reich. His escape into the dream world of *Auf den Marmorklippen* (On the Marble Cliffs), 1939, and *Heliopolis*, 1949, did not express an apathetic attitude toward what happened in the real world around him but demonstrated an effort on the part of the writer to maintain an indirect influence on society. His escapism was tactical rather than being caused by resignation. In later works Jünger leaned more noticeably toward skepticism regarding the future of mankind, but his philosophy still upheld the principle that hope leads farther than fear.

Skepticism regarding the possibilities that a writer can influence society, indeed uncertainty as to the direction that such influence should take, is also the prevailing attitude of Uwe Johnson (b. 1934). He is the only writer of reputation who has consistently dealt with the problem of the divided Germany and with what this division has done to the individuals who are torn between the conflicting ideologies of the two societies. Johnson himself went from East to West, but he refuses to renounce his basic agreement with socialist principles, although he appreciates the freedom that he can enjoy in the West.

His novels are by no means indifferent to political conditions, but they are not critical, that is to say, they do not involve partisanship. Even the titles sometimes indicate his own indecision or groping for the truth. The novel that secured his place among the outstanding writers of today was *Mutmas-sungen über Jakob* (Speculations about Jakob), 1959, in which he described the difficulties that people have in adjusting to the political system in the East as well as in the West. His second novel *Das dritte Buch über Achim* (The Third Book about Achim), 1961, deals with the inability of a journalist from the Federal Republic to understand and work within the framework of the socialist system. And in a subsequent book, *Zwei Ansichten* (Two Views), 1965, an elementary love story about two young people, different backgrounds originating in the Eastern and Western societies finally prevent their union. Johnson does not take sides; he does not accuse anybody; but he demonstrates the perplexity of the conditions in which we live. This attitude of neutrality has led him to a conclusion regarding the options left to a writer: to record as a chronicler of his time the experience of individuals in their interactions with events around them. A result has been the more than a thousand pages of the three volumes of *Jahrestage* (Days of the Year), 1970 to 1973. In these novels Johnson reaches an attitude toward society that almost reminds one of the objectivity of a scientific analyst.

If an aggressive condemnation of society like that of Heinrich Mann implies at least a remaining spark of hope for improvement, skepticism and resignation are certainly less positive about the future. They are mild forms of despair. And despair indeed can become the dominant attitude of the writer in his reaction to society. No other literature has produced a more desperate victim of society than Franz Kafka (1883–1924). Nowhere is the reaction of an author to society more extremely expressed than in the works of this Prague intellectual who wrote in German. Kafka was not a political writer. He did not concern himself with the conditions of society from an ideological standpoint, but he was profoundly involved in the problems that an individual has to face in trying to resist the restrictions that others impose on his freedom. It was the continual fight for power among people that obsessed him. He was weak and vulnerable, and his reactions to society were those of fear and defeatism. In some works like *Das Urteil* (The Sentence), 1913, society is represented by the family, especially the father; in novels like *Der Prozess* (The Trial), 1925, the threatening outside power is the bureaucratic machinery of the state; in still another work, *Die Strafkolonie* (The Penal Colony), 1919, it is the brutal judicial system for which the individual is nothing but a helpless victim. The anonymity and therefore the utter monstrosity of the repressive society is gruesomely described in *Das Schloss* (The Castle), 1926. Kafka was an extraordinary case bordering on the pathological, but in his panic and helplessness regarding the individual's dependence on modern society, he voiced a deep-seated trauma shared by many in some degree or other. For Kafka, there is no hope for the poor victim, and in spite of his visions of escaping through *Verwandlung* (Metamorphosis), 1915, or through shrinking in size, the victim always succumbs or is at least continually humiliated. Kafka's thinking, incidentally, was not limited to the endless difficulties that man creates for man. Especially in his symbolic shorter works he dealt with existential questions in an atmosphere of profound nihilism, as in *Beim Bau der chinesischen Mauer* (The Great Wall of China), written in 1918–19, in which the metaphysical aspects of man's life are viewed in macabre perspectives.

3. In contrast to the writer who allows himself to become despondent vis-à-vis the inhumanity of society, there is a different type of personality whose reaction evinces a much stronger character. Some of the top writers of our century have developed characteristic styles of irony and mild ridicule. This attitude is quite different from cynicism and even from satire that derives its effectiveness from distortion and exaggeration. Irony, on the other hand, chooses to paint human weaknesses so that the reader answers with a smile instead of with mephistophelian laughter. Irony involves the aloofness of the writer as a superior

observer of the human scene, and in this it differs from true humor that identifies itself with the frailty of others and still musters understanding and laughter.

But humor is rare, and irony is cheaper to come by, even though it requires a sharp eye and a witty mind. The greatest writer in this group, in fact "the Ironic German" himself, is Thomas Mann (1875–1955). In the tradition of German romanticism, irony became a subtle attitude of the artist that included his inner distance from his own work, and Thomas Mann belongs to this tradition. In such novels as *Die Buddenbrooks*, 1901, and particularly in *Der Zauberberg* (The Magic Mountain), 1924, he painted certain sections of the German society of his time with masterful strokes, bringing to life unforgettable characters, describing delightful episodes in the lives of typical representatives of the bourgeoisie, while now and then he stepped back from his work and "smiled down on it from the height of his intellectual summit." Thomas Mann's problem concerned the conflict of the artist with the expectations of society regarding its "healthy, normal citizens." This is a basic motif to which he continually returned. But the wider view about the inner weakness and morbidity of European society before and after the First World War became increasingly his concern and remained the topic of his novels. The smiling admission of the senselessness of life is the basic tenor of almost all of Mann's works, and one has the feeling that the author's irony is secretely enjoyed. Sometimes Mann set the story in his own time, as in the *Buddenbrooks*, the *Magic Mountain*, and *Doktor Faustus*; sometimes he went back in history, as in the Goethe novel *Lotte in Weimar*, 1939, and the colossal tetralogy *Joseph und seine Brüder* (Joseph and his Brothers), 1939–42. That opus constituted far more than a critical appraisal of the individual in society. It was, in his own words, "a humorous, mildly ironic, I would almost say: bashful story of mankind" (eine humoristisch getönte, ironisch abgedämpfte, ich möchte fast sagen: verschämte Menschheitsdichtung).

Among living German writers the attitude of irony, mockery, and the love of parody is not uncommon. One of the most widely read contemporary authors, Günter Grass (b. 1927), has a particular penchant for it. The time in which his two best known novels, *Die Blechtrommel* (The Tin Drum), 1959, and *Hundejahre* (Dog Years), 1963, take place is World War II and the immediate postwar years. There is enough for a writer to complain about in this era, but Grass chooses to look at the world through a grotesquely distorting mirror so that the unmistakable criticism of people and institutions becomes fascinating fiction with a peculiar blend of daring fantasy and witty persiflage. In the *Tin Drum,* the petit bourgeois milieu of a Danzig family is viewed from the bottom perspective of a dwarf who, at the age of three, refuses to continue to grow and henceforth develops some eerie faculties with which he tyrannizes the world around him. Grass's criticism of his time is serious enough, but his prevailing attitude is not hatred and contempt. He is a pensive critic who tries to help bring about changes in society. This approach has been clearly demonstrated not only in his novel *Örtlich betäubt* (Local Anaesthesia), 1969, in which he dealt with the protesting young people of the sixties, but also through his own activity for a political party in the Federal Republic. From press interviews, however, it becomes apparent that Grass, like his colleagues Martin Walser and Siegfrid Lenz, developed a certain pessimism and resignation in recent years that led him to doubt the role of literature in politics altogether. But Grass is not a nihilist. As he advances in years, there are indications that his sense of humor will prevail. His latest novel *Der Butt* (The Flounder), 1977, points in that direction. We will come back to it at the end of this survey.

Ridiculing society was also Martin Walser's (b. 1927) method of expressing his dissatisfaction with what he saw. He followed the development of his fictional hero, Anselm Kristlein, the typical member of the affluent postwar society, through several novels in which the author proved himself to be an ingenious master of the language and a witty storyteller. His first venture into social criticism was the novel *Ehen in Philippsburg* (Marriage in Philippsburg), 1957, followed by *Halbzeit* (Halftime), 1960, and *Das Einhorn* (The Unicorn), 1966. It has been mentioned before that Walser, in more recent times, has indicated a cautious skepticism about the actual role of writers in society. His latest novel, *Jenseits der Liebe* (Beyond Love), 1976, confirms this attitude. It is no longer the society that has to carry the burden of responsibility when the individual suffers. It is the individual himself who causes his own downfall. We witness in Walser a return to the psychological novel of the past, a withdrawal into the privacy of his individual problems.

4. Irony and mockery, as has been pointed out, mean that the writer has managed to keep a certain distance between himself and the object of his observation. This distance is maintained even more consciously by the objective analyst, the writer who avoids being emotionally involved. This sober philosophical attitude has yielded a number of very fine novels throughout the years, and the authors have succeeded in making their points no less clearly than have the loud protesters or the bitter satirists. A model case was mentioned when Uwe Johnson's *Jahrestage* was discussed. An earlier example was Hermann Kasack (1896–1966) with his novels *Die Stadt hinter dem Strom* (The City behind the River), 1947, and especially *Das Grosse Netz* (The Big Net), 1952. Here, as well as in the story *Der Webstuhl* (The Loom), 1949, Kasack describes in visionary scenes the gruesome consequences that mankind faces if technological development continues along the lines to which we have become accustomed.

Sober analysis of the affluent postwar society is also the background of Gerd Gaiser's (1908–76) critical novel *Schlussball* (The Graduation Ball), 1958. The boom of the "economic miracle" has left the inhabitants of a typical industrial city in

Germany hopelessly dominated by materialistic values, and behind a brilliant façade there is nothing but a vacuum.

Max Frisch (b. 1911) is a Swiss and also a cosmopolitan globe-trotter. As such he has an obvious predisposition for being a neutral observer, although his Swiss compatriots may find some passages of undisguised castigation of their parochial narrow-mindedness in his novels. But the general tone of Frisch's novels is one of curiosity. In his books *Stiller*, 1954, *Homo Faber*, 1957, and *Mein Name sei Gantenbein* (Let my name be Gantenbein), 1964), Frisch wonders what might have been if things had happened differently. Much like a research scientist, he likes to experiment with his material. For a writer, that means experimenting with the fate of his fictional characters. Frisch is a sagacious observer of society, but crusading for a better future is not his mission.

5. At times when the demands of society on the individual become extremely exacting, when everyone becomes the victim in one way or the other of what the authorities decree, many writers will rebel. They want to remind society of its limitations and proclaim the rights of the individual, unless, of course, they agree with the dictates of the authorities. Conditions of this kind prevail, for example, during a war. Society has always tried to silence the dissident writer, and protesting literature was banned or was only published abroad. But during the two great wars of this century there were many authors who felt impelled to accept the sacrifices that society demanded of them. Even Thomas Mann supported the ideology of the establishment during World War I, and, initially, also Alfred Döblin was in favor of the war. Especially during the postwar years, there was quite a number of writers who dealt with those trying times in attitudes of unquestioned loyalty to the hierarchical structure. Many war novels of the twenties and again of the fifties and after neglect the aspect of society and demonstrate instead the authors' determination to survive. They accept

their plights as necessities, not as an outrage of society, and thus their reaction is one of spite against the danger of living in these times rather than a complaint against the society that had spawned the danger. After World War I Ernst Jünger's *In Stahlgewittern* was but one of the many heroic war novels that were written in the nineteen twenties. After the Second World War the number of such fictionalized reports about the individual's fortitude under extremely adverse conditions was somewhat smaller, but, as literature, they sometimes reached a respectable level of quality and therefore merit attention. Gerd Gaiser wrote *Die sterbende Jagd* (The Last Squadron), 1953; Peter Bamm (1897–1975) was successful with his narrative documentation of medical personnel in combat, *Die unsichtbare Flagge* (The Invisible Flag), 1952; and belatedly, a former war reporter, Lothar Günter Buchheim (b. 1918) came forth with his impressive saga of the submarines, *Das Boot* (The Boat), in 1976.

Even an avowed antimilitarist like Alfred Andersch wrote war novels in which the will to survive outweighs the pacifist ideology. In *Kirschen der Freiheit* (Cherries of Freedom), 1952, he recounted the exploits of the deserter; in *Winterspelt*, 1974, it is the conflict of the officer who has to decide between sacrificing his men and surrendering.

Considering the tremendous impact that the two world wars have had on millions of individuals in Germany and elsewhere, it is not surprising that the war experiences produced a significant literary response. It is an old adage that times of extreme suffering bring out the worst as well as the best in man. The writers who reacted to extreme trial and tribulation by insisting on man's will to survive have found many readers among their contemporaries for whom this kind of reaction had a strong appeal.

6. Throughout history many people have found ultimate strength in religion or at least in the certainty that the universe is

benignly directed by a metaphysical order. With that conviction, individuals have gained power to discover meaning in
life, to accept the chaos that surrounds them, to develop attitudes of humility, love, and compassion toward their fellow men
and understanding of the conditions under which they have had
to live. A writer who is deeply religious may be critical of
society, but his works will always reflect his faith in the ultimate goodness of the world. In the twentieth century, as in
earlier times, there has been a strong element of religion in
literature. It is noteworthy that the biographies of several
writers of rank reveal that they are converts to catholicism.
This is the case with Alfred Döblin, Werner Bergengruen, Ger-
trud von le Fort, Eduard Schaper, Ruth Schaumann. Others like
Franz Werfel and Stefan Andres wrote their novels out of deep
religious convictions, even when they did not maintain close
ties with the church.

They all share the belief that the writer's task is, as Bergengruen said, to demonstrate the existence of a transcendental order
(das Sichtbarmachen ewiger Ordnungen). Evil in the world is
strong, man is weak and selfish, society is cruel. The only way to
cope is to have faith in God, to be humble before the mysteries
of life, and to be compassionate and loving toward others.

Alfred Döblin (1878–1957) was a physician among the poor
in Berlin. His novel *Berlin Alexanderplatz*, 1929, established
his fame, but in an earlier novel, *Berge, Meere und Giganten*
(Mountains, Oceans, and Giants), 1924, which is a utopian
description of a highly technical future, Döblin had shown his
characteristic effort to solve social problems through an awareness of metaphysical perspectives. Even the simple criminal
Franz Biberkopf in *Berlin Alexanderplatz* is eventually "born
again" in the recognition of his inner strength through love and
humility. After the second war, Döblin continued his attempts
to spread the message of Christian love and unbroken faith
in the meaning of life in spite of the chaos of the postwar world.
He reached an artistic summit in his last novel *Hamlet oder*

die lange Nacht nimmt ein Ende (Hamlet or the Long Night Comes to an End), in 1956.

Ernst Wiechert (1887–1950), whose novel of escapism *Das einfache Leben* was mentioned earlier, was also an undaunted religious writer who preached again and again that goodness and compassion are the strongest weapons against evil in the world. *Missa sine nomine*, 1950, his last novel, is the story of three brothers who meet after the horrors of the war and find consolation and strength to pursue a new life in their faith in God.

Franz Werfel (1890–1945), like Döblin a refugee from the Third Reich, had witnessed the dark powers of society in his own dramatic experience, but he never ceased searching for the good in man. "To be good is more than to be happy" was his belief, and his novels bear witness to this attitude. As his most explicit criticism of contemporary society we may consider his last novel, *Stern der Ungeborenen* (Star of the Unborn), 1946, in which he looked back on our era from a distant society a hundred thousand years from now. That utopian society is one without politics, without nations, without labor and social problems. The world is unified; there is only one language spoken by all. The humor of the situation becomes manifest when the author—a guest on leave from purgatory—is called upon to explain to future human beings the absurdities of his own time, that is, the world in which we live today. In the end the novel exposes the futility of technical progress. Man will always be human and will continue looking for salvation through his relationship with God.

Not surprisingly, women assume an important place among the religious writers of our century. The most fascinating among them was Elisabeth Langgässer (1899–1950). Her magnum opus is the novel *Das unauslöschliche Siegel* (The Indelible Seal), 1946, in which she gave a macabre description of the struggle between God and Satan in the heart of one individual, Lazarus Belfontaine, a Jewish merchant who had received the "indelible seal" of baptism when he married a Christian young woman. Society, political events, Europe's chaotic road to the abyss—all this provides the background for the psychological and religious turmoil in the mind of the hero who is ultimately saved by a mysterious act of divine grace that ends the devil's power over his life. It is an extremely ecstatic atmosphere in which Elisabeth Langgässer expressed the existential anxieties of our time. The artistic power of her writing puts her among the foremost German novelists of the twentieth century.

7. As our review of the novelists' reactions to society comes to an end, there is one group still to be mentioned: the true humorists. It was said before that they are a rare breed. To laugh at the world is easy, and there is nothing special about writing a satire, about being witty or ironic. But it is rare indeed to find an author who maintains the inner freedom of laughing without rancor and venom, without gloom and despair, of laughing at human weakness with optimism and sympathy.

At times we see a writer express occasional humor in an otherwise argumentative work, for example, Mann's *Magic Mountain* or Werfel's *Star of the Unborn*. In fact, glimpses of humor are to be found in many novels, with the possible exception of the outspoken ideological denunciations. But where is the novel that lets the reader participate in the author's sovereign reconciliation of the vicissitudes of life and invites him to join in the relief of laughter? Thomas Mann wrote such a novel. It was his last, and it remained uncompleted: *Bekenntnisse des Hochstaplers Felix Krull* (Confessions of Felix Krull, Confidence Man), 1954. Here Thomas Mann comes back to his old theme, the decadence of the bourgeoisie. But Felix Krull is not to be measured by the standards of the establishment. The author created this character out of sheer delight and playfulness. The whole of society is reversed, and, obviously, people can live in this reversed order and live pleasantly.

Another novelist who comes close to being a writer of true

humor is Arno Schmidt (b. 1914). He has been living like a hermit for many years in a village in North Germany. Initially, that is to say, in the years immediately following World War II, Schmidt appeared to be quite cynical. But gradually he adopted the role of the wise old man. Recently his books have become more and more difficult to read because of his experimental style that caused some critics to compare him with James Joyce. And there is indeed a certain affinity between the two. But once the formal obstacles of communication between author and reader have been overcome, Schmidt's fantastic ideas of future human societies offer abundant food for thought. Particularly impressive are the short novel *Die Gelehrtenrepublik* (The Republic of Scholars), 1957, the novel about outer space, *Kaff auch Mare Crisium* (Village and Mare Crisium), 1960, and the fictitious report *Schule der Atheisten* (School of Atheists), 1971. All three novels deal with conditions after a future war in which nuclear destruction has left only remnants of life on this globe. Pessimistic as such a background may appear, it takes a personality like Arno Schmidt to maintain his sense of humor in dealing with the people who have managed to survive the ultimate Armageddon.

Whereas Arno Schmidt has developed a sometimes cryptic language full of associations and implications about the subconscious, there is now a series of novels by a younger author, Walter Kempowski (b. 1929), who prefers the everyday language of the bourgeois family whose life in the thirties and afterward he describes in great detail. It is Kempowski's own family in the city of Rostock and his own youth that the author records. So far three novels have come out in the series; several more are expected to complete this history of a family in war and peace. The first one, *Tadellöser und Wolff,* 1971, was an immediate success and was followed quickly by *Uns geht's ja noch gold* (We are still well off), 1972. The third novel, *Ein Kapitel für sich* (Another Matter), was published in 1975. One has to know that the author spent eight years in Soviet prisons from

1948 to 1956 in order to appreciate the attitude of unshaken optimism displayed in this extraordinary chronicle of one of the most trying times that any family can experience. Kempowski is now living in West Germany. It may not be too daring to hope for future works from this author that would round out this literary monument of a historic period in a manner comparable to the timeless *Simplizissimus* by Grimmelshausen that recorded the horrors of the Thirty Years War.

The literary event of 1977 in West Germany was the publication of Günter Grass' latest novel *Der Butt* (The Flounder). Its reception indicated an immediate recognition of the novel's significance. Grass not only returned to the characteristic style that he had displayed with excellence in the *Tin Drum*, but he also proved that he matured from the role of a satirist to that of the great humorist. Thomas Mann had ventured to call *Joseph and his Brothers* a story of mankind. *Der Butt* is the story of mankind in Europe, the story of man and woman and their different roles in history. Clad in the symbolic form of the fairy tale about the fisherman and his wife, the novel leads us through the various historic periods up to the present, demonstrating the failures of men in their attempts to achieve a better society. The "Weltgeist," represented by the flounder, has been using the male as his instrument on the way to progress, but the male has been foolish and weak and has finally forfeited his leading role. The flounder turns to women, the women of today. They will henceforth be the recipients of his advice if they ask for it. Grass lets his readers know that he is not euphoric about this prospect. After all, he knows women. He has been dealing with them through history, for it was Grass himself who played the role of man in the various reincarnations in history, from the original fisherman to whom the fish appeared on the Baltic coast thousands of years ago to the present individual, the writer of this fantastic account. The symbolism of this novel may not instantly reveal itself, but its profoundness will not be lost on the scrutinizing reader.

3

CONTEMPORARY
GERMAN
THEATER

Jürgen Kalkbrenner

I

THE GERMAN EXPERT who recently stated, "There is no country in the world with as many theaters as Germany," may not have been motivated by modesty, but he did speak the truth.

The relatively large number of theaters in Germany reflects the diversified history of this country, which became a nation-state only in 1871. Earlier its contituent parts existed as some thirty kingdoms, principalities, dukedoms, and free city states, and its western portion today rightly calls itself the Federal Republic of Germany.

For the kings and princes and for the patricians in the free cities, theaters were instruments of cultural and political representation. The better the theater, the higher the reputation and standing of its protector and supporter. Some rulers took personal interest in the operation of their theaters; some limited their attention to the ladies of the cast.

Also the growing self-awareness of the German bourgeoisie

led to the creation of many theaters, often housed in monumental buildings that competed with those of the princes. This juxtaposition of court and municipal theaters proved altogether productive. When Germany became a republic after World War I, the court theaters became state theaters.

Except for the first half of the twentieth century, when the best theaters and the best actors were to be found in Berlin, there has never been and there is not now a specific city that can claim to be the center of German theater. Instead, many cities, big and small, compete for this title, the smaller ones often serving as stepping stones for talented actors.

Private theater companies and university theaters—familiar aspects of the American cultural scene—are exceptions in Germany. The majority of the theaters in the Federal Republic of Germany are operated and subsidized by municipal or Länder (state) governments. Often theater, opera house, and ballet are combined under one roof.

Most of the German theaters are repertory theaters. Instead of performing one play "en suite" until the box office slackens, they set up each year a "Spielplan," a repertory, consisting of several plays, German and foreign, classic, modern, and experimental. Except for a few traveling stars, actors stay in one place as members of a resident ensemble.

However, to cut costs small cities have started to pool their resources so that several cities may share one ensemble performing at different places.

The traditional diversification allows most of the theaters to develop their own identities. One may attract an unusually large number of qualified actors who are fascinated by the innovative talent of a director. Another may concentrate on classical drama, whereas its neighbor may acquire a reputation for its experiments in providing a platform for young playwrights. A fourth may appeal to foreign visitors because of its scenic setting (Heidelberg) or its annual festival (Recklinghausen).

In the 1973-74 season 28 million tickets, opera included, were sold, and in 350 cities of the Federal Republic of Germany regular theater performances were held. Although it is not guaranteed by the constitution, many Germans consider visiting a theater regularly an inalienable civic right. Few question the public duty of municipal and state governments to provide the necessary facilities. In fact, theater is seen and valued as an educational institution in the tradition of Friedrich Schiller who wrote an essay on "Die Schaubühne als moralische Anstalt" (The Stage as a Moral Institution).

Although heavily subsidized out of municipal and state funds, theaters are not instruments in the hands of the authorities for informing, instructing, educating, or manipulating the population. No *Intendant* (director general), no director would accept a post if he were subject to interference from budgetary or other authorities about the composition of the *Spielplan* or program. Because box office receipts and subscriptions cover only a quarter of the operational costs and taxpayers' money has to be used to supply the rest, it may happen that a city councilman will complain that he misses the lighter muses in the *Spielplan* or a politician will advocate a more "balanced" repertory. But the principle of artistic freedom for the management of the theaters is never questioned.

For the last twenty years the trend of repertories has been in the direction of literary relevance. A considerable portion of the public wants an intellectual confrontation with social topics and avant-garde artistic methods. Superficial entertainment, vaudeville and thrillers, has been taken over by film and television. The most frequently performed authors in 1973–74 were: Brecht, Shakespeare, Molière, Schiller, Nestroy, Feydeau, Beckett, Kroetz, Goetz, Lessing, Ibsen, and Hauptmann.

About half the plays performed on the stages of the Federal Republic of Germany are written by German-speaking authors, the other half being translations from foreign authors.

Often a German stage is the springboard to success for a foreign playwright.

Every year, between 100 and 120 new plays appear on the stage as either first performances or first performances in German translation.

The unusual, the experimental, the bold advance toward new artistic horizons share the stage with examples of 2,500 years of European theatrical history, the latter being a continual inspiration and challenge. Experiments are made not only in the form of new plays that contain novel themes and problems but also through a contemporary interpretation of the classics and by new methods of production.

A theater is faced with a number of conflicting demands: It is supposed to cater to diverse interests by producing a great variety of plays, and yet it must develop a continuous intellectual line. It is expected not to neglect the established tradition and yet be open to new adventures. The public wants to be informed about what is happening on the stages outside Germany. Anything of importance anywhere in the world is soon tracked down by one of the various German publishers, translated, and offered to the theaters. Their repertories, therefore, reflect social trends and the cultural climate of our time.

II

Plays performed on the stages of postwar Germany may be grouped loosely as follows:

plays confronting the immediate past, the twelve years of the Third Reich, its rise, and the fall that buried Germany under its ruins;

plays reviving the legacy of authors who had been banned from German stages during the Third Reich, such as Bertolt Brecht;

plays by foreign authors appearing for the first time on German stages, thus bridging the gap that had developed between the German and the international theater scene, for example, plays by Anouilh, Giraudoux, O'Neill, Wilder, Williams, and Miller;

plays reflecting a growing social and political awareness by criticizing society;

plays manifesting a rediscovery of the individual and his private problems.

The most impressive play that presented Germany in ruins after the end of World War II, frequently performed in make-shift theaters consisting of no more than patched-up ruins, was Wolfgang Borchert's "Draussen vor der Tür" (Left Out). Borchert, who during the war had served in a penal battalion for speaking up against Hitler, died of tuberculosis in a Swiss hospital in 1946, one day before his play was broadcast by the Hamburg radio network. The central figure of "Draussen vor der Tür" is Corporal Beckmann, released from the PW camps of Russia, a cripple, wandering through the ruins of a defeated Germany, searching to make sense of the sacrifices that his generation had been asked to make and looking for a place to live and work. Nobody wants him, not the arrogant ex-officer, now in charge of a firm, the stone-hearted landlady, the cabaret director who finds him lacking in manner and charm, not even the River Elbe in which he tries in vain to drown himself. God Father, a weak old man, complains that mankind no longer understands him. The final cry from Beckmann: "Gibt denn keiner, keiner Antwort?" ("Will nobody, nobody answer?") was, of course, the question raised by most of Borchert's and Beckmann's generation.

A similar if not greater impact on the German public, particularly on ex-soldiers, was made by Carl Zuckmayer's "Des Teufels General" (The Devil's General). Zuckmayer, who had been an officer in World War I, gained fame as a young playwright in the twenties. A full-blooded writer, his fingers on the pulse of people high and low, his humor thriving on the dialects of Germany's various regions, his social criticism blended with compassion for the individual, he met success after success. In his last play before he emigrated from Germany, "Der Haupt-

mann von Köpenick" ("The Captain of Köpenick"), he exposes
and debunks the influence of the military in imperial Germany.
The "hero," a poor shoemaker, Voigt, after having spent most
of his life in penitentiaries for petty crimes and being pushed
around for lacking proper papers, finally dons a second-hand
army captain's uniform, stops a patrol of soldiers in the streets
of Berlin, and marches them to the city hall of Köpenick, where
he hopes to obtain a passport. But he fails. Köpenick has no
passport office. The play is based on a real event that caused
the whole of Germany, including the Kaiser, to roar with
laughter.

"The Devil's General" is more serious. The play was written
in Vermont, Zuckmayer's refuge during his emigration. Based on
the fate of Ernst Udet, a World War I fighter ace, the play
centers around General Harras, a passionate professional soldier who, promoted to general by Hitler, sees his heroic dreams
come true when Germany's rearmament puts it on equal footing
with its neighbors. Yet Harras commits suicide while testing a
plane after realizing that he is serving the devil and has contributed to his deadly system of which he has himself become
a victim. Another central figure—more a hypothetical than a
real character—is Colonel Oderbruch who sabotages planes and
sacrifices comrades to save the country from being destroyed by
the war. Many of the younger generation among the theater-
goers who saw the play identified with Lieutenant Hartmann.
This young and idealistic officer has to come to terms with the
realization that his idealism is being misused for criminal ends.
The author and the play generated long and ardent discussions
at German universities, and "The Devil's General" heralded the
comeback of Zuckmayer to the German stage.

A third play of this group performed on many stages was
Max Frisch's "Nun singen sie wieder" (They are singing again),
the Swiss author's attempt to project despair and hope in a
world of war that engulfed innocent and guilty alike.

Among the authors unknown to the German stage until 1945

was Thornton Wilder, whose plays "Our Town" (Unsere kleine Stadt) and "By the Skin of our Teeth" (Wir sind noch einmal davongekommen) attracted considerable audiences. The value of the simple daily life manifested in "Our Town" revealed its essence powerfully among the ruins. The German title of "By the Skin of our Teeth," which reads "Wir sind noch einmal davongekommen" ("We were lucky to survive"), indicated the apocalyptic dimension that this play had acquired for its German viewers.

Steinbeck's "Of Mice and Men," Williams's "Glass Menagerie," and Miller's "Death of a Salesman" attracted similar audiences as did the plays of T. S. Elliot and Christopher Fry. In his versions of "Antigone"—a young woman stubbornly seeking death in order to preserve her identity and integrity—and of "Euridice"—hopeless love surrounded by a hostile world—Jean Anouilh presented to the younger generation in Germany characters with whom it could identify. Together with the plays of Sartre and Camus, whose themes were sociopolitical, the success of these plays demonstrated that the German theater once again had become part of the international theater scene.

Another milestone for the postwar German theater was the revival of Brecht's epic, didactic theater. For Brecht theater is meant to change society. His epic theater adopts a narrative form and allots to the spectator the part of an observer whose participation will be aroused, who will be forced to make decisions, and not be allowed to be emotionally involved. The plays proceed in jumps; scenes are mounted against each other to prevent the spectator from identifying with individual figures on the stage. The actor is supposed to show that he is not a hero but plays a hero. It is his task to make the spectator aware that he is acting a role and that he is not the character whom he represents. For Brecht theater has no magic function. He uses it as a didactic, moral, political instrument that does not provide the spectator with illusions but revolutionizes him.

In most of Brecht's plays man is not seen as a fixed individual but a process open to interpretation. His societal existence determines his thinking. In his later plays "Herr Puntila und sein Knecht," "Mutter Courage und ihre Kinder," "Der gute Mensch von Sezuan," "Galileo Galilei," and "Der kaukasische Kreidekreis," Brecht appears less didactic. In these plays he prefers historical material which he condenses into real plots and concrete subject matter. He relies on detail, atmosphere, and color. Theater again involves change, suspense, entertainment, and a touch of lightness. In "Mother Courage" the historical context is the Thirty Years War that ravaged Germany in the seventeenth century. In spite of the surrounding chaos, Mother Courage looks quietly after her business. She does not learn from mishaps, although she loses one child after the other. One of her sons, unaware that the war is over, continues to plunder and is hanged—yesterday a hero, today a criminal. The societal existence prescribes their thoughts, but each of these figures has his own private, shrewd little backdoor for himself.

After the war Brecht, who had immigrated to the USA, returned to East Berlin. Whether he saw the fulfillment of his political concepts in the communist regime remains, to say the least, doubtful. He survives as a genius of world fame, as a creator of characters and figures who, between the poles of anarchy and inhibition, move on a stage that Brecht chose to call "critical" theater.

Among the authors of the post-Brecht generation who regarded themselves as socially and politically engaged, Günter Grass portrayed Brecht himself in his play "Die Plebejer proben den Aufstand" ("The Plebeians Rehearse the Revolt"). The scene is East Berlin in 1953. A famous theater director, rehearsing a political play about the revolt of the plebeians in Rome, is interrupted by a group of workers about to revolt against the communist government, who ask the director for advice. But the director fails to provide the advice. He is unable to derive conclusions from the revolt that he is rehearsing on stage that could be applied to the real revolt that takes place outside for a double reason: Writing and directing a play is one thing, directing a revolution another. Besides, the theories of Marx and Lenin consider only the fight of the proletariat against capitalist oppressors. That a communist regime could become itself an oppressor, causing workers to protest against it, is a reality not foreseen in their theories.

Protest and revolt are also the themes of Grass's next play "Davor" (Uptight). A high school student intends to set fire to his Dachshund in front of a fashionable café in West Berlin, thus protesting the war in Vietnam. His teacher, whose former approval of revolutionary action has given way to insight into the futility of all violent acts, talks him out of his plan. We hear the philosophical voice of Grass propagating reform instead of revolution. The student ends up a conformist sitting in the chair of a dentist who is convinced that all the evils of the world will be cured once an international mental health system is established.

Other prominent names in the group of critical playwrights are Peter Weiss, author of the social–political play "Marat-Sade" and Peter Hacks who lives in the German Democratic Republic. One of the younger authors, Volker Braun, has discovered the "Arbeiterwelt," the world of the laborers. In his "Kipper" the daily life in factory and office is presented with extreme realism.

Franz Xaver Kroetz shows his sympathy with fringe groups of society. In his "Sterntaler," a family, refugees from the GDR, seeks in vain to achieve integration into its new social environment in West Germany. Kroetz feels compassion for his characters but reduces them—father a drinker, mother ill, son killed by police—to helpless objects and clichés.

As a reaction to this trend in German dramatic production, dominated by social and political problems, a number of authors, among them Tankred Dorst, Thomas Bernhard, and Peter Handke, have rediscovered the individual. Not the relationship between the individual and society but between individuals is the theme of their plays. Quitt, a company owner in Handke's "Die Unvernünftigen sterben aus" (The Unreasonable Ones are Becoming Extinct), realizes that the complications of his inner life mean more to him than do the balance sheets of his firm. For him this awareness of self is the real means of production. Yet as a businessman, he is unreasonable. Unable to solve the conflict between company and ego, he runs against a rock and dies out of desperation.

Romanticism, sensibility, and subjectivity are alive again on German stages—at least temporarily.

4

POLITICAL
LITERATURE
IN GERMANY

Bruno F. Steinbruckner

As in other modern societies, politics and literature in Germany have maintained various degrees of relationship and interaction. Both are components of our cultural existence, and it therefore seems only natural that between them should develop some form of communication. In considering specific works of literature for their "political" character, however, the application of the term "political literature" confronts one with the need to clarify the kinds of literature that may be defined as "political."

During the nineteen twenties strict distinctions prevailed between *Littérature* (*Poésie*) *pure* and *engagée* in German literary criticism.[1] Only "absolute art" could claim to be real literature, whereas political literature carried with it the odor of political propaganda. "Politics" was seen as clearly inferior to the art form of literature. During the years of national socialism in

Germany this view reversed itself when the main function of literature was seen as serving the prevailing ideology. Understandably, this clearly defined position of literature during the Third Reich left the term "political literature" with a rather negative connotation after 1945. In more recent years, however, during which the term "political" has itself experienced a process of redefinition, "political literature" has gained a more respectable place in literary criticism. Since it became apparent through the works of Heidegger and Sartre that "political reality" is to be considered part of the totality of human existence, the political content of a literary work does not necessarily have to be seen as a detriment to its aesthetic value, although the difficulty of judging the literary value of such a work remains.[2] It has also become obvious that one cannot speak of a "political literature" per se. One rather has to see literature of political content within the context of respective historical periods.[3] "Political literature" during the Middle Ages, for instance, differs considerably in its nature and in its goals from the "political literature" of the nineteenth century. Up to the Thirty Years War and even well into the eighteenth century "political literature" usually proclaimed the same general views as did the ruling dynasties, often even serving the interests of the rulers. At the end of the century of Enlightenment political writers began to emancipate themselves, and their objectives began to be independent from those of kings and dukes. Political norms that had been preserved by tradition became questionable and even subject to change.[4] The era of a modern "political literature," thus having been introduced, would in the future see writers air their political views in various forms, sometimes even disguised, if in disagreement with the official views of their rulers and governments. It is the political awareness of German authors and its reflection in their works since the end of the eighteenth century that constitute the subject of this brief and necessarily quite selective survey of German political literature.

The first powerful manifestation of a political will that dif-

fered considerably from the goals of eighteenth-century absolutism appeared in the works of a group of young writers
belonging to the literary movement of "Storm and Stress."
Whereas the novelists and dramatists of the baroque era had
depicted the absolute ruler as a benevolent tyrant, this new
generation of writers reminded the world in sometimes furious
monologues that even a despot, who derived his unlimited
powers divinely, was not allowed to act against reason or against
the basic principles of humanity. Both the young Goethe and
the young Schiller who became the most prominent writers of
"Storm and Stress" created powerful heroes who openly defied
tyranny. In Goethe's *Götz von Berlichingen* (1771), Götz, a
free knight, joins the rebellious peasants in their struggle against
their suppression by princes and bishops. Although he perished
in the process, his overwhelming desire for freedom and his
fiery temperament became a model for a generation. The emotional idealism of Götz stands in sharp contrast to the cold and
calculating schemes of his powerful opponents who used every
means available, even the erotic ambitions of one of his friends,
to bring about the downfall of the hero. Karl Moor in Schiller's
Die Räuber (*Robbers*, 1781) resorts to the perilous life of a
bandit because of the injustices he had suffered. As a "noble
villain" he surrenders himself to the court. In *Kabale und Liebe*
(*Intrigue and Love*, 1784), the corruption of the powerful at
a small court in Germany results in the death of two young
lovers. Contemporary events, such as soldiers being sold to
the British by the rulers of Württemberg and Hesse, appeared
as episodes in the plot, thus exposing the greed and irrespon-
sibility of the mighty. Schiller's directness and vehemence in
uncovering the abuses of the nobility originated largely from
personal experience. In his homeland of Württemberg, from
which he had to flee as a young man, despotic absolutism had
remained nearly unchecked during his youth, whereas a more
enlightened spirit of government was developing in Austria
under Joseph II and in Prussia under Frederick the Great.

The dramatists of "Storm and Stress," among them Friedrich Maximilian Klinger, Heinrich Leopold Wagner, and Jakob Michael Reinhold Lenz, did not limit their criticism to the abuses of their rulers. Society as a whole and its often inhumane conventions became the targets of their accusations: Symbols of social injustice or indifference, such as the unwed mother who kills her child and is punished by death and the debtor's prison, were central motifs of their plays.

Inspired by the writings of Johann Gottfried Herder, the writers of "Storm and Stress" began to rediscover Germany's history and culture, which the Enlightenment had relegated to the "Dark Ages." In Herder's and the young Goethe's view, the heroic age of the Germanic tribes and the Middle Ages were synonymous with originality and archaic strength and were much closer to the sentiment of the "people" than were the writings of their own century. Herder's initiatives in the direction of a feeling of national consciousness were picked up by the romanticists in the last decade of the eighteenth century and became an important pillar of their program at the turn of the century.[5]

The French Revolution as a cataclysmic historic event made a deep impression on the writers of "Storm and Stress." Although Schiller initially welcomed the revolution as a fresh start into new times (he was made an honorary citizen of Paris by the revolutionary government), he later condemned the brutality of the new regime. Later in his life, Schiller's quest for personal liberty and free development of the individual transformed itself into a concept of liberty through self-control, which Goethe had adopted shortly after his move to Weimar. Goethe, himself a high official of the court in Weimar, found it rather difficult all through his life to detach himself from the traditional political concepts of his time. For him, an extraordinary historic figure with the ambitions of a world ruler, in the person of Napoleon, for instance, remained definitely preferable to a future rule by the masses. Goethe's deep devotion to

Napoleon and his affinity for the conservative aims of the nobility later became the cause of bitter accusations by his contemporaries. In this light, one has to suspect that Goethe's remark about America having it easier should not be taken too seriously. He deeply mistrusted a future of total equality as a result of dangerous experimentation. During the last decade of his life Goethe hesitantly resigned himself to the developments of a new age that began to favor social change and question the merits of the traditional concepts of divine order.[6]

During Napoleon's rise to power, the romanticists, inspired by Herder's thoughts on German culture and history, further intensified in their works the feeling of a national cultural awareness.[7] Novalis gave the early romantic movement a programmatic foundation. In his essay *Die Christenheit oder Europa* (*Christianity or Europe*, 1799), he suggested a return to the universality of the Middle Ages, scolding the Reformation as one of the prime causes of the continuous disunity in Germany. The following century, however, he proclaimed as the era during which Germany would take spiritual leadership in Europe. Utopias like Novalis's "Christianity or Europe" had their roots in an overwhelming desire for a unified Germany, something the Holy Roman Empire had not been able to achieve since the late Middle Ages. When the old empire finally crumbled under the pressure exerted by Napoleon, the romanticists set for themselves a new goal: The much hated French emperor was to be brought down; a new German Reich had to rise from the ashes of the old. Many of them, including writers like Achim von Arnim, Joseph von Eichendorff, Joseph Görres, and Adalbert von Chamisso, took active parts in the wars against Napoleon. Friedrich Schlegel and Ernst Moritz Arndt contributed fiery poems and pamphlets, expressing their hatred against the French occupation. Napoleon himself emerged from these writings as the mythical incorporation of all evil, an anti-Christ to be purged from the surface of the earth. Much of the intensive feelings of national animosities between the

French and the Germans originated in the times of the liberation wars. The political song, an old form of resurrected expression, helped in popularizing the struggle against the French and the idea of a new Germany. Heinrich von Kleist, not usually considered a romanticist by literary historians, dedicated one of his powerful dramas to these ideas: His *Hermannsschlacht* (1821) glorifies the fight against an oppressor and suggests a future in national unity.

During the era of German romanticism, for the first time since Walther von der Vogelweide, enormous spiritual potential was freed and used for a defined political purpose. After Napoleon's fall, however, the rulers in Prussia and Austria had little use for the national enthusiasm espoused by the romanticists in a newly appeased Europe. They were carefully monitored by the police, and some were even persecuted. Their spirit, however, survived the restored monarchies of Europe, and it bore new fruit in our century.[8]

Although the main tools of the political writers of the liberation wars were the political poem and the political song, political journalism also played an important role in the attacks waged against the enemy. During the eighteen twenties a group of writers, who later became known as "the Young Germans," continued this journalistic tradition and used it skillfully in serving their ideas.[9] Adapting the "freedom theme" of Schiller and of the poets of the liberation wars, they proclaimed Germany's future in a unified and democratic state, freed from any domination by the dynasties. The most gifted of these writers, Heinrich Heine, was a master of political satire, which in his case often took the form of a poem or an epic in verse. In "Deutschland, ein Wintermärchen" ("Germany, A Winter Fairy Tale," 1884), he sharply attacked both the imperialist Prussian state and catholicism in Germany. In 1830 Heine had to flee Germany; he found a new home in Paris, as did his contemporary, Ludwig Börne. Having entangled themselves in the political questions of the day, the "Young Germans" weakened their thrust against the powers that they were fighting. Personal quarrels among themselves, which continued into the time of their exile, added to the ineffectiveness of their movement. Other than Georg Herwegh's "Gedichte eines Lebendigen" ("Poems of a Living Man," 1841–44), few of their works attained literary significance, although some poems written during this time attained a high level of dynamic expression—August Heinrich Hoffmann von Fallersleben's "Deutschland über alles," for example. This poem, written in 1841 during his captivity on the island of Helgoland, later became the national anthem of the Second German Reich.

Political suppression had rendered largely ineffective in Germany the attempts of the "Young Germans" to bring about democratization and the emancipation of the individual. In Austria the Metternich regime dealt with its opponents in a similar manner. The bourgeoisie, thus unable to express its political ambitions, reacted with cultural introversion. The *Biedermeier* era, enhanced by favorable economic conditions, brought an unprecedented level of cultural expression into the home of the burgher.[10] Among the intelligentsia, a persistent but muted liberalism that had its origin in the time of Joseph II led a peaceful but insignificant existence. Franz Grillparzer, himself a liberal thinker, had to earn his living as a bureaucrat while writing dramas for the Vienna court theater that were, of course, subject to censorship. Although Grillparzer had little respect for Metternich's police state and the capriciousness of the nobility at the Viennese court, his late dramas contain a powerful political message, reflecting a growing concern about the oncoming age of the masses. In *Ein Bruderzwist in Habsburg* (*A Quarrel in the House of Hapsburg,* 1848) and in *Libussa* (1847), visionary monologues proclaim a future of chaos and lawlessness. It was the abortive Revolution of 1848, with its rather bloody consequences in Vienna and in other German cities, that had led him as well as many other intellectuals of his age to embrace conservative ideals. Adalbert Stifter's late novels reflect a similar development: In *Der Nachsommer* (*Late Summer*, 1857) and *Witiko* (1865–67), he emphasized order and tradition as the most important ingredients of a meaningful existence. Even a satiric playwright such as Johann Nepomuk Nestroy, who usually avoided becoming involved in ideological controversies, rejected the Revolution of 1848 in his hilarious comedy *Die Freiheit in Krähwinkel* (*The Freedom in Krähwinkel*, 1848).[11]

There were others, however, who attacked the prevailing political order in Germany and Austria in a radical manner long before the revolution. Georg Büchner, who had to flee his native Hesse, was the founder of a secret society, the "Gesellschaft für Menschenrechte," and the editor of the *Hessische Landbote*, a pamphlet proclaiming radical socialist ideas. In his drama *Woyzeck* (1836), the hero appears as the victim of a merciless class structure.[12]

After immigrating to America, Charles Sealsfield (Karl Postl) anonymously published a book entitled *Austria as It Is* (1828) in which he compared the liberal democracy of the American system with the suppression of the Austrian police state. This book, factual on many accounts, was instrumental in creating a rather unfavorable image of Austria in the Anglo-Saxon countries during the nineteenth century.[13]

In Switzerland, where democracy had a long tradition and where political suppression was not a burning issue, the conservative cause found a powerful voice in Jeremias Gotthelf (Albert Bitzius). Unlike Grillparzer and Stifter, Gotthelf, an eloquent Protestant pastor from ·the Emmental, did not resign himself to the role of a gentle admonisher in the face of an unsettling political future. In his novel *Jakobs des Handwerksburschen Wanderungen durch die Schweiz* (*Journeyman Jacob's Travels through Switzerland*, 1846–47), he declared open warfare on the new socialist ideas. He settled his accounts with the Bern government, which had been strongly influenced by the new ideologies since the eighteen thirties, in *Zeitgeist und*

Bernergeist (*Spirit of the Times and Spirit of Bern*, 1852). In his major work *Der grüne Heinrich* (*The Green Henry*, 1854–55), Gotthelf's fellow countryman Gottfried Keller also rejected the revolutionary ideas with which he had sympathized in his youth. Keller's late novel, *Martin Salander* (1886) vehemently criticized the imminent age of mass society and its proletarianizing effect on the individual.[14]

Free of revolutionary visions but fully aware of the irreversible development of the new democratic principles, Theodor Fontane gave a masterful assessment of the Prussian society of his time in his great novel *Der Stechlin* (1898). In this portrait of an old Junker family, he demonstrated that new times and political philosophies had rendered obsolete the species of the landed gentry.[15]

Disturbed by growing urbanization and by the social conditions in the cities, some writers sought remedies in the open country. Influenced by Gotthelf and Keller, Berthold Auerbach wrote his *Schwarzwälder Dorfgeschichten* (*Village Tales from the Black Forest*, 1843–53) in which life in the country is seen as wholesome and natural and in sharp contrast to the dehumanizing existence of a city dweller. The Austrian Peter Rosegger expressed his view of the city as the root of all evil in numerous prose pieces, most of which glorified country life in a highly idealistic fashion and advocated a return to nature as the only way of reversing the decadence of society.[16]

Although not a *Heimatdichter*, the Bavarian Ludwig Thoma wrote a highly political novel entitled *Andreas Vöst* (1905) in which an industrious farmer who refuses to submit to the selfish will of the village priest is brought down by the intrigues of his revengeful enemy. The times of the *Kulturkampf* and the emergence of the *Bauernbund*, whose leaders intended to break the hegemonial powers of the Bavarian Center party in the rural areas, provide effective background for the story. Thoma involved himself in numerous political controversies as a writer and editor of the satiric journal *Simplicissimus*, which Albert

Langen founded in Munich in 1896. With great vigor the writers of the *Simplicissimus* attacked the regime of Wilhelm II for its bungling foreign policy and for its hypersensitivity to criticism at home. Although not the only satirical periodical in Germany around the turn of the century, the *Simplicissimus* was one of the most famous.[17]

The literary movement of European naturalism found its most famous German representative in the younger Gerhart Hauptmann. The best known of his early dramas, *Die Weber* (*The Weavers*, 1892), described vividly both the poverty and the political agony of a class of people caught between the exploitation by early capitalism and the advent of total industrialization. It should be remembered at this point that industrialization in Germany began considerably later than in England and France. The newly created social situation of an uprooted proletariat and its detrimental consequences for the individual are, therefore, not reflected in German literature until the late eighteen eighties. Although not intended as a political drama, according to the author, *The Weavers* was certainly understood as a message against capitalism and its political supporters. Hauptmann was celebrated as a hero of the international workers movement and his play was censored by the government. More than fifty years later, shortly before his death in 1946, he was still honored by the Soviet occupational forces as the author of The Weavers.[18]

During the two decades preceding World War I the narrow-mindedness and satiety of the German bourgeois became targets for several talented writers of literary expressionism. One of the most poignant expressions of political criticism against the middle class is contained in Carl Sternheim's cycle of eleven plays, entitled *Aus dem bürgerlichen Heldenleben* (*From the Heroic Life of the Bourgeois,* 1911–18). The numerous dramas of Frank Wedekind and Georg Kaiser are also aimed at the hypocrisy and smallness of the bourgeois. The most demolishing portrait of the philistine in Wilhelm II's Germany was written by Heinrich Mann.[19] The main hero of his novel *Der Untertan* (*The Subject*, 1914), Diederich Hessling, is a petty opportunist who appears as the epitome of the unscrupulous climber who would sacrifice every principle to gain advantage over his adversaries.

As in the other nations of Europe, World War I prompted a number of German writers to involve themselves in polemic poems and essays against the enemy. Most of them, however, were of mediocre caliber, although writers like Stefan George, Hugo von Hofmannsthal, and Rudolf Alexander Schröder also wrote contributions for the cause of their countries. Hugo von Hofmannsthal's main concern was his fear for the survival of a political entity, namely, Austria-Hungary, which symbolized for him the cradle of culture in central and eastern Europe. Indeed, he never recovered from a state of depression that followed the defeat of Austria and Germany and the subsequent abolition of the two monarchies.

When Heinrich Mann published an essay on Emile Zola in 1915, attacking the cruelty of war and the insensitivity of some writers who still supported it, he provoked his brother Thomas Mann to publish a long reply, which also took the form of an essay, entitled *Betrachtungen eines Unpolitischen* (*Observations of a Non-Political*, 1918). This work represents a vigorous defense of German conservatism and numerous attacks against the *Entente*. Aiming at his brother Heinrich, Thomas Mann coined the term *Zivilisationsliterat*, meaning the unprincipled writer who would even help an enemy in time of war. Naturally, the essay caused a deep rift between the two brothers.

Thomas Mann changed his political conviction shortly after the end of World War I. In his essay *Von deutscher Republik* (*Of the German Republic*, 1923), he spoke eloquently for the new form of government in Germany. His newly acquired ideological creed found its most refined expression in his novel *Der Zauberberg* (*The Magic Mountain*, 1924). Hans Castorp, the hero, is to be seen as a (partially autobiographical) representative of German youth at the time of World War I. Having spent seven years under the influence of two teachers, one representing the ultraconservative position, the other, the liberal socialist, Castorp chooses to follow the way of his second mentor, although history itself seems to give more credence to the first. After his emigration, Thomas Mann became a vocal opponent of the Hitler regime both in his essays, such as *Vom kommenden Sieg der Demokratie* (*Of the Coming Victory of Democracy*, 1938), and in his addresses that were broadcast by the BBC in London during World War II. In his late novel *Doktor Faustus* (1948), the tragic fate of the German nation serves as a background for the plot.[20]

After the end of World War I several German writers who had taken an active part in the war as soldiers began to assess their experiences in an attempt to come to grips with the phenomenon of "war." Ernst Jünger gave an exact account of his war experiences in *In Stahlgewittern* (*Storms of Steel*, 1920), although not condemning war entirely, as did Carl Zuckmayer in his book *Als wär's ein Stück von mir* (*Memoirs*, 1969). Certainly the most famous of all books about war, Erich Maria Remarque's *Im Westen nicht Neues* (*All Quiet on the Western Front*, 1929), portrays war as the most inhumane of experiences. Other writers, such as Ernst Bertram, Erwin Guido Kolbenheyer, and Josef Weinheber, the latter a lyric poet of rare talent, glorified the battle and transformed it into a mythological experience. Literature of such a nature was, of course, welcomed by the rulers of the Third Reich, whose *Reichsschrifttumskammer* saw to it that anything not agreeing with the official line of the new regime that proclaimed a "new heroism" was taken out of circulation. Literary works criticizing the new state or showing an inclination toward socialist ideas were labeled "degenerate art" and officially forbidden. Many authors emigrated and continued their opposition to Hitler's Germany from abroad. Others remained and took refuge in the *innere Emigration*, which usually had to take the form of total silence.[21]

The most famous emigrant writer other than Thomas Mann was undoubtedly Bertolt Brecht who found it natural that literature should openly express political ideas. Brecht's early dramas *Trommeln in der Nacht* (*Drums in the Night*, 1922) and *Baal* (1922) reflect his political creed, which occasionally revealed anarchic tendencies, immediately after World War I. Brecht's devout Marxism began to become evident in *Die heilige Johanna der Schlachthöfe* (*Joan of Arc of the Stockyards*, 1932) and later dominated other plays, such as *Die Gewehre der Frau Carrar* (*The Guns of Mrs. Carrar*, 1937) and *Herr Puntila und sein Knecht Matti* (*Mr. Puntila and his Servant Matti*, 1948). His play *Der aufhaltsame Aufstieg des Arturo Ui* (*The Preventable Rise of Arturo Ui*, 1941) was aimed at Hitler's dictatorship. Brecht also used various forms of lyric poetry to express his political views, often requiring the reader to join him in sophisticated intellectual games.[22]

After World War II, to a much greater extent than in any other time in history, German literature tried to master the political experience of the immediate past. Most of Heinrich Böll's novels, for instance, deal with the war's tragic implications on people as well as with political opportunism. Günter Grass's *Die Blechtrommel* (*Tin Drum*, 1959) the most famous novel written by a German author after 1945, scourges the timeservers among the middle class in Hitler's times. In his drama *Der Stellvertreter* (*The Deputy*, 1963), Rolf Hochhuth severely criticized the alleged passivity of the church in the face of the annihilation of the Jews. Max Frisch reminded the German middle class of its past mass hysteria in his play *Andorra* (1962). Although the war and the question of guilt still dominated German political literature in the nineteen sixties, other issues such as the division of Germany and the ideological regimentation in East Germany began to be subjects of interest for German writers, as evidenced in Uwe Johnson's novels *Mutmassungen über Jakob* (*Speculations about Jacob*, 1959) and *Das dritte Buch über Achim* (*The Third Book on Achim*, 1961), and

Christa Wolf's *Der geteilte Himmel* (*The Divided Heaven*, 1963).[23]

In the absence in the West of dangers through ideological domination or of political suppression, writers direct their criticism at the issues of the cold and impersonal governmental bureaucracy of the modern state (Thomas Bernhard), the pettiness of society in a small country (Max Frisch and Friedrich Dürrenmatt), and the complacency of the citizen in the society of the economic miracle (Peter Handke). Handke certainly discovered an original dramatic technique to drive home his point in his *Publikumsbeschimpfung* (*Insulting the Audience*, 1966). Judging by the benevolent reactions of his German audiences to the insults hurled down from the stage by the actors, one tends to suspect that the author is accurate in his assessment of the West German citizen's lethargy. During a performance of the play in Barcelona in the early seventies, the audience reacted in a different manner: The viewers shouted insults back at the actors.

NOTES

1. Benno von Wiese, *Politische Dichtung Deutschlands*. (Berlin, 1931), 10, and Fritz Strich, "Der Dichter und der Staat," F. S., *Dichtung und Zivilisation*. (Munich, 1928).

2. Wolfgang Mohr/Werner Kohlschmidt, "Politische Dichtung," *Reallexikon der deutschen Literaturgeschichte*, vol. 3, 2nd ed. (Berlin, 1967), p. 157.

3. Peter Stein, *Politisches Bewusstsein und künstlerischer Gestaltungswille in der politischen Lyrik 1780–1848*. (Hamburg, 1971), p. 18.

4. *Ibid.*, p. 19.

5. Cf. Roy Pascal, *The German Sturm und Drang*. (Manchester, 1953).

6. Cf. Walter Horace Bruford, *Culture and Society in Classical Weimar, 1775–1806* (Cambridge, 1962), and Arnold Bergsträsser, *Goethe's Image of Man and Society*. (Chicago, 1949).

7. Cf. Paul Kluckhohn, *Persönlichkeit und Gemeinschaft. Studien zur Staatsauffassung der deutschen Romantik*. (Halle/Saale, 1925).

8. Wilhelm Kosch, *Deutsche Dichter vor und nach 1813. Befreiungskampf und Burschenschaft im Spiegel der zeitgenössischen Dichtung.* (Stuttgart, 1925).

9. Eliza Marian Butler, *The Saint-Simonian Religion in Germany. A Study of the Young German Movement.* (Cambridge, 1926).

10. Cf. Eilhard Erich Pauls, *Der politische Biedermeier.* (Lübeck, 1925).

11. Cf. Otto Rommel, ed., *Der österreichische Vormärz, 1816–1847.* (Leipzig, 1931).

12. Hans Mayer, *Georg Büchner und seine Zeit,* 2nd ed. (Wiesbaden, 1959).

13. Eduard Castle, *Das Geheimnis des grossen Unbekannten.* (Vienna, 1943).

14. Cf. Jean-Daniel Demagny, *Les idées politiques de Jeremias Gotthelf et de Gottfried Keller et leur evolution.* (Paris, 1954).

15. Cf. Joachim Remak, *The Gentle Critic. Theodor Fontane and German Politics, 1848–1898.* (Syracuse, 1964).

16. Cf. Georg Maurer, "Zum Problem der Heimatdichtung," G. M., *Der Dichter und seine Zeit.* (Berlin, 1956), pp. 108–124.

17. Cf. Harry Pross, *Literatur und Politik. Geschichte und Programme der politisch-literarischen Zeitschriften im deutschen Sprachgebiet seit 1810.* (Freiburg im Breisgau, 1963).

18. Cf. Hermann Barnstorff, *Die soziale, politische und wirtschaftliche Zeitkritik im Werke Gerhart Hauptmanns.* (Jena, 1938).

19. Cf. Ulrich Weisstein, *Heinrich Mann. Eine histor.-krit. Einführung in sein dichterisches Werk.* (Tübingen, 1962).

20. Cf. Max Rychner, "Thomas Mann und die Politik," M. R., *Welt im Wort.* (Zurich, 1949), pp. 349–394.

21. Cf. Herbert Wiesner, "Innere Emigration," *Handbuch der Gegenwartsliteratur.* (Munich, 1965).

22. Cf. Martin Esslin, *Brecht. A Choice of Evils; A Critical Study of the Man, His Work and His Opinions.* (London, 1959).

23. Cf. Marcel Reich-Ranicki, *Deutsche Literatur in West und Ost. Prosa seit 1945.* (Munich, 1963).

NOTES ON
CONTRIBUTORS

Ralf Dahrendorf is director of the London School of Economics and Political Science. In 1944 he was arrested by the Gestapo for anti-Nazi activities at school and was sent to a concentration camp. He received his doctorate in philosophy and classical philology from the University of Hamburg and in sociology from the University of London. He has taught at the universities of Saarbrucken, Hamburg, Tübingen and Constance and was visiting professor at Harvard and the University of Oregon. Before joining the EEC in 1970 as commissioner in charge of external relations and trade, he served as representative of the FDP (Free Democratic Party) in the *Landtag* and the Bundestag, and subsequently as parliamentary secretary of state for foreign affairs. His many publications include *Society and Democracy in Germany.*

Viola Herms Drath, long-time Washington foreign correspondent and publicist and author of numerous university textbooks on German affairs, studied philosophy and Germanic literatures at the University of Nebraska where she received an M.A. She has lectured at a number of American universities, among them USC and the University of Nebraska and now teaches at American University. Among her latest publications is an analytical study entitled *Willy Brandt: Prisoner of his Past.* Her comments on the political and cultural scene have appeared in *Commentary, National Observer,* the *Chicago Tribune, Harper's, Frankfurter Allgemeine Zeitung, Handelsblatt, das Parlament,* and other publications here and abroad.

Charles Foster, executive secretary of the Committee on Atlantic Studies and secretary-treasurer of the Conference Group on German Politics, has served on the faculties of the College of William and Mary, Indiana University, and De Pauw University. He studied political science at Harvard, joined the United States Office of Education as a specialist in social science and teacher training in 1966. He is also academic adviser to the Atlantic Council of the United States and has contributed to numerous publications.

Niels Hansen, minister of the embassy of the Federal Republic of Germany, studied at the universities of Göttingen, Hamburg, Heidelberg, Zurich, and at Geneva where he earned a doctorate of laws and became assistant on the faculty for Roman law and the history of law. Becoming a career foreign service officer for the FRG, he served as deputy chief of mission in Lisbon and Berne, as deputy consul in New York, and minister counselor to the permanent mission at the United Nations in New York before he was assigned to Washington.

Peter Hermes, State secretary with the German Foreign Office, studied law and political science at the universities of Munich and Vienna. His education was interrupted by World War II and five years (1945–50) in a POW camp in the Soviet Union. He joined the Federal Foreign Office after obtaining his LL.D. in 1952 and was attached to the German Consulate General in San Francisco and in Basel, the embassy to the Holy See, and the OECD mission in Paris, where he was responsible for trade and agricultural affairs. As ambassador-at-large, he headed the delegation for trade agreements with the USSR, the People's Republic of China, Poland, Rumania, Bulgaria, Hungary and the offset negotiations with the USA. In 1973 he was promoted to head the division for foreign trade and payments policy, development policy, and European economic integration. In addition he served as chairman of the OECD trade committee and deputy of the German delegation to the German–Soviet economic commission.

Jürgen Kalkbrenner has been cultural counselor at the embassy of the Federal Republic of Germany in Washington for the past seven years. He received an LL.D. from the University of Kiel and did postgradaute work at the University of Washington. He joined the German Foreign Office in 1955 and was assigned to Nairobi and later to Ankara. In Brussels he served as assistant to the then president of the EEC, Walter Hallstein. His publications include a study of Thomas Jefferson's explorations of the region along the Rhine and Moselle.

Catherine McArdle Kelleher is a professor in the Graduate School of International Affairs at the University of Denver and a faculty associate of the Center for Political Studies of the Institute for Social Research. She taught at Michigan, Barnard, Columbia, and the University of Illinois at Chicago Circle. She has held Fulbright, Ford, and Marshall Fund fellowships and has published a number of articles and books on German foreign policy and the problems of European security, notably, *Germany and the Politics of Nuclear Weapons,* and is working on a book about *The End of the Mass-Army in Europe.* She also served several times as a consultant to various governmental agencies, most recently on President Carter's National Security Council, and on private research institutes, in Europe and in the United States.

Robert Gerald Livingston, president of the German Marshall Fund in the United States, received his Ph.D. in Russian, Byzantine, and Balkan history and South Slav literature from Harvard. After teaching Russian history in the overseas program of Maryland University, he served in the State Department from 1956 to 1974. As a visiting fellow of the Council on Foreign Relations and staff member of the National Security Council, he concentrated on European and German affairs. His last foreign assignment was deputy chief of the political section in Bonn. His articles and essays have appeared in *Foreign Affairs, Foreign Policy,* and a number of other scholarly publications.

Peter C. Ludz, internationally recognized authority on the German Democratic Republic, is professor of political science at the University of Munich. Ludz received his Ph.D. from the Free University of Berlin and has taught at Bielefeld, Columbia, the New School for Social Research, and McGill University. Since 1970 he has served as political adviser to the West German government and divides his time between teaching assignments in the United States and at Munich. Among Ludz's most recent publications are *Die DDR zwischen Ost und West* (The GDR between East and West) and the *DDR Handbuch.*

Hugo Mueller, professor of German and linguistics, now emeritus, and long-time chairman of the department of language and foreign studies at American University, received his Ph.D. at Hamburg University. He also taught at Georgetown University and is the author of numerous books and articles on literature, linguistics, and the methodology of foreign language teaching.

George Schwab is professor of history at the City College of New York and chairman of the CUNY Conference on History and Politics. He is a member of the doctoral faculty at the City University Graduate School and the board of directors of the National Committee on American Foreign Policy. He also taught at Columbia where he received his Ph.D. Among his latest publications are *The Challenge of the Exception: An Introduction to the Political Ideas of Carl Schmitt* and a translation and introduction to Carl Schmitt's *The Concept of the Political.* He is co-editor of a volume on *Detente* and editor of *Ideology and Foreign Policy.*

Frederick Spotts studied at Swarthmore, the Fletcher School of Law and Diplomacy, and Oxford University, where he was awarded a Ph.D. He entered the Foreign Service in 1960 and was assigned to the political sections in Paris, Rangoon, and Bonn. He was a member of the State Department's Bureau of Political-Military Affairs before becoming special assistant to the deputy under secretary for management and his subsequent transfer to the US embassy in Rome. His book *The Churches and Politics in Germany* was published in Germany under the title *Kirchen und Politik in Deutschland.*

Wendelgard von Staden studied economics at the University of Tübingen as well as at the Académie des Sciences in Paris and the University of Southern California in Los Angeles. After graduating from the German Diplomats' School in Speyer, she became a foreign service officer in the Auswaertiges Amt. She served as attaché at the German embassy in Berne and as first secretary at the embassy in Washington.

John M. Starrels studied political science at the University of California in Berkeley, San Francisco State University, and at the University of California in Santa Barbara where he earned his Ph.D. in 1972. He lectured at the Foreign Service Institute, participated in the State Department's scholar–diplomat program, and teaches at George Washington University. He is co-author of *Politics in the German Democratic Republic* and has contributed to various scholarly journals. He is currently engaged in research on comparative public policy—America and Western Europe.

Bruno F. Steinbruckner is professor of German studies and chairman of the department of language and foreign studies at American University. He has studied and taught German literature and philology at the University of Innsbruck where he earned his Ph.D. He is a consultant in research at The George Washington University and has contributed articles on German literature and philology to scholarly journals here and in his native Austria.

Werner Steltzer is Director of Inter Nationes, Bonn. A World War II POW, he studied law at the University of Frankfurt, became an editor of the *Neue Zeitung* in Munich and Frankfurt, and later at the Norddeutsche Rundfunk. He served as founder and director of J. Walter Thompson's department of public relations in Germany and director of the information center in Berlin. Several special missions for the government led to an assignment as director for press and public relations in the Ministry for Economic Cooperation.

INDEX